Jürgen Rohweder, text

Peter Neumann, photography and design

# QUIETER, DEEPER, FASTER

## Innovations in German Submarine Construction

E.S. Mittler & Sohn

Hamburg · Bonn

This book is dedicated to my father

Dipl.-Ing. Helmut Rohweder

Captain (ret'd), Submarine Chief Engineering Officer and awardee of the Knight's Cross

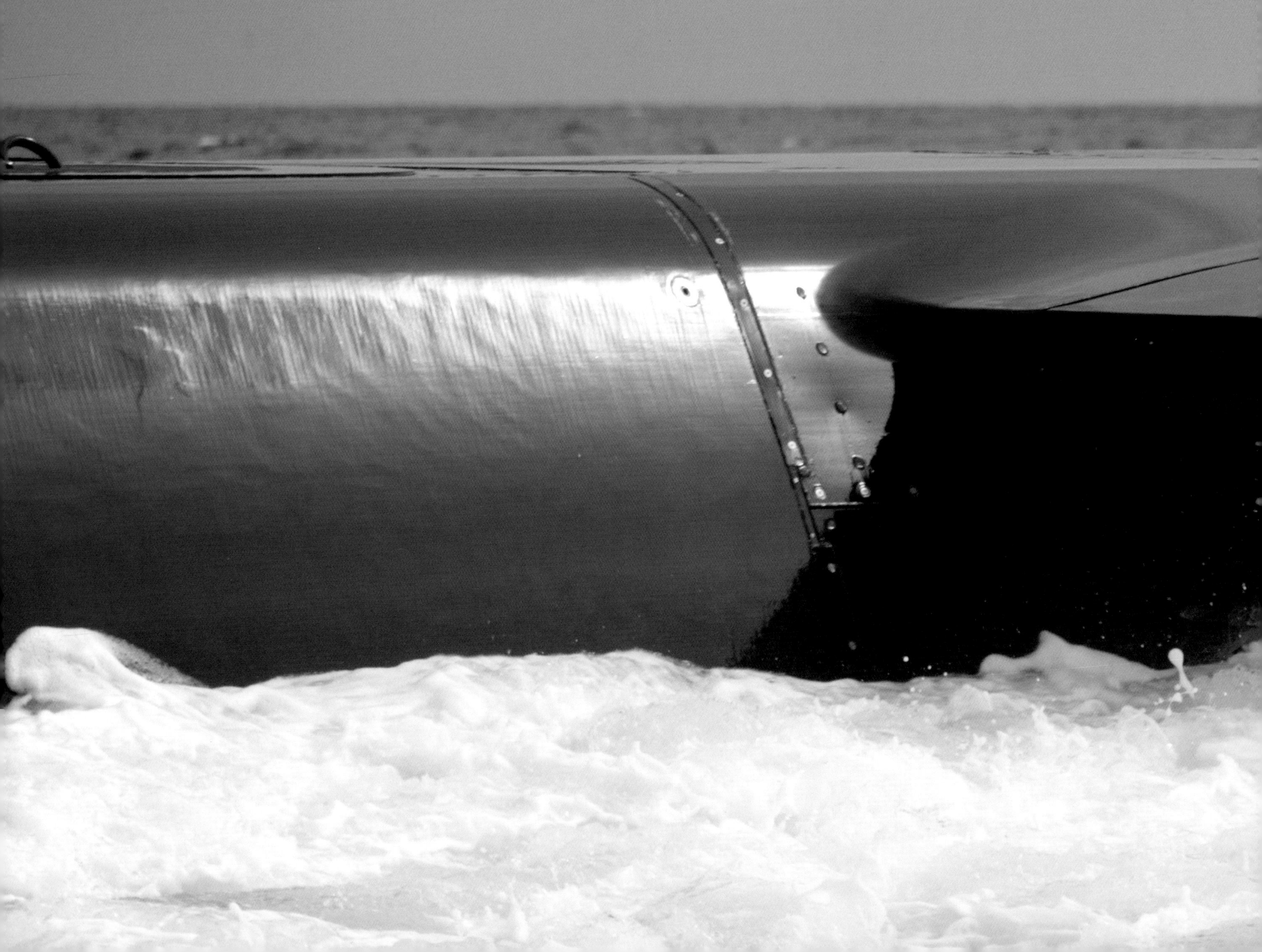

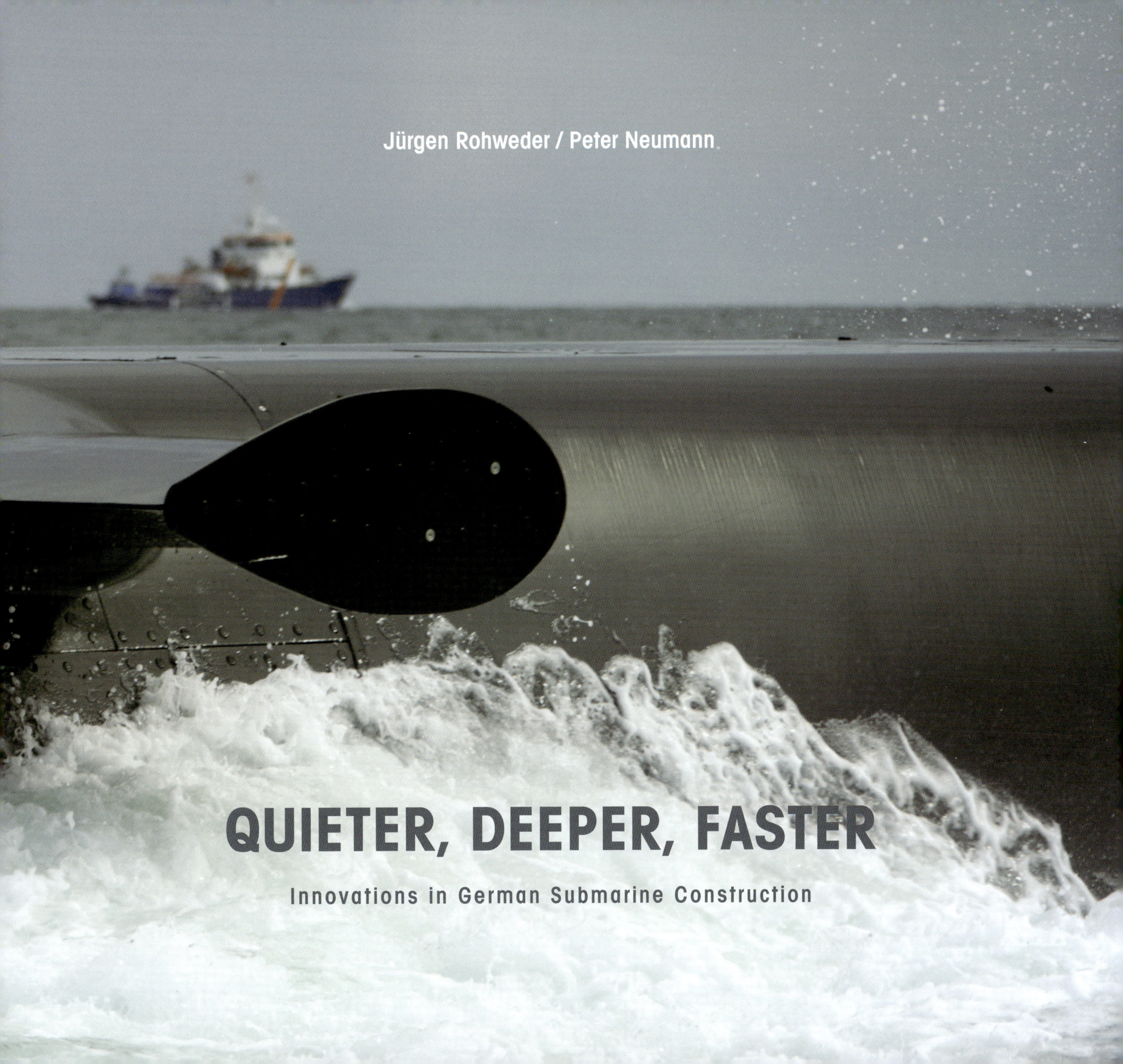

Jürgen Rohweder / Peter Neumann

# QUIETER, DEEPER, FASTER

Innovations in German Submarine Construction

**PUBLISHING DETAILS**

**QUIETER, DEEPER, FASTER** Innovations in German Submarine Construction

Bibliographic information of the German National Library:
The German National Library lists this publication in the German National Bibliography; detailed bibliographic data can be found on the Internet at http://dnb.d-nb.de.

ISBN: 978-3-8132-0912-9

© 2015/2016 by Mittler in Maximilian Verlag GmbH & Co. KG
All rights, in particular that of translation, are reserved.

Overall design/production: YPS Hamburg, Peter Neumann

Printed in Europe

# Contents

|     | Preface and thanks. | 7 |
| --- | --- | --- |
| 1.  | Leviathan wakes | 14 |
| 2.  | The roll of the submarine in modern scenarios | 23 |
| 3.  | Germany builds submarines | 35 |
| 4.  | The Class XXI submarine – A revolution at sea | 46 |
| 5.  | Germany builds submarines again | 58 |
| 6.  | Submarines "Made in Germany" | 78 |
| 7.  | The second German revolution in submarine construction: the Fuel Cell | 94 |
| 8.  | The Fuel Cell embarks | 110 |
| 9.  | The Class 212A becomes reality | 116 |
| 10. | HDW Class 214 submarines – Fuel Cell technology for the world | 138 |
| 11. | Still on Paper: HDW Class 210mod and Class 216 Submarines | 146 |
| 12. | Tomorrow's submarine technology today | 154 |
| 12. | A future within competitive markets | 162 |
| 14. | List of submarines built in Germany since 1960 | 164 |
| 15. | List of footnotes | 170 |
| 16. | Bibliography | 171 |

# Preface

I have dedicated this book to my father. He served as Chief Engineer on submarines in the Second World War and afterwards, was involved in setting up the Federal Republic of Germany's new submarine force. He was not a preacher of submarine myths. He was above all an engineer with heart and soul – engineering and technology in general always fascinated him, and he passed this enthralment on to his sons.

The development of seafaring, the mastery and exploration of the seas, the discovery of new continents, and the establishment of maritime trade routes have – just as the wars sea control – been accompanied by and dependent on the technical development of water craft. And they still are today.

Submarines have fascinated people throughout the world for a long time. On the one hand, because they can voyage into unknown depths far beneath the surface of the seas. But on the other, submarine wars in two world wars have created a special warrior myth shrouding submarines – and not only in Germany.

Today, this has changed into the myth of technology. Without doubt, the submarine is a weapon – good or evil, depending on the hand that wields it. But it is also pure technology. And thus the techniques and technologies used in submarines that we see today, are comparable to those used in space.

Today, German submarine technologies count among the leaders in the world. The Germans were not the first to have introduced submarines into their navy, but it wasn't long before the most technically demanding boats were being designed and built in German shipyards – a pursuit which has always involved ground breaking innovations and continues to this day.

This book attempts to show why this is the case. I have many people to thank. For his many suggestions and critical reviews, I particularly thank Hans Saeger. I extend a big thanks to all my colleagues at HDW and ThyssenKrupp Marine Systems, who during my stint at HDW expertly and patiently explained submarine building to me and gave me the opportunity to experience it first-hand. I thank Dr. Ute Arriens very much for her friendly support, she was always a big help to me in obtaining images and information. Further warm thanks go to Gabi Kolberg, who has proofread the text with a sharp mind and eye. And finally, a very big thanks goes to my friend Peter Neumann, to whom I am bound by many beautiful books, and who took a closer look at the German to English translation.

*Jürgen Rohweder*

*Stein in October 2015 / April 2016*

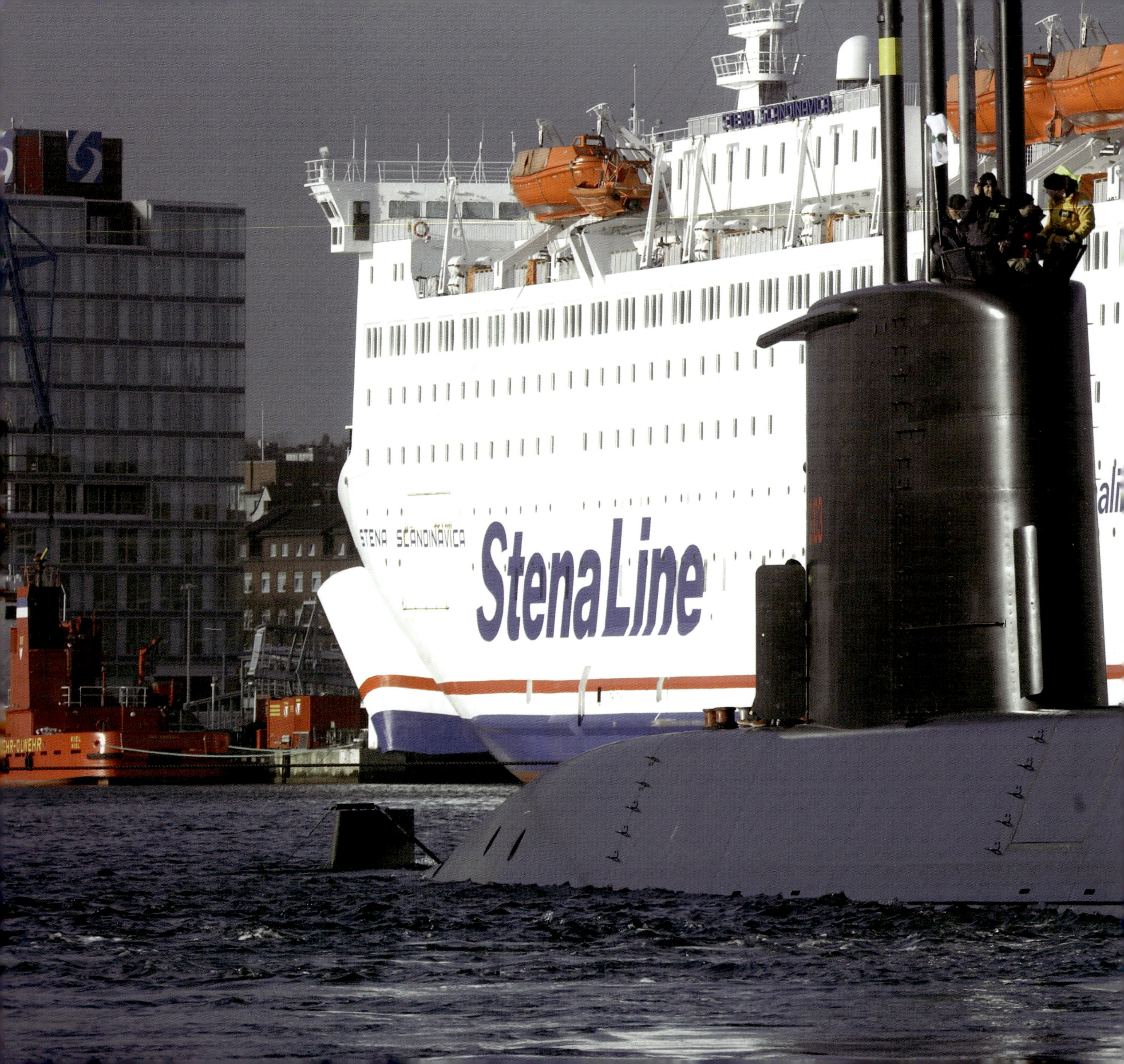
STENA SCANDINAVICA
StenaLine

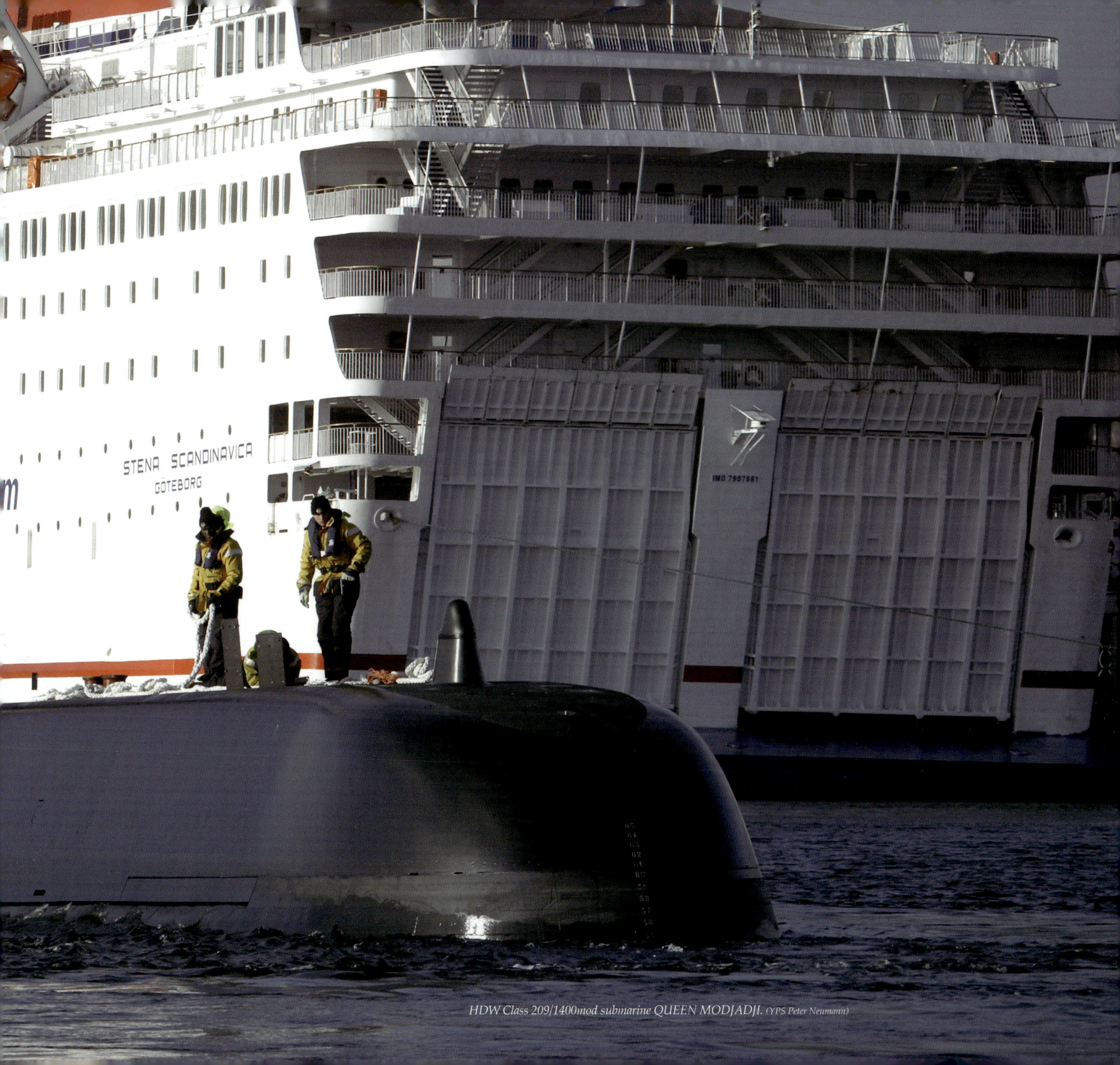
STENA SCANDINAVICA
GÖTEBORG

*HDW Class 209/1400mod submarine QUEEN MODJADJI.* (YPS Peter Neumann)

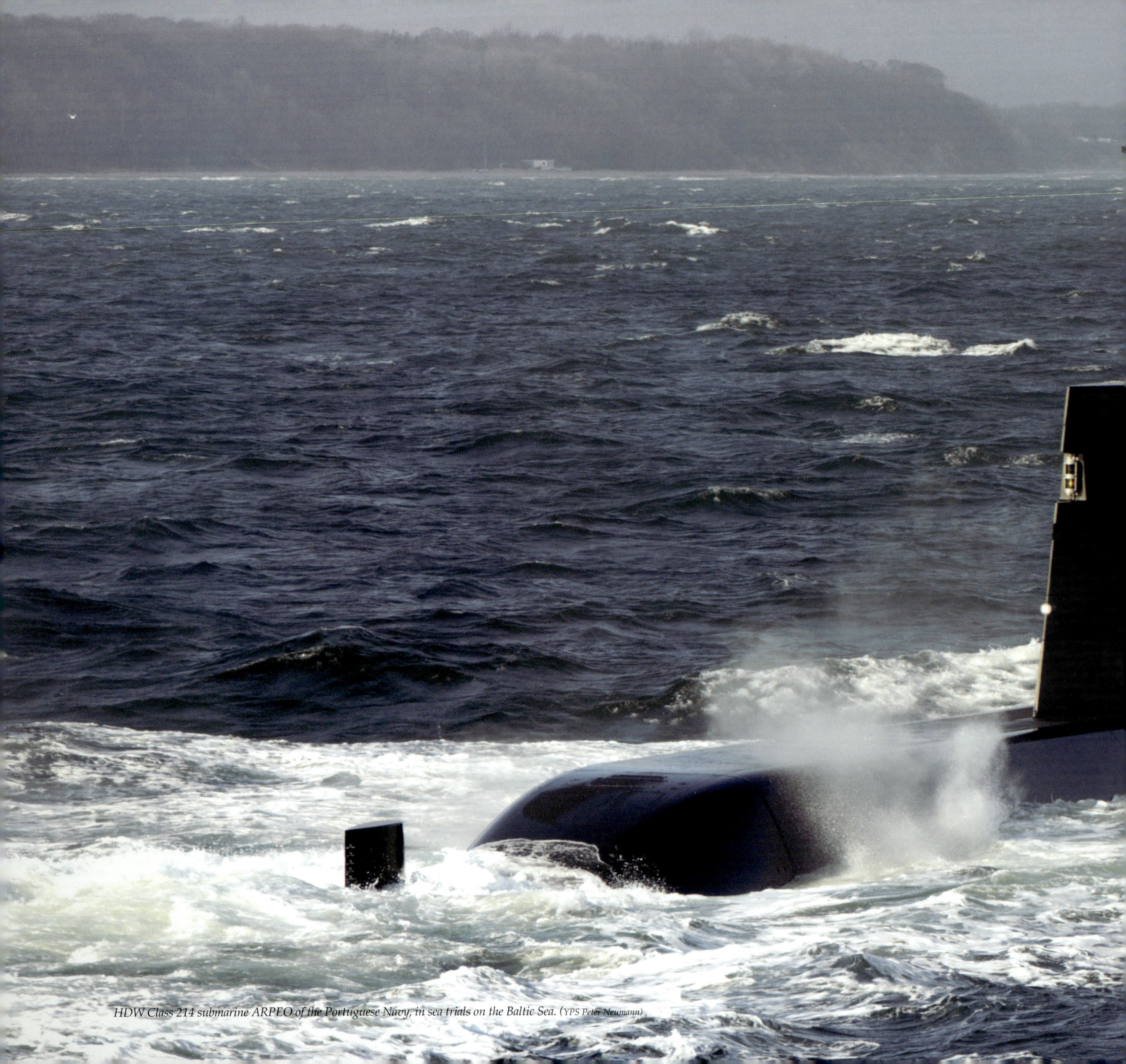

*HDW Class 214 submarine ARPEO of the Portuguese Navy, in sea trials on the Baltic Sea.* (YPS Peter Neumann)

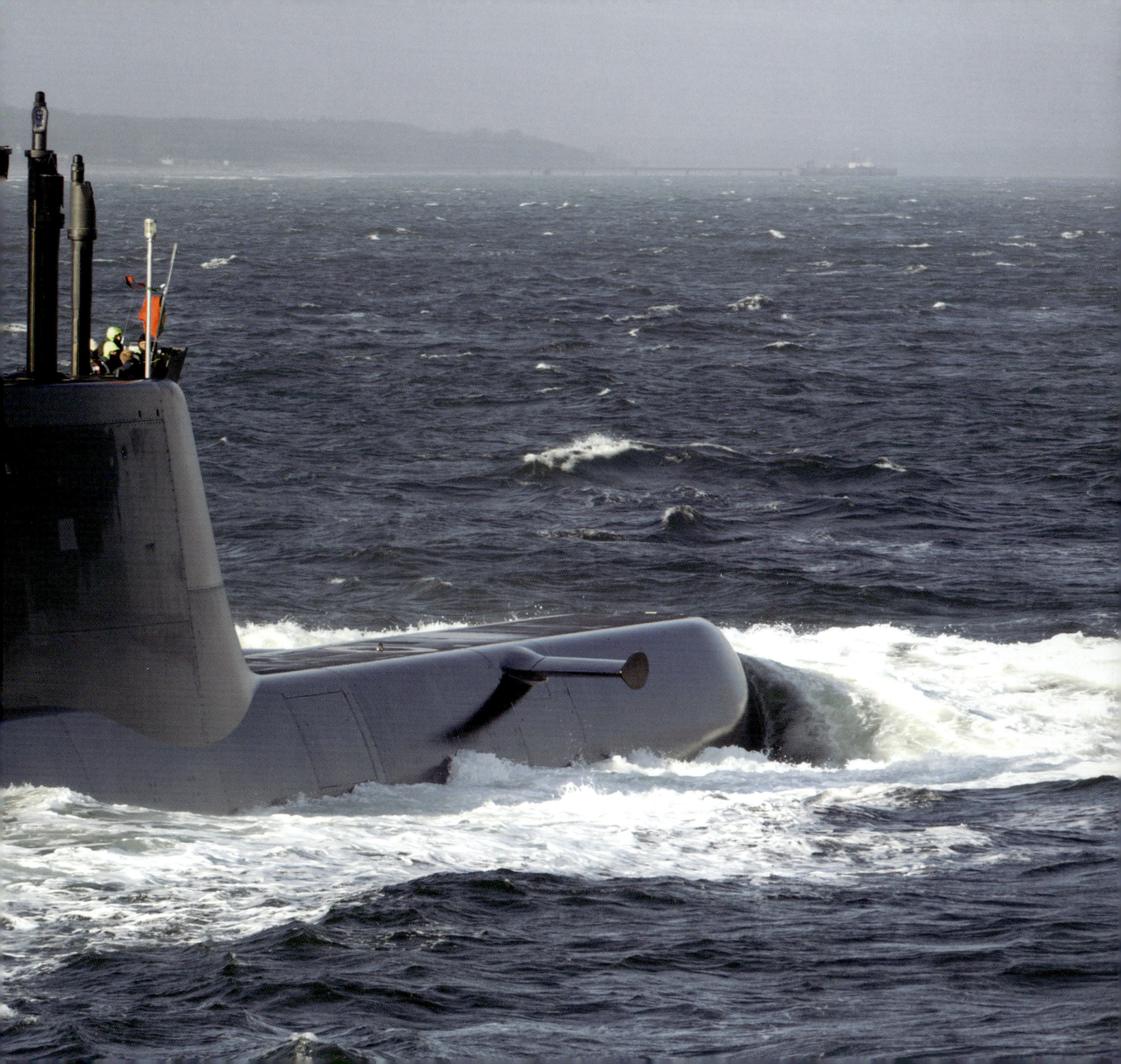

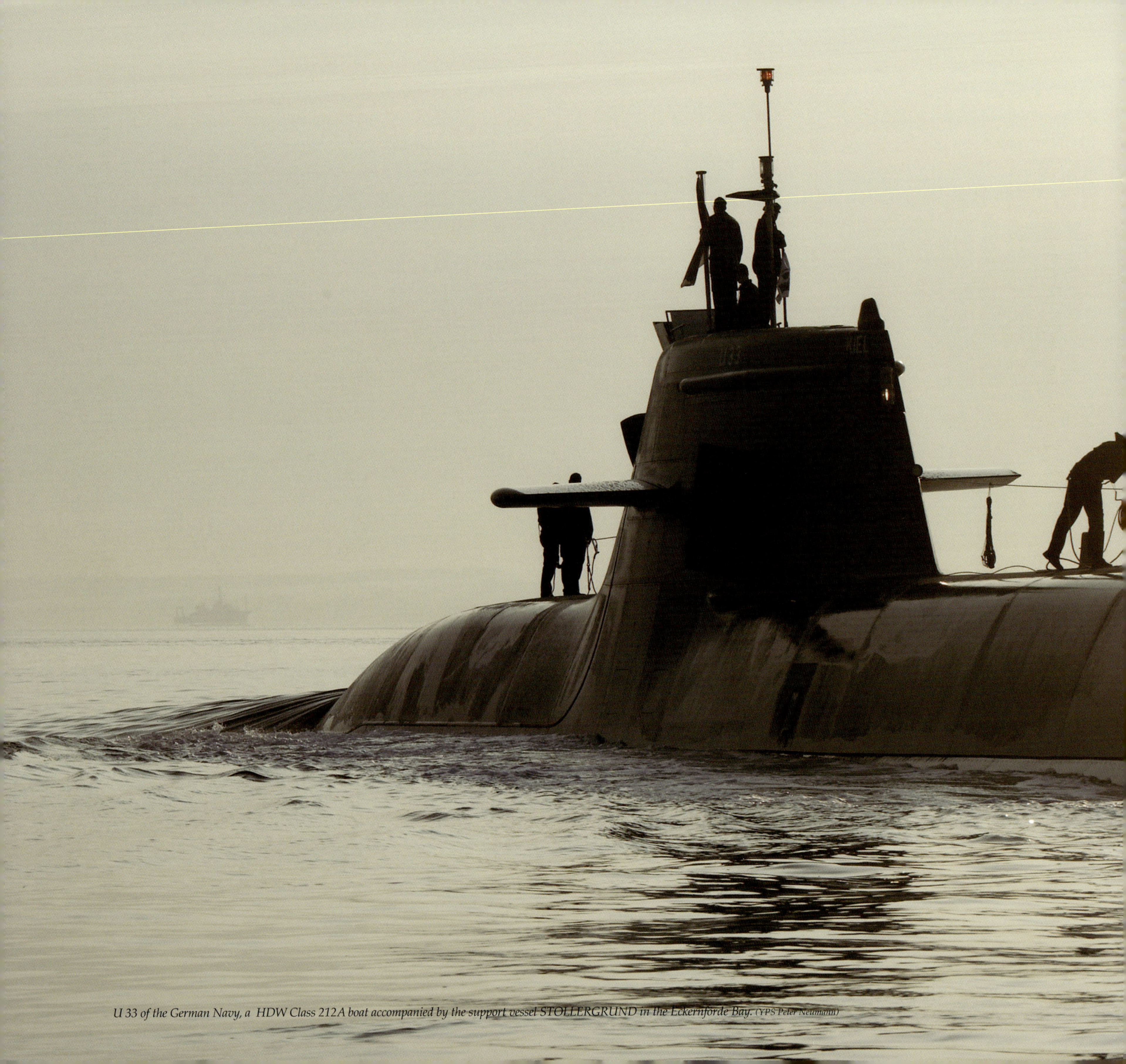
U33
KIEL

*U 33 of the German Navy, a HDW Class 212A boat accompanied by the support vessel STOLLERGRUND in the Eckernförde Bay.* (YPS Peter Neumann)

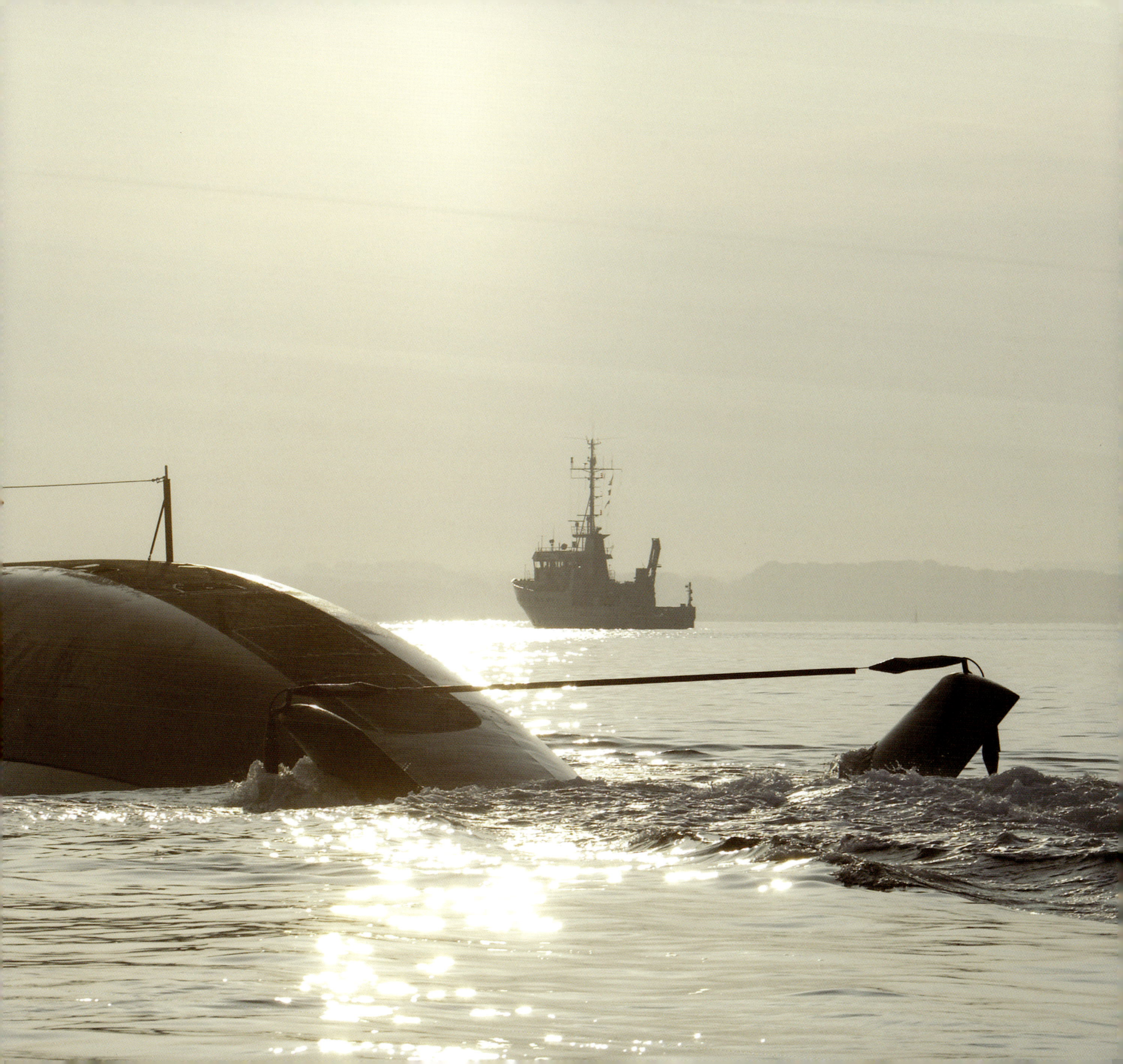

*"Can you pull in Leviathan with a fishhook or tie down its tongue with a rope? … If you lay a hand on it, you will remember the struggle and never do it again! … No one is fierce enough to rouse it … Who can strip off its outer coat? Who dares open the doors of its mouth, ringed about with fearsome teeth? … Its back has rows of shields tightly sealed together … Flames stream from its mouth; sparks of fire shoot out. … When it rises up, the mighty are terrified … The sword that reaches it has no effect … It makes the depths churn like a boiling caldron … Nothing on earth is its equal; a creature without fear." Book of Job 40:25–41:26*

# Leviathan Wakes

At a press conference in September 1945, Chester W. Nimitz, five-star Admiral and Commander in Chief of the US Pacific fleet said: *"Warships are the ships of yesterday, aircraft carriers are the ships of today, but submarines will be the ships of the future."*[1] For his naval comrades on all Seven Seas coasts, who were still thinking along the lines of conventional naval warfare and had the greatest respect for the impressive size and strength of the above-surface mammoths, this was probably a very bold forecast.

Certainly, the submarine had played a significant role during two previous world wars, but ultimately in World War II the joint forces of the allies – surface vessels and aircraft – had decisively beaten the dreaded German Wolf Pack. In the end, the technical superiority of submarine defence outweighed the technical superiority of the German standard submarines. Only the initiated had seen that a new submarine type with completely new capacities had emerged in Germany – one that would redefine the role of the submarine. The transition from the former submersible surface ship to the genuine submarine was benchmarked with the German Types XXI and XXIII submarines. The use of such boats called for a complete rethink of the strategic role which a modern submarine was going to play in the future.

Strategies are always dependent on the technical possibilities. In reality, therefore, the journey from the first diving boat of the 18th and 19th century to the modern submarine was very long. Leonardo da Vinci had already made designs for a submarine in 1515, and in 1580 the Englishman William Borne published the description of a diving boat. In 1654, the Frenchman de Son designed a semi-submersible, the Rotterdam Boot. It was probably the first submarine for military purposes, as it was to attack unobserved enemy ships and ram a hole in their hulls. In 1776, the American David Bushnell built the first submarine, TURTLE, which was actually intended during the American Civil War, to at-

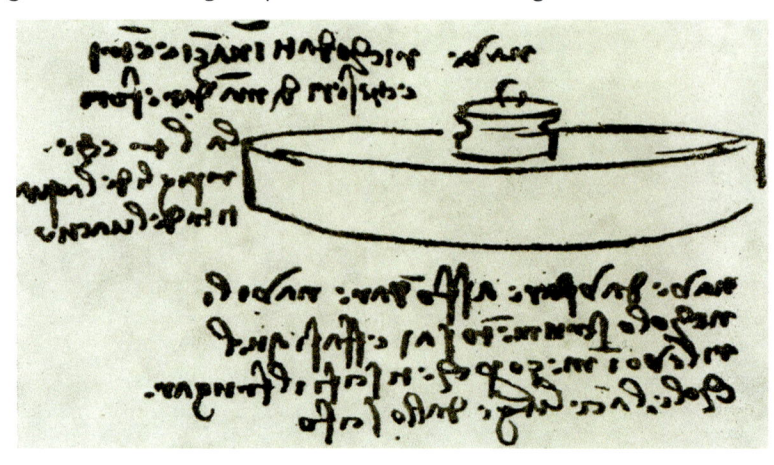

*Leonardo da Vinci: Sketch of a diving vessel, 1515.*

tack a warship, drill holes in it and insert a bomb fitted with a self-timer. However, the attack on a British warship anchored in New York's port failed as the drill could not penetrate the hull. At least Sergeant Ezra Lee, who was at the helm of the boat, came back unscathed.

The strategic benefits of a submarine were described in 1797 for the first time by the American Robert Fulton: *"If warships were to be destroyed with such novel, such hidden and such unpredictable resources, the confidence of seafarers would evaporate and the fleet would give up in despair from the first moment of the attack."* [2] It was the first formulation of the theory of deterrence by submarines. Fulton lived in Paris and supported Napoleon in the sea war against England. He made an offer to the French for a submarine with which he hoped to destroy the Royal Navy. So, at his own expense, he built the NAUTILUS, which he also wanted to helm himself. In compensation, he demanded a payment for each English ship he destroyed. He built the submarine (which was to give its name to the first American nuclear submarine), and conducted several successful diving trips with it. He managed to dive down to 8 metres and remained submerged for up to

Plate the First
half an inch to a foot
Robt Fulton
1806
A
B
C
D
E
F
G
H
I
J
K
L
M
N
O
P
Q
R

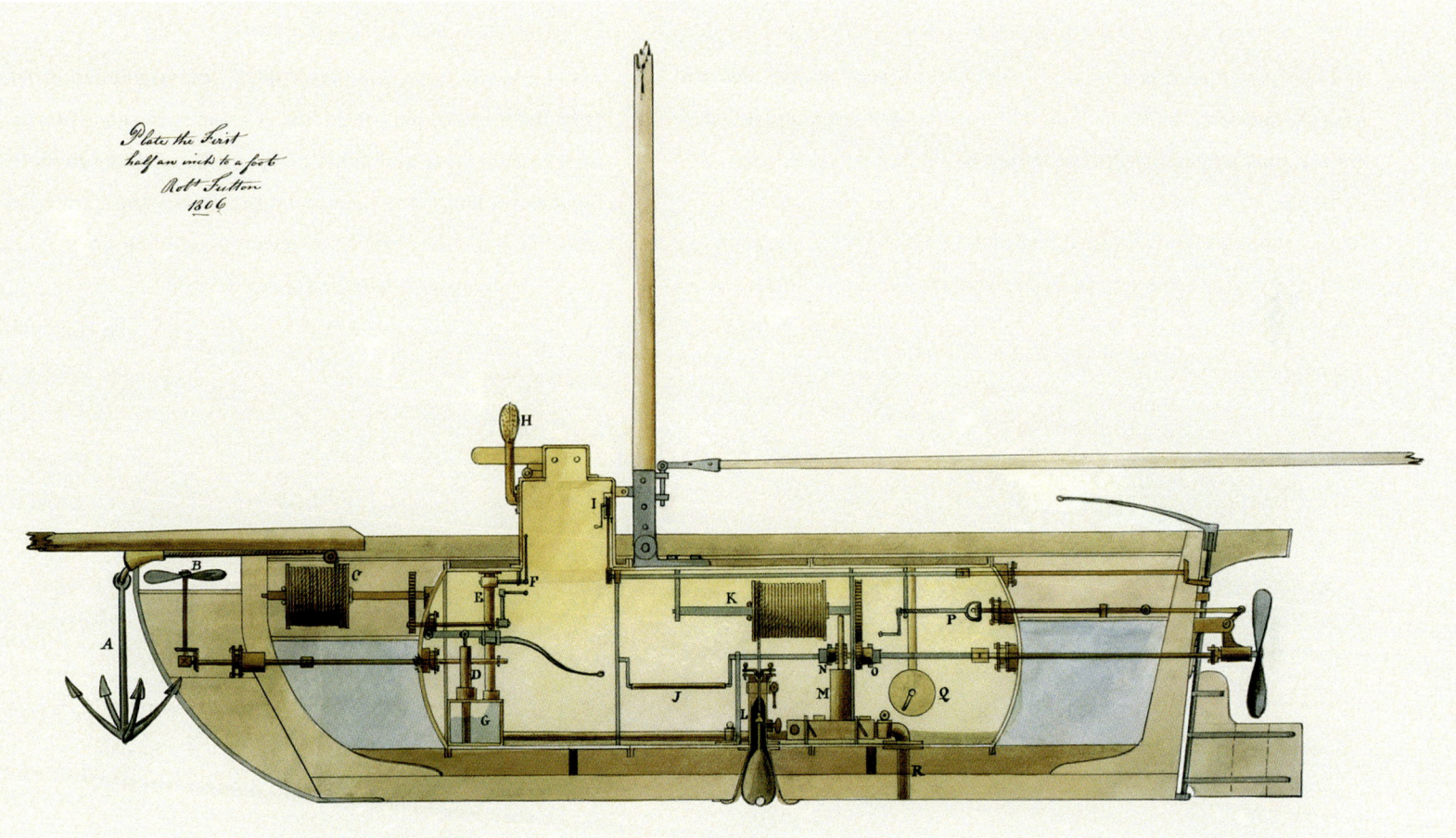

*Design of a submarine by Robert Fulton dating from 1806.*

six hours. A tube reaching up to the water surface – a forerunner of the snorkel – provided air. The hand-operated NAUTILUS, in practice a further development of the TURTLE, sustained an underwater speed of 4 knots with laborious manual work; above water, a mast and sails enabled easier travel.

Fulton, whom the French Government had awarded the rank of Rear Admiral, tried several unsuccessful attacks on English ships. British sailors saw the NAUTILUS coming and simply moved of the way. Thus the French Navy lost interest in the vessel, and a new Minister of the Navy thought that the NAUTILUS could perhaps be useful against Algerian pirates. However, French interests were focused on the wide ocean. Nevertheless, 70 years later, Jules Verne gave the NAUTILUS an immortal monument with his novel "20,000 Leagues under the Sea", and thereby became one of the founders of the submarine myth, which continues to this day.

There were early ideas for the construction of submarines in Germany. Count Wilhelm of Schaumburg-Lippe, who had built Wilhelmstein island fortress in Lake Steinhuder near to Hanover, where he also established a military academy, ordered in 1772 the design of a fish-shaped submarine. Named HECHT (pike), the adventurous vehicle built of oak and fitted with a flexing tail fin was supposed to have been driven submerged in Lake Steinhuder for 12 minutes. Today, a model of the HECHT displayed on the tourist island recalls the early ideas and plans of its designer Jakob Chrysostomus Praetorius, who even planned to travel to Portugal unnoticed with the vessel, within six days to take letters, items or people to safety, if the fortress were to come under siege.

The German-Danish war of 1848 to 1851 was the occasion to give a new impetus to German submarine inventiveness. Gustav Winkler, a Prussian government surveyor hailing from Halberstadt, submitted to his government a draft for a submersible that could be of use to the military, but the government made clear that it wanted to have nothing to do with it and referred him to the German National Assembly in Frankfurt/Main where the Navy Committee discussed his project in 1848. However, they

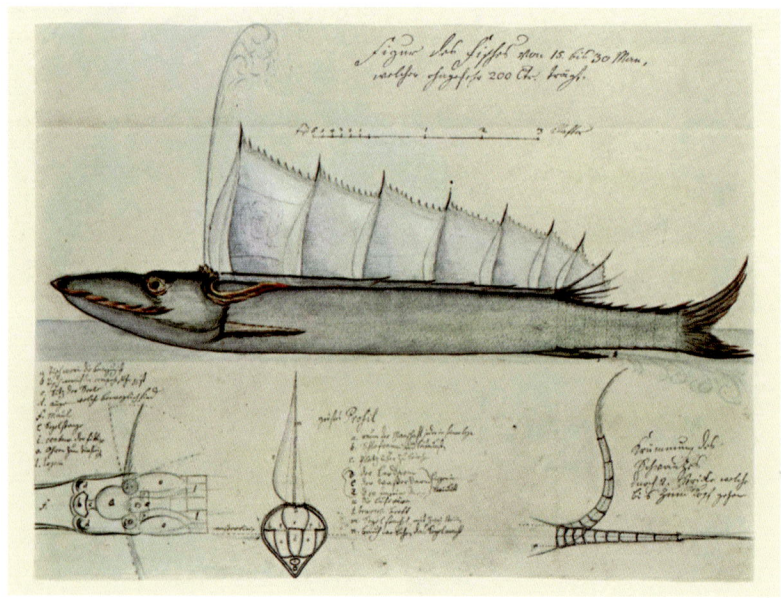
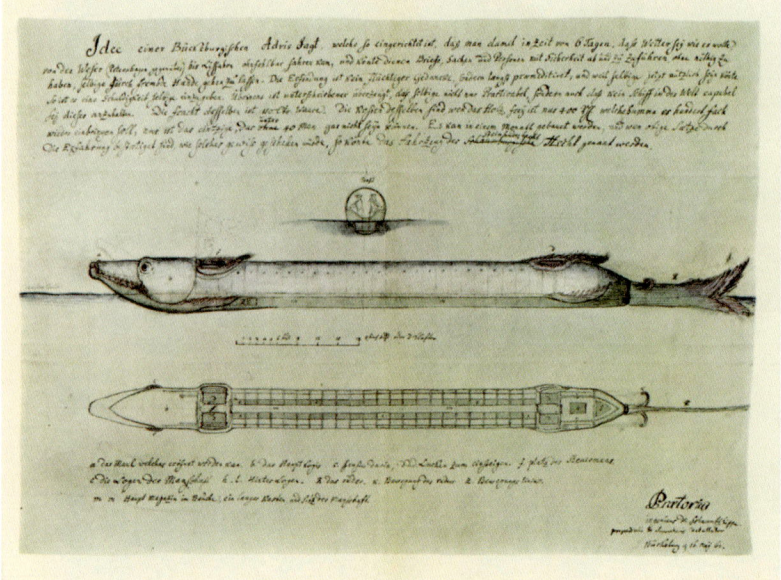

*Only a model remains: the design of the STEINHUDER HECHT from the year 1772.*

lacked the funds to even build a test boat, and the project was put on the back-burner. The draft is still technically interesting. Externally, the 6-metre boat is similar to modern midget submarines. Moreover, Winkler had abandoned manual operation. He intended to use a kind of explosive-driven machine as the drive – a decisive conceptual step in the future of the modern submarine.

The Bavarian corporal Wilhelm Bauer had more success. In 1848, the skilled and technically gifted wood turner had joined the 1st Royal Bavarian Artillery Regiment "Prince Luitpold" and took part in the German-Danish war as a corporal in the 10th field battery of the regiment. In 1850, he switched to the Schleswig-Holstein army and, inspired by his observations of attempts to blow up the bridge crossing the Alsen sound in 1849, proposed to his superiors that explosive charges secretly be installed under water on bridges, or on ships of the enemy. The vehicle for this was a submersible – the "BRANDTAUCHER" – the Fire-Diver.

Technically speaking, the boat was a quantum leap, and many regard it to be the world's first "modern" submarine. In fact, the draft had many innovations not featured on its predecessors, and which today can still be found on modern boats.[3] In addition to diving and control cells, the BRANDTAUCHER had a trim weight. To measure the depth, it used a pressure gauge and a water glass; this principal was later known as "Papenberg".

Das Innere, von oben gesehen.
Äußere Ansicht.
Das Innere, von der Seite gesehen.
Der Bauersche Brandtaucher.
Länge: 7,90 m. Breite: 2,00 m. Höhe: 3,00 m.
S Archimedische Schraube.
W Schraubenwelle.
R Steuerruder.
A Steuerapparat.
T Treträder.
Z Zahnradsystem.
P Pumpen.
K Verschiebbares Balanciergewicht.
B Eisenballast.
V Ventile für das einzulassende Wasser.
M Öffnungen für das auszupumpende Wasser.
F Mit Glas verschlossene Fenster.
G Mit Gummi verschlossene Öffnung zum Hinausgreifen, um Sprengminen an den feindlichen Schiffen zu befestigen.
L Einsteigeluke.

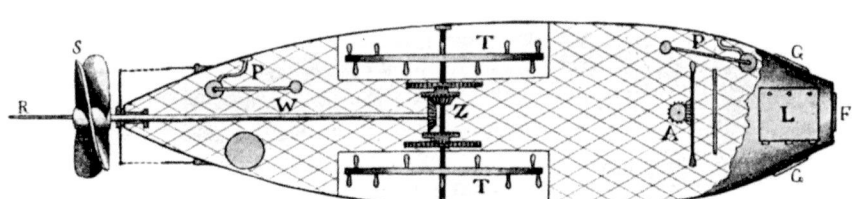

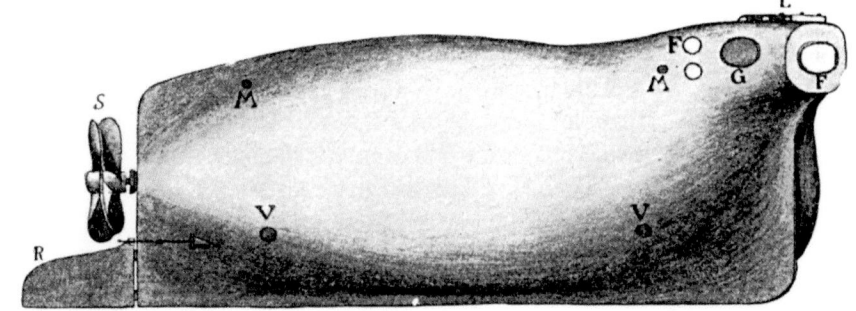

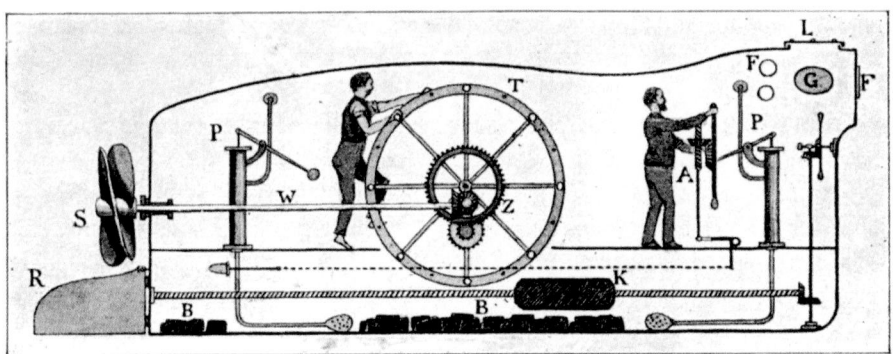

*The BRANDTAUCHER in a contemporary depiction.*

In later designs, Bauer introduced detachable ballast weights to facilitate emergency ascents, depth and side rudders, and air replenishment through a kind of snorkel. Bauer had also recognized that the treadmill drive was all but advantageous, and in later years undertook the first attempts to introduce petroleum engines and steam turbines.

As is well known, the BRANDTAUCHER sank during trials as the commission examining the design did not think the boat should be built as solid as Bauer envisaged – and it lacked funds anyway. Necessary machine parts therefore could not be installed by Schweffel & Howaldt in Kiel, contrary to the original concept – in particular the planned diving and control cells – and *"important parts of the apparatus had to be replaced by other, simpler but less satisfactory ones"* [4], as the later report of the accident notes. It acquits Bauer of any blame for the submersible's demise.

After the end of the German-Danish war, Wilhelm Bauer returned to his Bavarian homeland and worked feverishly on new designs that were based on his experience with the BRANDTAUCHER, and he developed the original design further. He had them patented in England and succeeded in getting the contract to build a submersible for the Russian Navy. Named SEETEUFEL, it was built in St. Petersburg and launched in 1856. The boat made 134 successful underwater trips until it sank owing to an operating error. We note in passing that the SEETEUFEL's most spectacular dive took place on occasion of Tsar Alexander II's coronation in 1856. Dived, it had a four-piece brass band playing the Russian national anthem so loud that it could be heard above the surface.

*Wilhelm Bauer*

In the end, the achievements of Bauer and his submersible were so impressive that competent Russian officers, after the diving trials in the roads of Kronstadt, summarised the results as follows: *"Finally it can be said that the submarine concept has been fully validated, but its construction goals, are in practice, far from having been reached. Since, however, the tests have shown that the main elements of the task have been resolved, one can hope for an improvement of boat construction which will lead up to an incomparably better result of submarine travel."* [5]

At least the BRANDTAUCHER demonstrated for the first time the practical deterrent effect of submarines. After Danish spies spread rumours over the BRANDTAUCHER, the Danish fleet, which blockaded Kiel's port during German-Danish, withdrew as quickly as possible, and returned back to the opposite side of Baltic.

Militarily, however, the submarine still only played a role in the minds of visionaries for a long time to come. Technically and strategically, submarines were initially a long way from playing a serious role in maritime warfare if they were to remain human-powered and deploy mines attached to spars as a weapon. Their appearances in the American Civil War remained episodes, although they gave rise to intensive further development of the submarine force. Confederates units definitely achieved success with the sinking and damaging of Union ships, and engineers and inventors in Europe and the United States turned to developing submarine drives and effective torpedoes which, for the first time, would made the submarine capable of serious deployment.

In 1897 the Irish-American inventor John Philip Holland made the decisive step towards implementing an effective submarine engine as the first



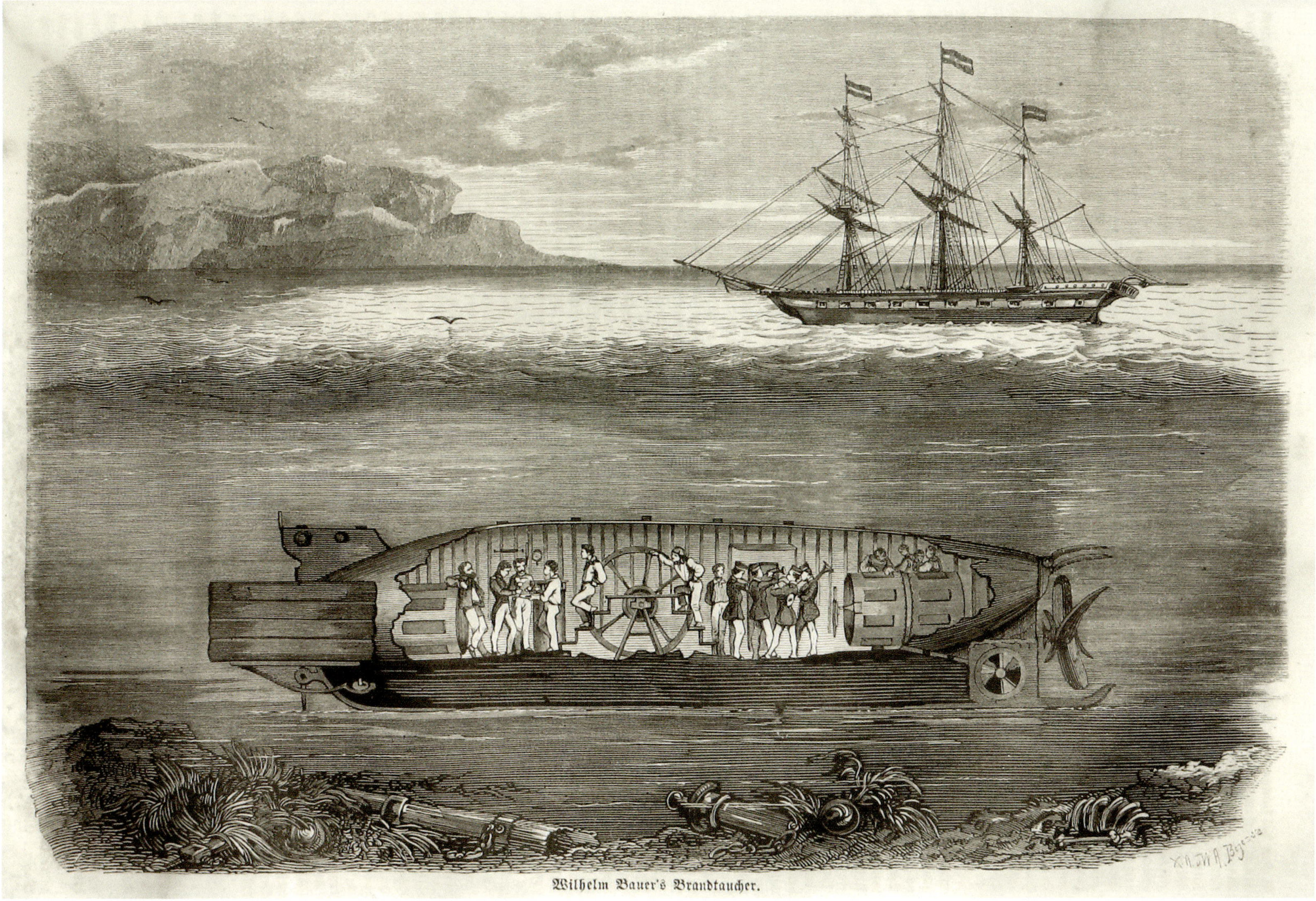
Wilhelm Bauer's Brandtaucher.

*This is how "Die Gartenlaube", a German newspaper, depicted the musical voyage of Bauer's SEETEUFEL in 1863. It is erroneously called BRANDTAUCHER in this picture.*

person to install an internal combustion engine below deck, which powered the boat above the surface and replenished batteries for submerged travel. The US Navy bought the boat after extensive testing in 1900 and deployed it as USS HOLLAND – the prototype for a whole range of other boats in various American and European navies. It was the "Holland" class that made the breakthrough for operational submarines.

The first submarines still used hazardous petrol as fuel. As it is highly inflammable, boats suffered plenty of smaller and the one or other large explosions. The first German submarines preferred petroleum as fuel, which not only had an acrid smell, but also developed highly visible, dense white fumes. Diesel, which came on board around 1910, became the reliable and safe energy source.

Only after the self-propelled torpedo be introduced did submarines become strategically usable. Sinkings had indeed been achieved by Robert Fulton with a spar torpedo in trials, and in 1805 he blew the DOROTHEA, a brig, out of the water within 20 seconds.[6] And during

*The USS HOLLAND was bought in 1900 at the suggestion of the then Deputy Secretary of the Navy, Theodore Roosevelt, and deployed by the United States Navy.*

the American Civil War, the world's first submersible to be used in war, the Confederate submarine HUNLEY sunk the Union troops' HOUSATONIC with a spar torpedo in 1864. However, HUNLEY went down too. According to recent theories, not because of the explosion, but rather as the crew perished from a lack of oxygen.

The self-propelled torpedo was (and still is) the right weapon for submarines, and the Whitehead torpedo, named after its builder Robert Whitehead, an English engineer, was prototype for all modern torpedoes.

He presented an initial version of it in 1866, powered with compressed air, now that after previous experiments – such as clockwork or flywheel drives – had proved ineffective. Two counter-rotating screws ensured a straight track – the first torpedoes could not be steered, that had to wait for later. After launching, early torpedoes ran straight ahead until they had reached their targets – or their fuel was consumed.

With the motorised and torpedo-armed submarine, a warship was created which introduced a new dimension of naval warfare strategies.

*The first submersible in the world to be used in war, the CSS H. L. HUNLEY, sank the HOUSATONIC of the Union troops with a spar torpedo on 6 December 1864.*

However, it necessitated a rethinking in the minds of senior naval officers accustomed to thinking in terms of big grey ships sailing stormy seas. New thinking was hard on them. Furthermore, they were caught up in a moral dilemma, demonstrated by the example of the Royal Navy, which had commissioned five submarines in 1900.[7] The old school admirals considered covert warfare to be principally illegal. Gentlemen fought, in their opinion, face to face and wore easily identifiable uniforms. So, the advocates of the submarine promised to proceed with caution and initially examine the *"value of submarines in the possession of our enemies"*. Rear Admiral A.K. Wilson made himself immortal with the much quoted dictum on the submarine: *"underhand, unfair and damned un-English"*. And so he advised the government to treat all submariners as pirates and simply hang them.



However, time and development quickly superseded the doughty Admiral. Despite the old ethical prejudices against submarines, the maritime world saw a sizeable submarine fleet on the seas on the eve of the First World War: England possessed the world's largest submarine fleet, with 74 units in service, 31 under construction and seven in planning. France followed with 62 boats in service and nine under construction, Russia had 48 boats in service, Germany had 28 in service and 17 under construction, the United States had 30 in service and ten under construction, Italy 21 in service and seven under construction, Japan 13 in service and three under construction, and Austria six in service and two under construction.[8] A total therefore of 282 commissioned submarines, with 79 to follow shortly, and the delivery of seven further was written in the stars.

However, nobody at the time knew how exactly to deal with the boats. No nation had developed methods for discovering submarines and attacking them after discovery. The answer to that question was critically important. Only a few weeks after the outbreak of the First World War, U 21, a German submarine sank the British cruiser PATHFINDER with only a single torpedo. The entry of the submarine into sea war had irrevocably changed naval warfare. The age of the submarine had dawned.

1
2
3
4
5
6
7
POYET

Fig. 1. — Torpille automobile Whitehead. — 1. Magasin. — 2. Chambre à secret. — 3. Réservoir d'air comprimé. — 4. Chambre des moteurs à air comprimé. — 5. Flotteur ou chambre de flottaison. — 6. Mécanisme de commande de rotation des hélices. — 7. Hélices et gouvernails.

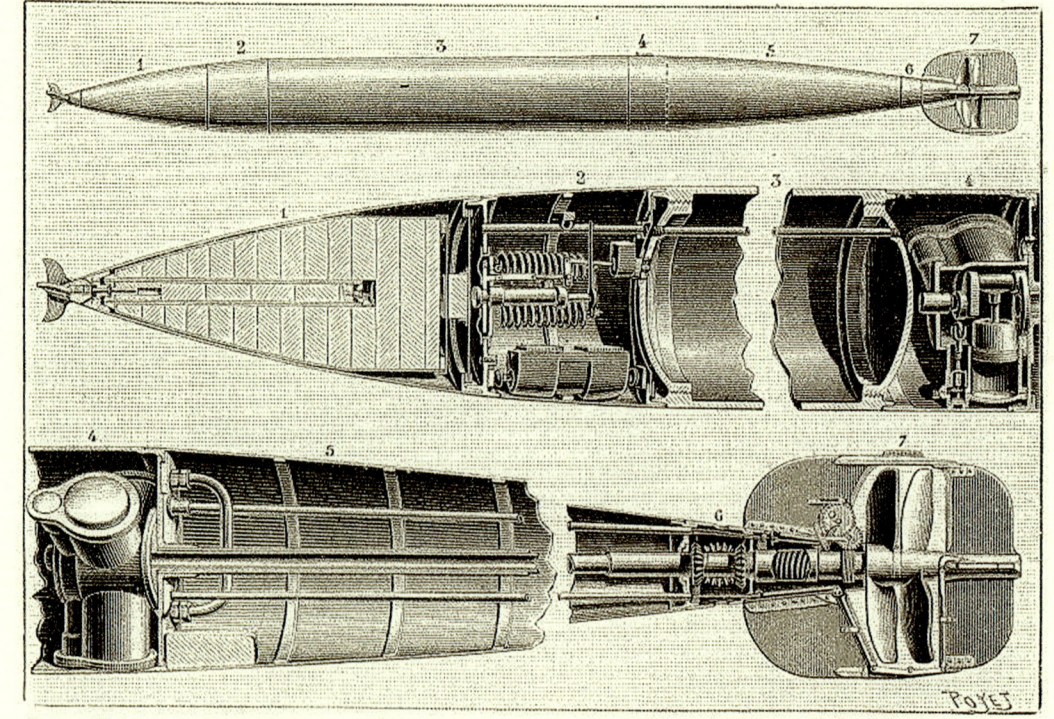

*The mechanism of the Whitehead torpedo, as published in the newspaper "La Nature" in 1891.*

# The Role of the Submarine in Modern Scenarios

Today, worldwide 41 navies have approximately 450 submarines, and this number is growing. Most navies are modernising their submarine fleets, increasing them, or both. By the year 2021, over 150 submarines will be added.[1] This will cost over USD 210 billion on today's calculations. Of this amount, the United States will spend USD 80 billion, the European countries together account for 70 billion, regional tensions in Asia will be responsible for spending of over USD 50 billion, and in Latin America primarily Brazil and Argentina are bearing the brunt of expenses to the call of USD 10 billion. In December 2013 this market study was underlined with two announcements: the Russian Agency RIA Novosti reported on 24 December the commissioning of the strategic nuclear submarine ALEXANDER NEWSKI (project 955 Borej), to be allocated to the Russian Pacific fleet and stationed on the Kamchatka peninsula. The third Borej class boat, WLADIMIR MONOMACH, will also be stationed here. Russian President Vladimir Putin wants to bring eight nuclear submarines into service by the year 2020.[2]

Two years earlier, the Washington Post reported that Pentagon planners were recommending in a study the deployment of one or more attack submarines in the Pacific as China's conduct in Yellow Sea was becoming increasingly aggressive,[3] well reflected in the dispute over the Senkaku Islands. For this reason, Japan and Australia are planning to increase spending on new submarines, and in December 2013 the Singapore Navy ordered two ultra-modern HDW Class 218 SG submarines in Kiel. So, it is hardly surprising at all, that ever more countries which so far had no submarines, are equipping themselves to protect their coastal and maritime areas in the face of the ongoing and emerging global conflicts of all kinds. China's rising defence spending – connected with the increasing threat of the Chinese Navy, and particularly the tensions around the integrity of islands in the Pacific Ocean – has meant that states in the Asian region are planning on higher spending on submarine capacities to counter the threat. Both Japan and Australia intend to enlarge their submarine fleets in the next ten to fifteen years.

Why submarines? In the past 100 years, the submarine has evolved into a solid and valuable strategic and operational part of a fleet as it is extremely flexible in use, and is a valuable addition to the other strategic resources of a nation's armed forces. In the past, the deployment and tactics of submarines have continuously evolved in step with technological progress.

The first submarines, navies acquired around the turn of the 20th century, were comparatively simple boats which largely functioned as surface ships. They sailed above the surface to their operational areas and only submerged to launch torpedo attacks. Similarly, escapes were also conducted dived after attacking. They could sink an enemy ship with some experience and a bit of good luck as their simple torpedoes could only run in a straight line. Today we would use a modern term to refer to this attack strategy: Anti Surface Warfare (ASuW)[4]. There were not very many countermeasures to it, and only the convoy system offered some degree of protection during the First World War.

In principle, nothing had changed in this strategy as the Second World War broke out. As earlier, the main task of submarines was to search for enemy war or merchant ships, and if possible sink them with a torpedo; submarines dived only to attack or escape. The main weapon was still the torpedo, albeit in an improved form. However, times for submariners had become tougher. Above all, German submarines that were being detected. The Allies had developed effective means to locate and combat submarines with radar and patrol aircraft. In the "Black May" of 1943, the Kriegsmarine, the German Navy, suffered the loss of 43 submarines. The answer was the introduction of the snorkel, which allowed submerged underwater travel and made the boat more difficult to detect. In addition, the Kriegsmarine developed better tactics and techniques to protect their boats. However, despite being called a "submarine", these submarines were still only submersible surface vessels. Thus the Kriegsmarine took

*Convoy WS-12 on the way to Cape Town in November 1941. A Vought SB2U Vindicator reconnaissance bomber searching for submarines.* (US Navy Naval Historical Center)

the decisive step to a real submarine with the Type XXI, whose design and construction was ordered by Admiral Karl Dönitz in 1943. The design of the 1,800 tonne Type XXI was so advanced that, after the Second World War, it became a model for all following submarines used by the navies of the United States, Great Britain and the Soviet Union. The small 250 tonne Type XXIII, a coastal submarine, which, in contrast to the Type XXI, was still employed at war's end, was created according to the same principle. The same design features finally were also shared by the Type XXVII – the midget submarine "Seehund" – of which around 300 boats had been built towards the end of the war. It was an act of desperation, this immature design was more dangerous for the crews than for the Allies.

In addition, German engineers examined a number of ways – apart from the snorkel – to develop genuine air-independent propulsion plants for submarines: the Walter turbine which used hydrogen peroxide as fuel, and the closed cycle diesel, whose waste gases were cleaned, enriched with oxygen and then fed back to the engine. These developments, however, remained stuck at the trial stage.

After the end of the Second World War, submarines remained an integral part of all major navies. During the Cold War, which more or less promptly started after active hostilities had ended, submarines had clear-cut tasks: they were to combat landing forces or high-value targets. In addition, conventional submarines could lay mines unobserved. Submarine attack was not one of their strengths, but the boats were capable of own defence. Their capacities were limited as their passive sensors only had a small ranges detection, and maximum speeds dived, essential for anti-submarine activities, were only available for short periods. Active sonar was only deployed if they had been detected by another submarine.

Sensors and armament were primarily designed to attack surface targets. Also, collecting information and reconnaissance missions were limited as periscopes and radar warning receivers of the time had little coverage and thus in-depth analysis was weak. Finally, communication back to the land base was difficult, boats could transmit and receive information via radio-telephone and radio-teletype, but could not pass the full accrued intelligence on. This was tactically only available to the boat itself. Improvements had to await the introduction of satellite communications[5].

*U-3008, Type XXI, and two Type IX boats in Wilhelmshaven, June 1945.* (US Navy)

On 30 September 1954, the US Navy commissioned the world's first nuclear submarine, USS NAUTILUS, and this vessel was a game changer for naval warfare. The reactor gave the submarine totally new qualities – it was a boat that could stay submerged for months and maintain high speeds in the depths of the ocean. Proof was provided in 1958 when USS NAUTILUS sailed under North Pole, and in 1960 as USS TRITON circumnavigated the globe dived. The only restrictions were the amount of provisions and the state of crew morale. Breathing oxygen was extracted from sea water.

The US were not alone for long with nuclear submarines, the Russian Navy was hard on the heels of the United States Navy, and in 1958 commissioned its first nuclear submarine, the K-3 LENINSKY KOMSOMOL. It was a typical product of the arms race with the United States, for all its performance it was immature, prone to breakdowns and dangerous for the crew. Still, the navies of the two great powers had recognized the strategic value of submarines fitted with the new drive and were pushing its development at all costs – especially in the USSR. The nuclear submarine became the Leviathan of the Cold War and took maritime warfare into a new dimension.

However, the USS NAUTILUS and its Russian successor were still equipped with torpedoes, the weaponry of the Second World War, but the big step that changed them into modern nuclear submarines was introduction of ballistic missiles. On 30 December 1959, the United States Navy put the USS GEORGE WASHINGTON (SSBN-598) into service – the world's first nuclear submarine armed with ballistic missiles. Again Russian response came quickly as the Soviet Navy put its first "Hotel" Class – the infamous K 19 – missile submarine into service on 12 November 1960. The successful launch of two Polaris A1 missiles in July 1960 was the a pivotal moment for nuclear submarines as they demonstrated their sovereign prowess. They could remain undetected and ensure that a first strike would not checkmate own nuclear capabilities. In addition to ballistic missiles, the navies of the 60s were already deploying cruise missiles. The submarine, as part of the nuclear deterrence philosophy of the Cold War, had now become a strategical instrument of great powers, which included Great Britain and France.[6] Today, further navies rely on nuclear submarines, together with India and China six in all – the seed sown by Admiral Hyman Rickover has flourished.

The superpowers' nuclear-powered submarines played a prominent role during the Cold War. The United States deployed 41 boats with ballistic missiles in the following years, and 104 hunter and attack submarines.

*Rear Admiral Hyman George Rickover, US Navy, is regarded as the "Father of the Nuclear Navy" and as Director of Naval Reactors managed their operations for decades.*

(US Naval Historical Center, 1955)

*Launching USS NAUTILUS on 21 January 1954.* (US Navy)

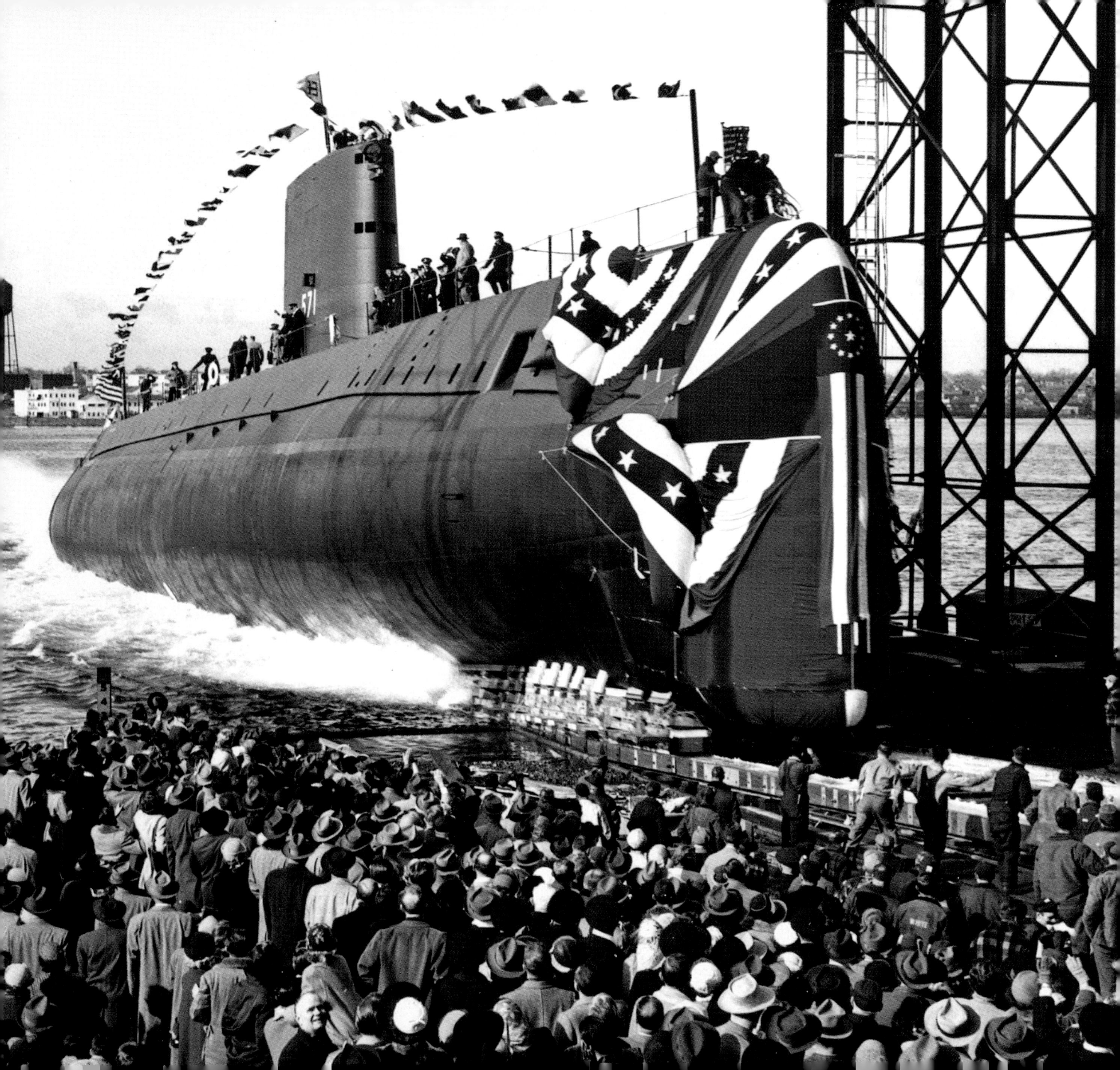
571

The figures for the Soviet Navy are far higher as the USSR attached higher priorities to their submarine force [7]. Seen from the outside, the superpowers in the Cold War played cat and mouse with each other. This harmless abstraction might perhaps conceal the fact that they conducted a secret, dogged fight, which, however, was not to escalate into open conflict. Both sides conducted numerous covert and highly risky operations to collecting as much information about each's foe as possible. And that did not rule out occasional serious confrontations. Collisions between American and Russian submarines did happen, and some accidents sometimes ended tragically.

Bizarre events happened, such as when the Russian diesel submarine that ran around off a Swedish naval base; this *faux-pas* went down in history as "Whisky on the rocks". But the nuclear submarine remained a constant threat to the world with its secret launch bases in the dark depths of the Seven Seas.

During the Cold War, submarines fulfilled Admiral Chester W. Nimitz's prophecy of 1945. They became the ships of the future. Maxim Worcester wrote: *"Dominion over the sea is today rather under than above the surface. The Falklands War clearly proved this in 1982. This short war in the South Atlantic showed that even well manned and modern surface vessels cannot defend themselves against high-performance jet fighters, and certainly not against nuclear-powered attack submarines."* [8] And he continues: *"The era of the submarine as a dominant weapon at sea has begun..."*

## CHALLENGES IN THE 21ST CENTURY

In the 20th century, the submarine grew into its role with the growing technical achievements and skills as well as increasing experience. In the 21st century, it will have to live up to it. In the last hundred years, it has already played a decisive role in various conflicts which took place on the stage of conventional warfare and conflict resolution – most recently in the Cold War. In the future, however, it will need to take on tasks which are untraditional and differ from conventional warfare – to sink enemy ships or to block sea lanes.

The world's security situation has changed dramatically. After 11 September 2001, politicians and the general public have had to come to terms with the fact that, although the Cold War is over, neither has peace come about, nor has promised democracy, freedom and prosperity for all. The opposite has occurred: in the last two decades, we have experienced serious political and military crises and armed conflicts in Europe, Africa, the Middle and the Far East. They still continue, and threats have by no means disappeared. The Cold War was predictable, and had a certain kind of stability and thus security. The players were known and to a certain extent predictable in their actions and reactions. The global conflict between two ideological camps, controlled by two all-powerful superpowers in the West and East, pushed local conflicts into the background. Understanding and compromise between the two camps was possible. A prime example was how it was ultimately possible to avert the dramatic Cuban missile crisis.

The globe has become less safe since the end of the Cold War. Our once well organised world, with its closely interwoven economies, is now exposed to new threats which know no national boundaries. The battle for shrinking resources has begun. Oil production has peaked and the struggle for remaining reserves has long been conducted behind closed doors. The natural resources under Arctic ice has incited desire amongst all of the Arctic Ocean's stakeholders. This is becoming a dangerous hotspot.

China's aggressive expansion into the Red Sea, for similar reasons, has put the entire region on alert, with the result that neighbours are dramatically upgrading naval forces – not least with modern submarines. The wave of conflicts has produced massive streams of refugees around the world, and religious and ethnic intolerances ensuring further violence. Now the effects of climate change are beginning to show, and this will have an impact on international security. And finally, an old phenomenon is coming back to life, which were attributed to times long past: piracy. It is now crueller, better organised and better equipped than ever before. Threatening sea lanes is a direct attack on the closely intertwined global economy; 90 % of all goods are transported by sea.

New actors have appeared on the scene. We are facing a global asymmetrical threat posed by so-called "rogue states", but also by terrorist organisations and global crime which has long been organised. They have no concern or respect for the Hague international treaties, they are unpredictable and they operate in the dark with every possible means against any target. These campaigns are not only aimed against soldiers, but against defenceless civilian populations – women, men, children and the elderly are not spared. And it also does not adhere to law and order. These "new wars" are reminiscent of the Thirty Years' War, and are far removed from the regular wars of the last century.

The Cold War was characterised by the confrontation of two large, solidly cemented blocks with differing ideologies, and in military terms by the doctrine of nuclear deterrence of the superpowers. After its end, strategists had to think again. The number of conflicts has increased all over the world, but at lower contention levels. This leads to the doctrine of thinking "from the sea". About 70 per cent of the world's population live on or in the vicinity of the sea. So, it is understandable that the largest part of all existing or potential threats and conflicts are at, or within easy reach of the sea. Navies therefore also have their share of prevention, conflict resolution, or the battle against terrorism and piracy, as well as the protection of own coasts. Unlike during the Cold War, the field of battle is now no longer in the midst of the vast oceans, but directly off coasts in shallow waters.

These littoral waters are not the deployment field of the Cold War's nuclear submarines. Here these beasts are the dinosaurs of a past era – they are simply too big. Rather it is the smaller, non-nuclear submarine that can operate close to under the coast for the operations in the littorals. Even the United States has got the message, and that "Admiral Rickover's boys" and the singular use of nuclear submarines – quite right in the Cold War – are antiquated in the face of new threats and scenarios. The United States are now contemplating whether returning to conventional submarines. But they no longer have experience to build them – or alternatively deploy "host submarines", nuclear submarines supported when needed by small submarines. This may explain the fact that the US Navy has conducted trials with a borrowed Swedish submarine.[9]

## THE MODERN SUBMARINE

The submarine has grown into its new role. No other independently operating ship has comparable properties of deterrence or threat. Its outstanding features are stealth, initiative, ability to survive, freedom of movement in three dimensions, flexibility, and endurance. Taken together, this produces a deployment advantage and potential at sea, which will deter even a superior opponent – and not only in theory.[10/11]

The submarine is the perfect stealth ship. It operates under the surface of the sea, in a medium that is generally non-permissive to discovery of the boat, or to countermeasures. Once submerged, it is virtually invisible to all antisubmarine defence forces with the exception of the most powerful. Its invisibility gives it around-the-clock protection and significantly helps it to successfully carry out mandates. The importance of these properties has increased to the extent that nations have taken to building regional and global maritime monitoring systems. The monitoring of the sea with aircraft, satellites, surface and underwater sensors makes it almost impossible to hide forces on the ocean's surface. And that increases the value of the stealth properties of submarines.

The covert use of a submarine is fundamental to its military value. But at the same time, it also means that the boat can be used and locally unnoticed in times of increasing political tension, without thereby exacerbating the crisis. Once the crisis passes, it can be quietly withdrawn again. Initiative means the ability of the submarine to prevent an opponent from knowing where it is located and how many more submarines are in the vicinity. That gives it the advantage of surprise, because the master has the freedom to decide if, when or how he will reveal himself to the opponent.

Survival capacity is the ability to operate in a hostile environment with no or little risk. A submarine needs only dive to dodge most threats. Surface warships are, by contrast, exposed to attacks with underwater weapons, ground and air forces – but not the submarine. This relative invulnerability allows it to work without accompaniment. The survival capacity of the submarine also proves itself in the context of weapons systems that still in development, but could have severe consequences for surface ships, such as electromagnetic pulse and high power microwave weapons that can inflict heavy damage or even destroy microcircuits, radar equipment, computers, sensors, communications networks and other electronic systems. Further thermobaric rockets and bombs are already in use, which generate enormous heat and pressure at relatively small sizes, and finally work is going on to develop sonic weapons and high speed projectiles which use electromagnetic instead of chemical drives. Generally speaking, submarines are invulnerable to such weapons.[12]

Submarines are characterised by great endurance in use. They can journey to their deployment area and stay there for a long time, without the need of replenishment. American nuclear-powered submarines usually have supplies for 90 days and remain underwater for 60 or more days. They can even carry supplies for up to 120 days. Smaller conventional submarines achieve considerable underwater stays too. For example, the commander of the Argentine submarine ARA SAN LUIS reported that he could go on patrol for at least 60 days with his conventional diesel-electric 1,200 tonne HDW Class 209 boat during the Falklands War. The gap between the nuclear submarine and the conventional submarine is filled by submarines with air independent propulsion plants (AIP) – based on either a Fuel Cell, the Stirling engine or the MESMA turbine. The Fuel Cell is the most powerful system. ThyssenKrupp Marine Systems/HDW estimates the underwater travel capacity of types 212A and 214 to be at about three weeks, whereas the specialist press reports 50 days and far beyond. Submarines can stay at sea far longer than surface ships without having to replenish on board fuel supplies.

The submarine has freedom of movement in contrast to surface vessels. It can move with relative impunity from place to place and choose the point of deployment – including places where surface warships cannot be used. And in these areas the submarine can change its location at will, as the tactical situation requires. Finally, a submerged submarine is immune to bad weather and rough seas. Its properties of stealth, endurance and mobility give the submarine the opportunity to exert influence over large sea areas, even if its weapons can only reach a relatively small part of the theatre of operations. Since, however, surface warships do not know the location of the boat, they must suspect it everywhere and operate with corresponding caution. They are in a relatively weak position.[13]

Thanks to its sensors and weapons systems, the modern submarine is incredibly flexible. That is particularly beneficial in use in shallow water off coasts at depths of up to 200 metres. There, surface vessels are increasingly exposed to asymmetric or terrorist attacks. Here in particular,

*Submarine in covert operation off the coast.* (YPS Peter Neumann)

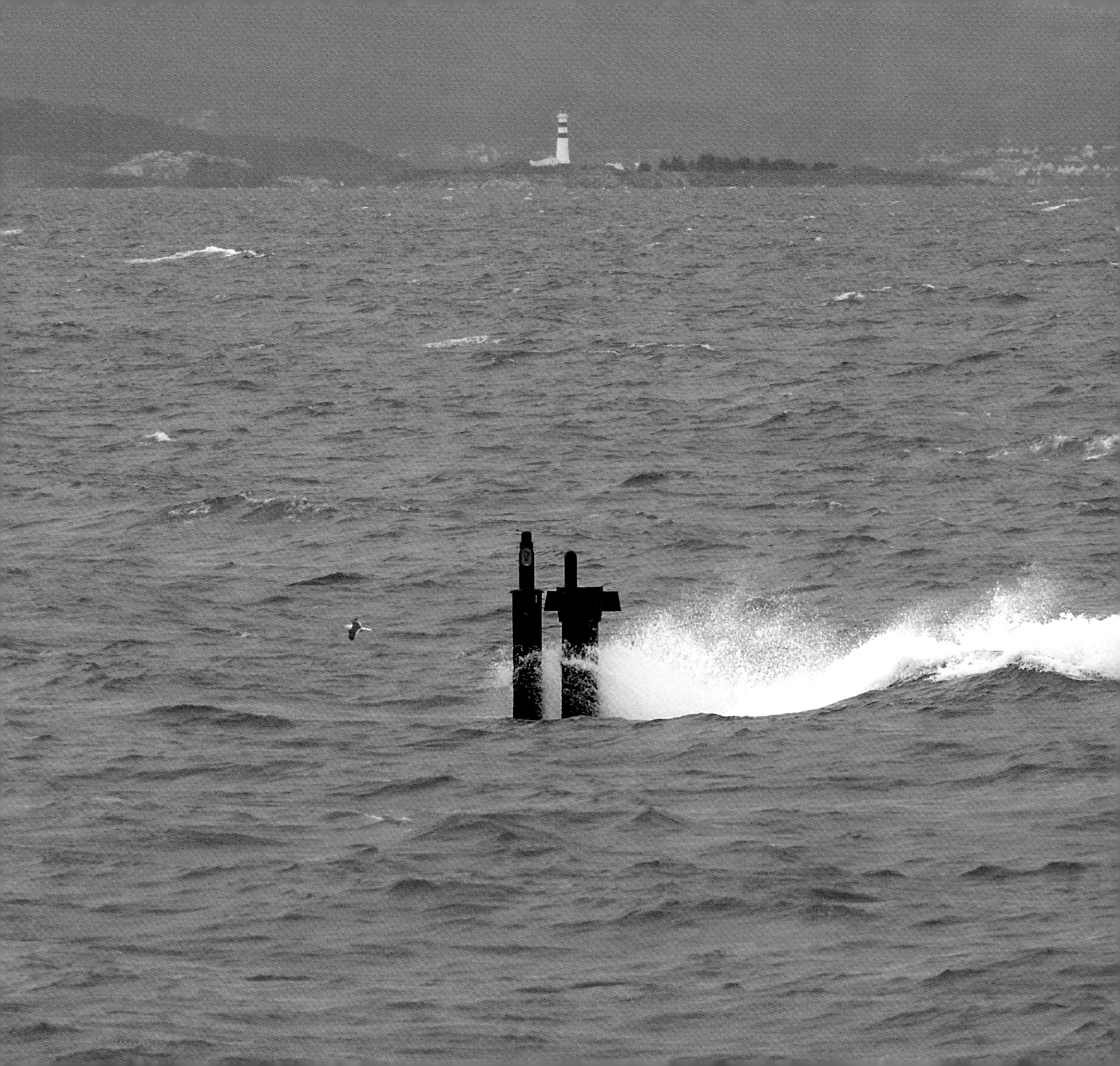

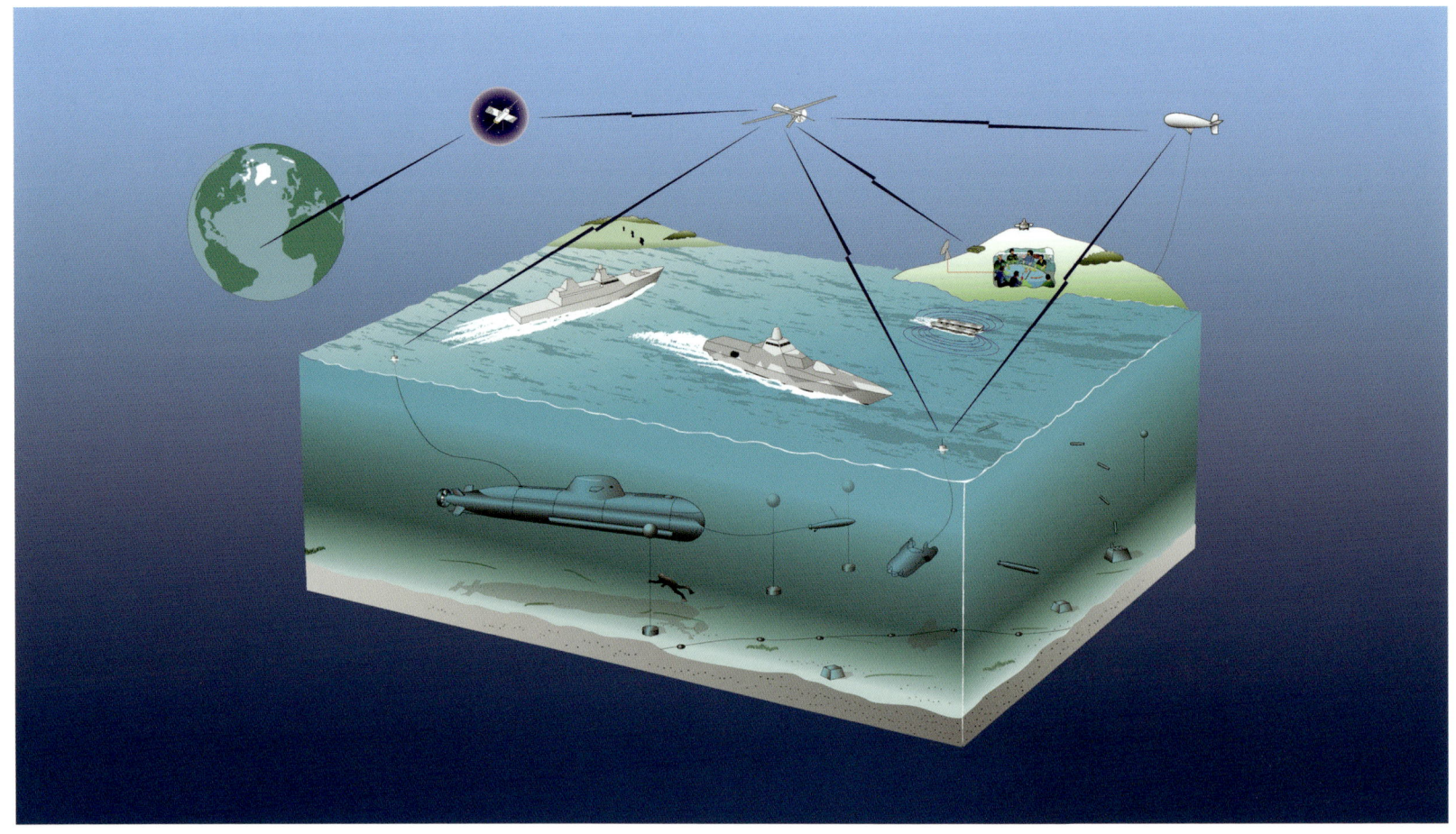

*The role of the submarine in modern scenarios.* (Source: Kockums)

conventional non-nuclear boats have the edge over nuclear submarines. And they can perform their tasks with relatively low risk. These include:

▶ Covert observation and reconnaissance in coastal waters,
▶ Police and civilian surveillance and intervention in collaboration with other institutions for combating piracy, smuggling, drug trafficking, illegal fishing and organised crime, etc,
▶ Patrols to monitor ship trading routes and disputed Exclusive Economic Zones (EEC) of individual nations,
▶ Collect undetected covert electronic intelligence, for example from frequencies and transmitters that can be monitored only at short distances.
▶ Conduct tactical and strategic operations against land targets, in the future also with sea-to-ground missiles of different sizes, ranging up to cruise missiles,[14]
▶ Conduct mine laying and seeking missions, support land commandos or deploy or unmanned vehicles, and finally conduct so-called "ground mapping" – the exact cartographic recording of coastal sea beds in preparation of landing operations.
▶ Furthermore, in a single mission, a submarine is not limited to one of the tasks, but can typically perform several assignments at the

same time, or one after the other, depending on what the strategic, operational or tactical situation requires. It can also adjust flexibly to a change of location.

The Second World War was the age of the "Wolf Packs". They have passed. Today, the submarine is a lone wolf. The former Knights of the Depths, enshrined in submarine myths, have become IT specialists on highly complex and computerised systems. And this is precisely what allows the boat to operate alone – albeit in the context of diverse and global communications with its deployment location and in collaboration with other maritime, land and air forces. The term "Network Centric Warfare", in which the boat is integrated, describes a concept in which all reconnaissance, leadership and active systems are networked and therefore have information superiority. It integrates all parts of the armed forces, allows them to achieve the effective cooperation of all units and ultimately gives them superiority in joint operations.

Modern submarines appear to be at first look expensive. Critics complain that even poor countries are acquiring increasing numbers of boats. They overlook the fact that these states are increasingly threatened on their coasts. And the fact that only a few boats are needed to defend themselves against aggressors of all kinds makes the submarine asset significantly less expensive in relation to otherwise necessary costs for a powerful surface fleet. Regardless of this, the acquisition and maintenance costs of even an AIP submarine over its lifetime are much less than for a large surface unit. This does not mean that submarines can completely replace a fleet of surface vessels. Rather, experience suggests that a mixture of submarines and surface ships create a highly effective team. The submarine therefore makes sense as an integral part of a navy, and on that basis, has a future.

Today, the greatest value of the submarine is not its great ability to attack, but its deterrent force. The mere assumption of one or more submarines loitering in a sea area will be sufficient to prevent attacks or even wars. 2,500 years ago, Sun Tzu knew *"Those who render the opposing army helpless, without letting it come to a fight, are the truly excellent ones."*[15] This has been shown in the history of warfare again and again. An early example is the history of Bauer's BRANDTAUCHER in the German-Danish war of 1851, in which, although the boat had only just completed its first test run, the rumour of its existence was enough to force the Danish fleet to back off blockading Kiel. Such examples can be repeated indefinitely.

The submarine is a means of sending diplomatic signals. Its presence can be announced officially through its services, discreetly through diplomatic channels, or through the media when public attention is desirable.[16] This can be used for the escalation as also the de-escalation of conflicts. For example, take the Cuban missile crisis. The United States ordered the USS ABRAHAM LINCOLN, a nuclear submarine, to put to sea from Scotland, where the Russians promptly discovered it, which was doubtlessly the intention. On the one side, this served a military purpose, but it was also a strategic signal to put pressure on the USSR. Ultimately, the crisis was resolved peacefully. And finally, there are persistent rumours about the Israeli DOLPHIN class submarines, which are claimed to be able to fire cruise missiles with nuclear warheads. Experts assume that the rumours might be true, but there is no solid evidence. It is certain that these rumours, no matter whether true or not, are useful to remind Israel's opponents of the need for restraint and thus avoid a war.

The fact that today over 40 nations have submarines underlines the value of the modern submarine – and more are being added. It is not only a varied and versatile instrument of maritime management and national security, but also supports the foreign policy of a nation on a wide range of tasks.[17]

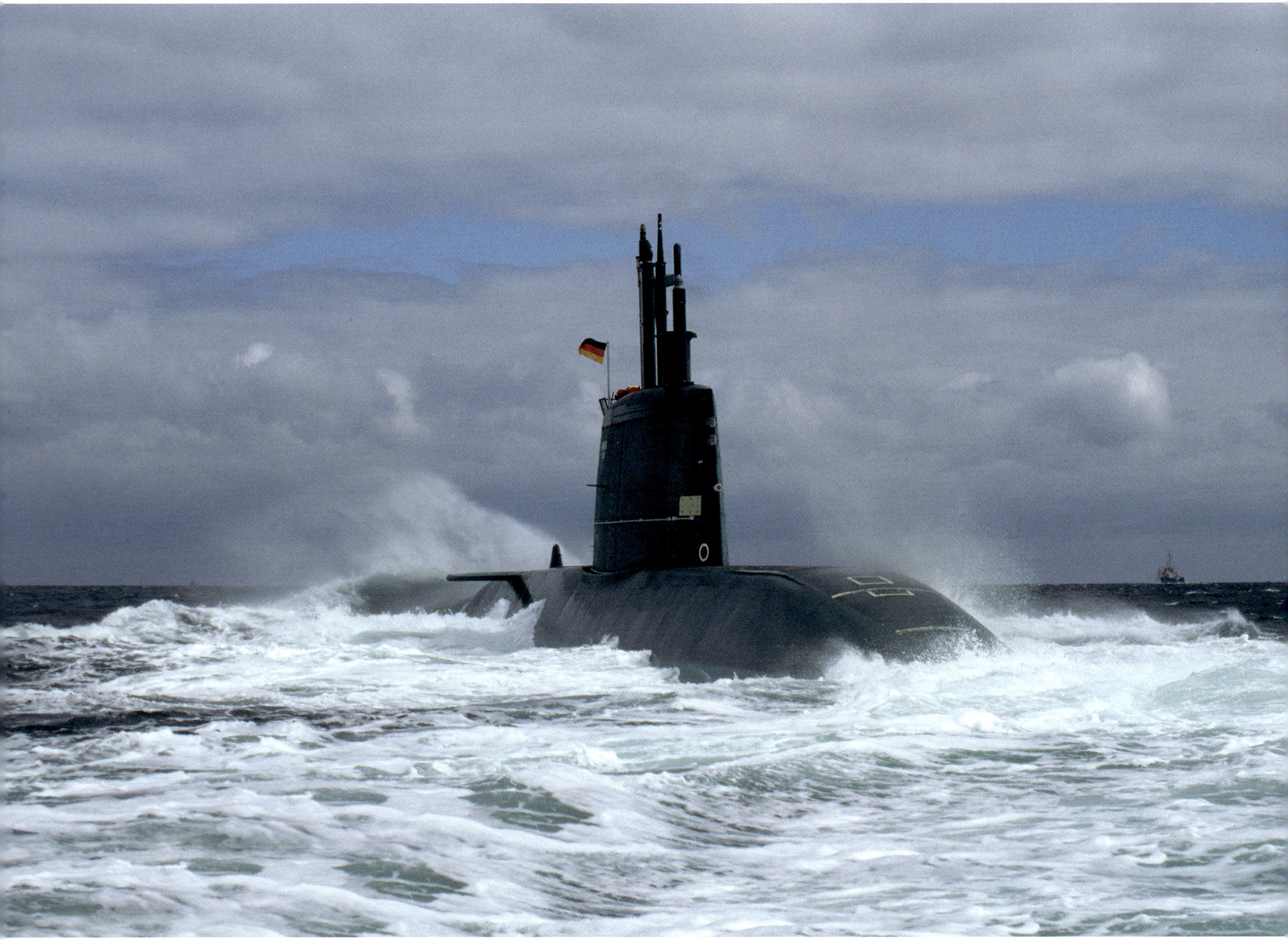

*The DOLPHIN Class submarine – fitted with cruise missiles?* (YPS Peter Neumann)

# Germany Builds Submarines

Around the turn of the 20th century, the submarine was already an inherent part of the many navies' fleets and no longer the technical curiosity of enthusiasts, dreamers and inventors. In particular, the American Civil War had been the nucleus for underwater vehicles, which were able to prove their suitability for military operations for the first time. This created a huge boost for the development of new types of submarine, and evermore navies deployed these boats as a supplement to their fleets.

Shortly after the beginning of the 20th century, already twelve nations had taken up the new arms race. England, America, France, Holland, Italy, Greece, Japan, Portugal, Russia, Spain, Sweden and Turkey participated in it with great zeal.[1] This was not the case with the young Imperial Navy, which didn't know where to begin with the new boats. Instead it relied on large cruisers and ships of the line, complemented with fast torpedo boats. The abstinence against the new weapon is generally attributed to Grand Admiral Alfred von Tirpitz, who created the German high seas fleet. But he was not alone in his assessment. For example, the then-prestigious German shipbuilding expert Carl Busley opined as late as 1899 that: *"The still present and fairly significant technical inferiority of undersea vehicles, which cannot easily be mastered particularly as regards their low longitudinal stability, secure them no great prospects for the future. ... It can therefore be only right for the German naval administration, if it has not yet engaged in costly and protracted trials with submarines, but has confined itself only to the construction of battleships, cruisers, and sea-going torpedo vessels."* [2] Regardless of the fact that it is rumoured that Admiral von Tirpitz pushed him to make this statement, the facts seemed to bear out Busley.

Actually, it appears that only two submarines, and possibly a third were built in Germany up to 1900 after BRANDTAUCHER [3] – with less than moderate success. A small submersible fitted with a steam engine, designed by Friedrich Otto Vogel, and suitable for surface and underwater travel, was built between 1867 and 1870 at the Schlick shipyard in Dresden. But apparently it did not do much more than conduct trials on the Elbe.

In 1897, the Howaldtswerke built under hull number 333 an "experimental vessel" according to the proposals of a German naval officer – probably the torpedo engineer Karl Leps – which also was not much of a success, apart from the fact that Kaiser Wilhelm II is supposed to have seen it on the Kiel Bay, surfaced in 1901. It never made manned dives. And because there was understandably no interest in this boat, it ended up in the scrapyard.[4] The alleged existence of a third boat of which a photo – possibly from 1891 – exists is mysterious; it was supposedly taken at the Howaldtswerke, but no further information is available.

This was not the end of German submarine dreams, however, which led to at least 181 proposals and offers of the Prussian, North German and Imperial Navy between 1861 and 1900.[5] On the contrary, they came true when the Krupp Group of Essen, which had recently taken over the Germaniawerft in Kiel, took up the case. It saw good prospects for profitable business deals with submarines, and its foresight turned out to be right. This great opportunity emerged in 1902 when the Spanish engineer Raimondo Lorenzo d'Equevilley-Montjustin offered Krupp not only his services, but his own submarine design. Previously he had spent some time employed at the major French designer Maxime Laubeuf, who had heralded a new era in submarine building with his NARVAL submarine. Its double-hull concept was the basis of most submarines all over the world until after the Second World War.

D'Equevilley therefore brought profound know-how and promising hardware when he moved to Krupp. The result was – we remark in passing – a series of suspicions and speculations, especially of course in French circles, that d'Equevilley had taken French submarine plans to Germany.[6] This suspicion, which the Germaniawerft of course rejected, has been to this day neither confirmed nor excluded. Krupp signed a long-term contract with him, and the construction of the first submarine, FORELLE, began in 1902. Although Kaiser Wilhelm II and Prince Heinrich visited the boat in the year after that – Prince Heinrich even personally helmed it on a diving trip – the first customer was the Russian Navy, which was impressed by the handling characteristics of the boat. In 1904, it bought three more of the approximately 200-tonne submarines, KARP, KARASS and KAMBALA in addition to the small FORELLE with its displacement of 15.5 tonnes.

*Experimental boat FORELLE in 1902 during trials on the Kiel fjord.* (Archive TKMS/HDW)

*Trial submarine, Howaldtswerke build nr. 333 in Kiel, 1897.* (Archive TKMS/HDW)

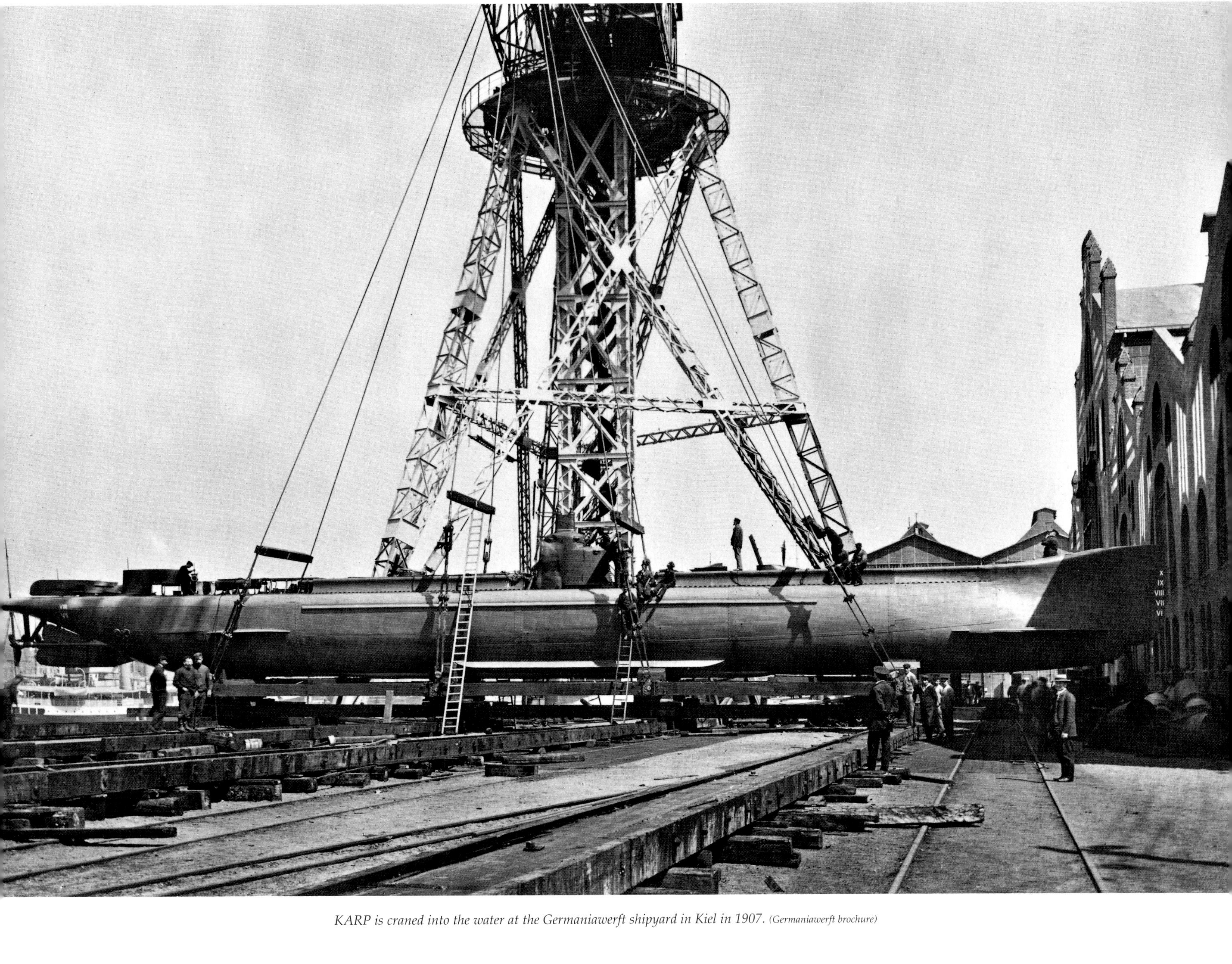
X
IX
VIII
VII
VI

*KARP is craned into the water at the Germaniawerft shipyard in Kiel in 1907.* (Germaniawerft brochure)

Meanwhile, the Navy was officially still not much in favour of submarines. Their Torpedo Inspectorate, however, had its eye on the boats after the successes of the French submarine force, participated in test runs on the FORELLE and proposed the construction of an experimental submarine for testing purposes. To start with, it was biting on granite. But resistance slowly crumbled. Although Tirpitz still in 1904 brushed off the Parliamentarian Wilhelm von Kardorff, who dared publicly to ask him the question why the Navy had not previously thought of the construction of submarines, to which he succinctly answered that he did not think much of submarines.[7] But in fact he commissioned the Technical Department of the Imperial Navy secretly to seek out a suitable younger official who should construct a submarine in the German Imperial Naval Office. The naval architect Gustav Berling received the order and was assigned to the Torpedo Inspectorate. And in 1904, the Navy commissioned the Germania shipyard to build a submarine based on the plans of the Russian KARP Class – the later U 1, the first submarine of the Imperial Navy; in service in 1906.



Things, however, remained there at first. Three other boats were to be built at the Imperial Shipyard in Danzig and the Germaniawerft sought further orders from the Navy, but was stonewalled as it was reluctant to give its design documents to a shipyard which was that successful in the international submarine business. Whatever, the Germaniawerft nevertheless succeeded in bringing ashore a number of contracts on foreign accounts, such as boats for the Austria-Hungarian Empire, Italy and Norway. But the main reason lay in the person of the foreigner d'Equevilley, who had made enemies not least through his clumsy tactics.[8]

At the suggestion of Berling, he was replaced by the naval architect Dr.-Ing Hans Techel in 1907. He had begun his career at the Germaniawerft in 1895, and after a detour through the Howaldtswerke from

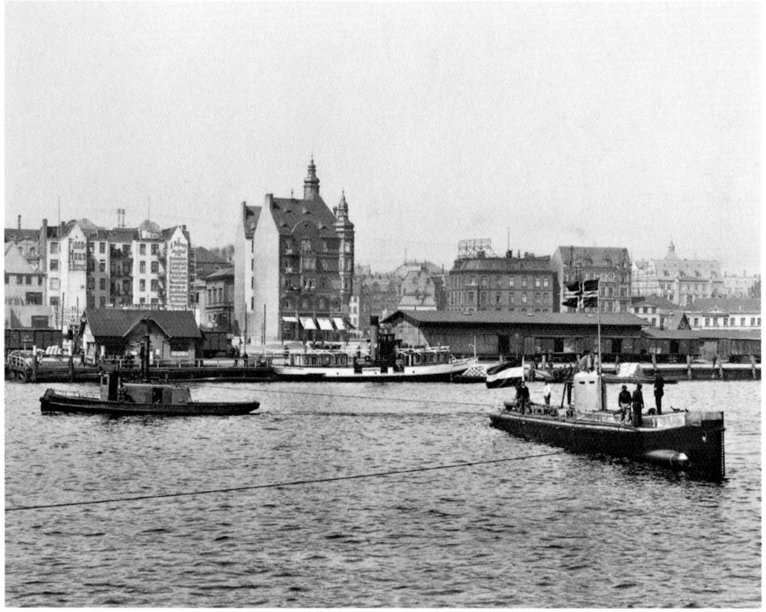

*KOBBEN, built in 1908 for the Norwegian Navy, after launching in Kiel's harbour.*

*(Germaniawerft brochure)*

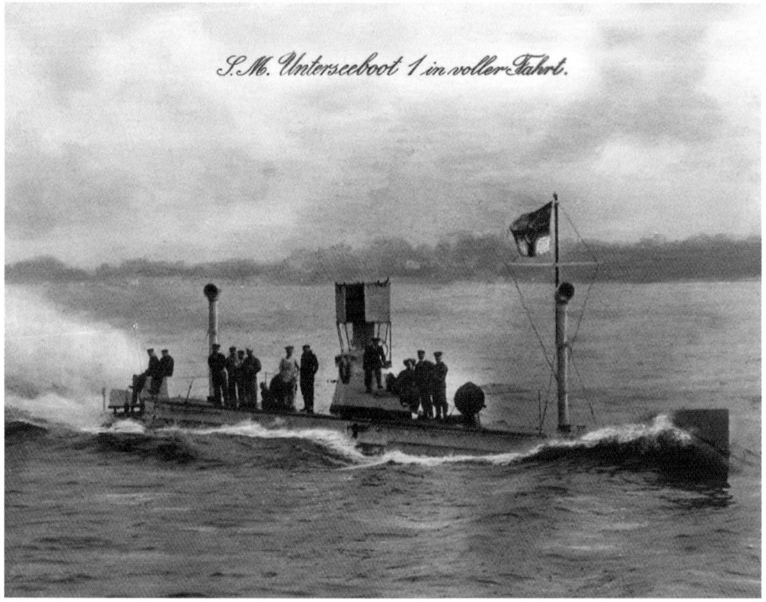
S.M. Unterseeboot 1 in voller Fahrt.

*The first submarine of the Imperial Navy, U 1, in 1906.*

*At the stern exhaust vapour of the petroleum engine. (Contemporary postcard)*

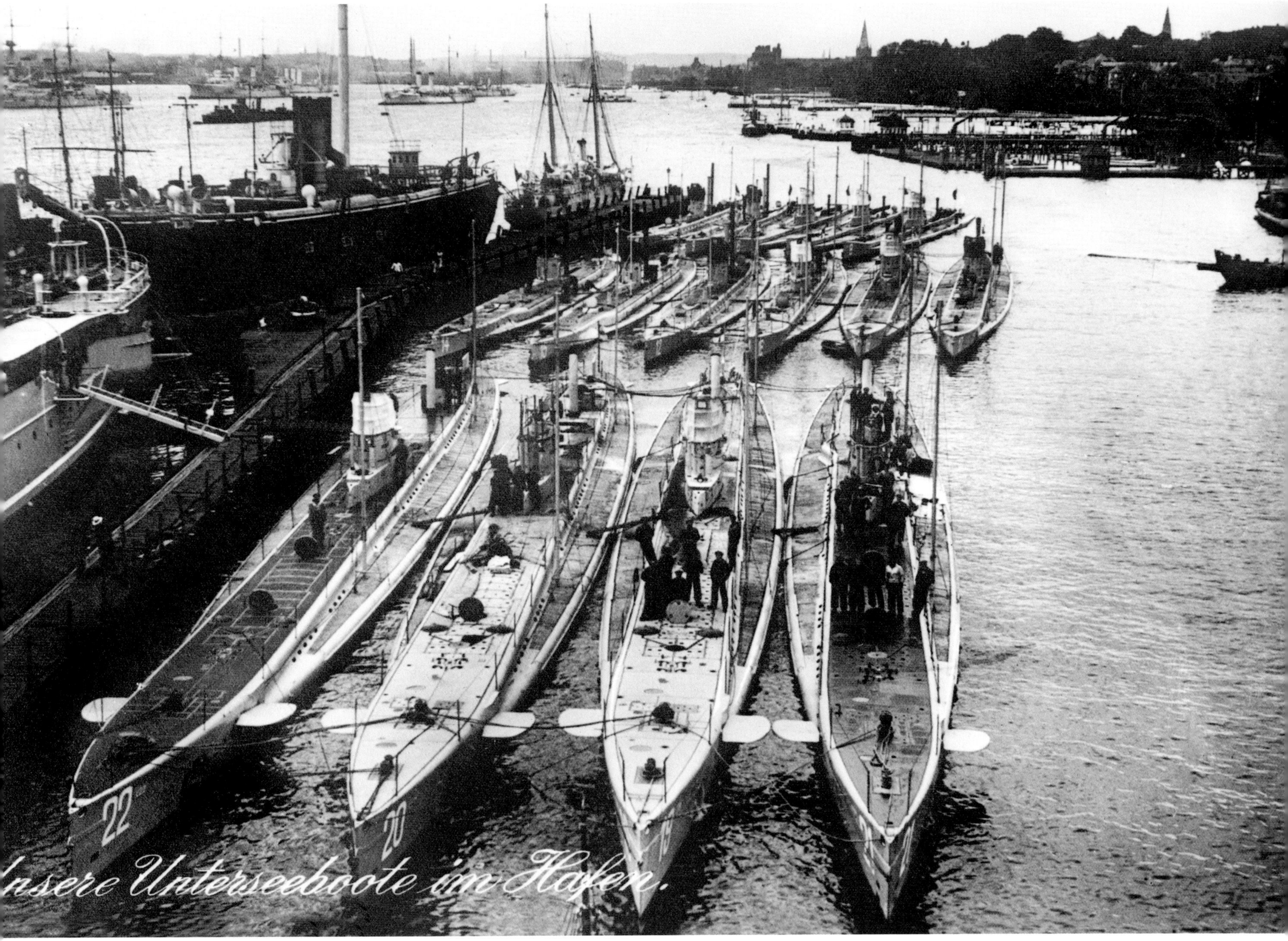
nsere Unterseeboote im Hafen.

*Submarines of the Imperial Navy in 1914 Kiel's harbour. In the foreground U 19 to 22 – the first submarines of the Imperial Navy to be equipped with diesel engines.*

1901 until 1907, where he mostly worked on warships, had returned to Germania. The success story of modern German submarine construction starts with this unusually gifted man, who forced the rapid development of new submarine designs which cumulated in technical progress – the boats became bigger and more powerful. At the same time, Techel's appointment encouraged a successful cooperation between the Germania shipyard and the Navy. During the First World War, he and capable, imaginative designers working in his office, developed numerous different submarine types for especially at the Germaniawerft, but also for AG Weser in Bremen, Vulcan AG in Stettin and Blohm+Voss in Hamburg.

And at the end of the war, Germany had arguably the world's most powerful submarine industry with particularly sophisticated constructions. This however changed nothing about the fact that the war had been lost and the Versailles Treaty ordered the extradition of the German submarine fleet to Britain, and the scrapping of non-extraditable boats. Article 191, moreover, stipulated that Germany was prohibited to continue the construction and acquisition of submarines – even for merchant purposes.

Nevertheless, between the two world wars, German know-how had a direct and indirect influence on the development of submarine construction worldwide. The only exceptions were Britain, and to a lesser extent the Soviet Union. All major navies of the victorious Allies – Britain, France, Italy, Japan and the United States had received copies of the latest German submarines under the provisions of the cease-fire and the Treaty of Versailles. The plans were thoroughly investigated and analysed to determine whether the designs were suitable to be implemented in own developments. And in some cases, various German submarines re-entered service with afore mentioned navies for them to gather experience. In particular, France and Italy were strongly influenced by the medium sized vessels and the UB III types as they developed their own first post-war submarines. The German submarine cruiser had even greater impact. The highly seaworthy French REQUIN class benefited particularly from the design of this submarine cruiser. The big US Navy boats also owed much to the German templates – including, their diesel drive chains – and German engineers were deeply involved in the development of the early Japanese KAIDAI and JUNSEN classes.

## SUBMARINE BUILDING IN DISGUISE: INGENIEURSKANTOOR VOOR SCHEEPSBOUW (IVS), THE ENGINEERING OFFICE FOR MARITIME CONSTRUCTION

For Germany, the Treaty of Versailles' terms meant not only the renunciation of a submarine defence, but were also a major blow to the shipyards. Thus now the Navy and the shipyards therefore looked for ways to circumvent the Treaty and maintain and expand the design and development capabilities of German designers. But what ultimately mattered, was to have modern boat designs for the time when Germany would once again be permitted to have submarines, and to build them.

Thus began the secret development of a new generation of German submarines. The players did not suffer from bad consciences as the Treaty of Versailles' terms were generally regarded as unjust and too harsh. Furthermore, the Navy considered it to be intolerable that it had no submarines to ward of sea attacks; it saw Germany exposed to risks that other nations could exploit the favourable opportunity and take over German islands, coastal towns and fishing bases.

The Treaty of Versailles stipulated the delivery of German submarines to the victorious powers, or the scrapping of them, but it said nothing about the construction documents and construction plans. So the German shipyards promptly retained what they had. And in addition

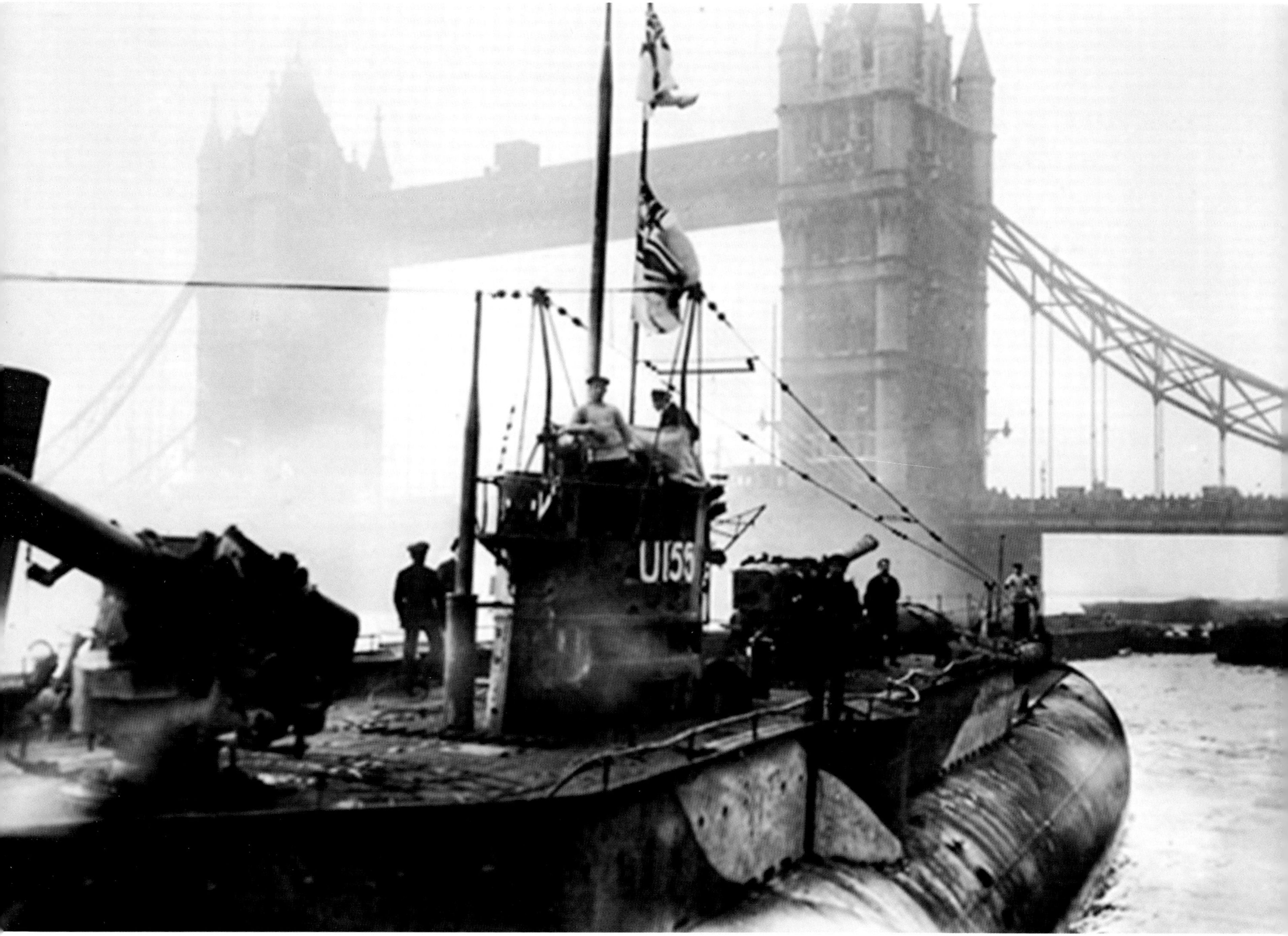
U155

*Submarine Cruiser U 155, formerly the merchant submarine DEUTSCHLAND, after the transfer to England in 1919 in front of Tower Bridge in London.* (Photographer unknown)

to these invaluable documents, they still had a base of skilled engineers, designers and experienced workers.

Thus German shipyards began, with the approval and support of the Navy Board, the trade with blueprints, engineers and consultants with neutral and friendly nations – and to develop and eventually exploit existing know-how. Japan became the first customer in 1920. Under the partly personal leadership of Dr. Hans Techel, the Japanese Navy built the submarines I 1-3 and I 21-24 at the Kawasaki plant in Kobe. And experienced retired German naval officer took part in the sea trials, with the approval of the naval administration.

In 1921, Argentina hired the former head of the Flanders Submarine Flotilla together with two former submarine designers as civilian consultants to help set up their own submarine flotilla. They planned the design and building of ten boats. In 1924, Japan built three mine-laying submarines in collaboration with Blohm + Voss. And finally, Sweden and Italy used German submarine expertise in 1922. Even Spain, which also wanted to have a strong submarine force, showed interest.[9]

The news of the attractive naval business with Argentina led to the formation of a consortium led by Krupp Germaniawerft, AG Weser and the Vulcan shipyard. But, according to the terms laid out in the Treaty of Versailles, fulfilling the buoyant demand, that in addition to submarine building, included redesign and development was going to be difficult as it was forbidden inside Germany. But as boats could be built abroad, without risk of prosecution, the Netherlands promptly offered itself as a seat for a new company – especially as it had not signed the Treaty of Versailles. The innocuously named "N.V. Ingenieurskantoor voor Schepsbouw" – Engineering office for Naval Construction – IvS for short, was set up in 1922 by Krupp's shipyard Germaniawerft, and together with AG Weser and AG Vulcan all three granted the company with a seat in The Hague a modest initial investment of 12,000 guilders – each paid in a third. Dr. Techel became Technical Director, and an ex-submariner, Commander (retired) Ulrich Blum, was assigned with the commercial management. As the company's registration suffered under political delays and bureaucratic obstacles, an interim office was opened in the premises of the Germania shipyard in Kiel. Only after a Dutch straw-man had been found who was prepared to register the company in Holland under his name, did IvS move to The Hague in 1925 with 11 employees.

Meanwhile, the once brilliant prospects had started to loose their sparkle as Argentina changed plans, Italy lost interest and Spanish plans for the construction of 40 submarines exposed IvS to merciless competition with America, England, France and Italy. In order to save the Spanish deal, the German naval administration appointed the able and submarine-savvy Lieutenant Commander Wilhelm Canaris as representative, especially as his Spanish was fluent. But in 1925, Spain rejected its plans. Despite 53 quotations to various interested parties, IvS had not won a single order since opening office in the Netherlands.[10]

But it did still have hope for an order from Turkey for the construction of two 500-tonne submarines, which would be designed and built in the Netherlands. However, the financial risks and burdens and risks of this transaction were unsustainable for the consortium partners.

And now the Navy entered the game with a secret fund of the Sea Transport Department with enough liquidity. As the Navy could not officially be a shareholder of IvS, the Sea Transport Department founded a shell company called "Mentor Bilanz", and thus the Navy surreptitiously became the IvS' fourth owner.

The Navy was, we remark in passing, not alone in its efforts to circumvent the Treaty of Versailles's terms. The Reichswehr leadership did everything possible to secretly re-arm, unnoticed by the overseers of the Inter-Allied Military Control Commission. For example, it conducted illegal large scale weapons tests in the Soviet Union with tanks, aircraft and artillery. Lenin was very grateful for the large sums of cash and the support with which the German Empire – albeit anything but altruistic – had paved his way to power. The launching of IvS fits in with this picture.

IvS speeded up with the money from the Navy in its pocket. Turkey could now place binding orders for two submarines, which were developed out of the First World War UB III type. This type of submarine, a medium-sized coastal boat with a displacement of 505/620 tonnes, and its further development (together with the UC III) was particularly interesting to the Navy, which foresaw in them the future of a German submarine force in the event that the restrictions of the Treaty of Versailles should be lifted.

Thus during 1927, numerous apparently retired navy personnel could be seen working on the completion of the boats in a Dutch shipyard.[11] They were gaining valuable experience, and would gather more on delivery to Turkey.

The same thread fits to a Finnish order placed in 1926 for three 500 tonne boats, which were to be further developed from the UC III type. This design was a medium sized submarine of nearly 500 tonnes, with a combined torpedo and mine armament. Accommodation for 20 mines in shafts fitted to the pressure hull was a novel feature for a submarine of this size.[12] With this order, IvS had created a powerful submarine type, which was far ahead of the WWI UC III type.[13] Three years later, IvS received yet another order from the Finnish Navy. This boat with 99 tonnes displacement was at that time the smallest class of submarines in the world. Here too a German crew was on board for the tests. Named SAUKKO, this boat was build to operate in the Lake Lagoda, shared between Finland and Russia.

*Launching of the Finnish 500 tonne submarine VETEHINEN 1930 in Turku.*
*(Photographer unknown)*

## THE ROAD TO THE MODERN GERMAN SUBMARINE FLEET

The prospect of doing business with the Spanish Navy, which was engaged in an ambitious submarine construction programme, paved the way for the later Type VII submarine. The first attempt in 1924 failed, however. But three years later, the collaboration with a Spanish industrialist, Don Horacio Echevarrieta, who had excellent connections to the Spanish Royal family, presented the unique opportunity to build a larger submarine according to the proposals of the German naval command.[14] A design of the Imperial Navy, which was to replace the UB III, served as the basis. This resulted in the design of a 755 tonne boat E 1, which was characterised by a more powerful engine and a wider operating range as compared to the original design.

Construction was delayed for various reasons, especially owing to the bankruptcy of the Spaniard, so that sea trials could begin in 1931. It was again attended by active and inactive German naval personnel, of which some were to play a significant role in the German submarine force later. And of course IvS also had its designers on board. The

German Navy's interest in the class was so strong that it covered the vast majority – about 85 per cent – of the construction costs, while Echevarrieta paid the rest.

The Spanish Navy did not get the boat, however, since the overthrow of the Spanish monarchy ruled out the planned purchase. The German Navy could not keep it either as Treaty of Versailles's terms still banned possession. Ultimately it was sold at loss to Turkey.

IvS was assigned building supervision of the project "Liliput", or CB 707, at the Crichton-Vulcan yard in Turku, Finland. It was a 250 tonne boat which was launched 1936 as VESIKKO, after future German submarine commanders had been trained on it. The German Navy had a particular interest in boat type, as it corresponded to its wishes and requirements for a future German submarine force. And this boat was a step towards the future Type II of the Kriegsmarine.

In 1932, the Imperial Navy decided on a reconstruction program for a modern and powerful navy. This decision also included the setting up of a submarine flotilla comprising further developed IvS designs E 1 and CV 707, later the Type I and Type II submarines. However, the process could only begin after Britain had given its consent. Preparations, however, were



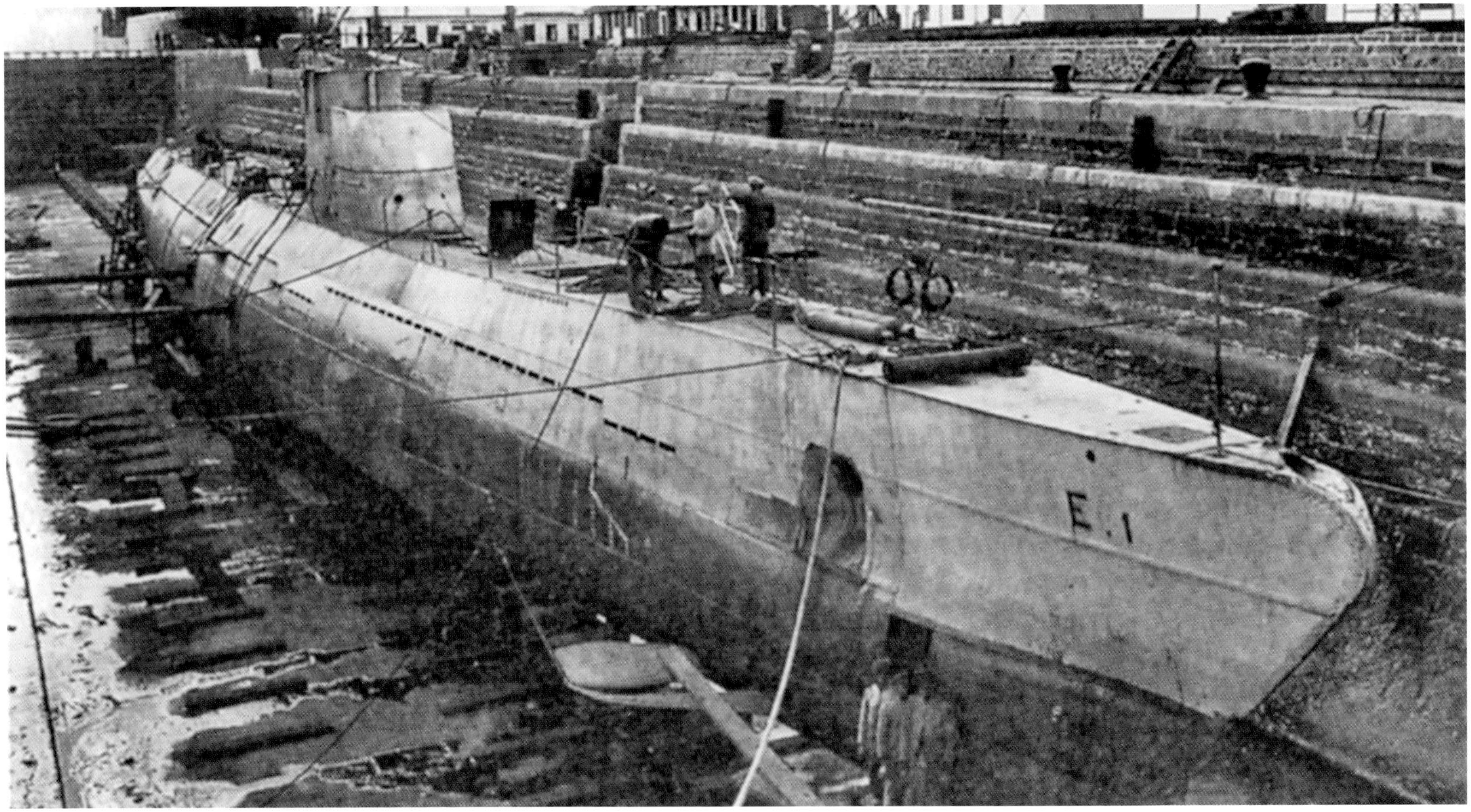
E.1

*E 1 at the shipyard in Spain.* (Wikipedia)

to start immediately, so that the shipyards would be able to begin with building boats without delay on the unknown day X. During negotiations it became apparent that England was aiming at limiting the total tonnage of the fleet, but not the number of boats, and thus a medium size boat was needed which should be as combat-ready as soon as possible. An IvS design was available already in 1934; it had been developed it from CV 707, given a more powerful drive, a stronger armament and saddle tanks, and was similar in almost all details to the later Type VII boats.[15] Thus the prototypes of the first three German submarine types after the First World War were in place, and construction could begin, for which two Kiel shipyards, the Germaniawerft and Deutsche Werke Kiel had been earmarked.

At the same time, the naval administration had decided to follow up the first six Type II boats with six more improved version units, the Type IIB. In 1934 the shipyards set up design offices to accompany and supervise monitor construction. This required experienced submarine designers, which in the circumstances, could come only from IvS, who took over the task leadership for the yards and Imperial Navy. Another office named "Schiffbaukontor GmbH Bremen" (Shipbuilding Bureau Bremen Ltd) was set up at AG Weser in Bremen, where the Type I and VII boats were to be developed.

Germany was at this time still not allowed to build submarines. It is doubtful that First World War victors had not noticed IvS's activities. In fact, given the large number of submarines IvS had successfully built in many countries, it's actually impossible. Rather, it is a reasonable suspicion that they kept their eyes shut – at least as long as IvS activities were not particularly visible. But they became public as New York Times reported on 7 September 1934:

*In a report to the Electric Boat Co., Capt. Paul Koster, a former officer of the Dutch Navy and former representative of the above company in Europe, stated that Inkavos (Note: the telegraphic address of IvS) was in his opinion, a German company which is organised for the purpose of keeping the German Navy informed about the submarine designs of all countries ...*

*"Mr Techel is the soul of the whole thing", Mr Koster continued and suggested it should be necessary to prod the former Allies to force Germany to comply to the provisions laid down by the Versailles peace agreement.*[16]

This was embarrassing, and only after a month did the Völkische Beobachter (the newspaper of the NSDAP, the National Socialist German Workers' Party) publish an official disclaimer stating that the alleged design office in The Hague did indeed exist. However, it was controlled by a Dutchman and his son [sic!], who used the assistance of two unemployed German shipbuilders to supply shipbuilding plans to any nation that would pay for them.

It was detrimental to the secret preparations for submarine building in Germany, and even more for the negotiations with Great Britain. Consequently, the Navy withdrew in 1935 as a shareholder of IvS and Deschimag took over two-thirds and the Germania shipyard one third of its shares. In The Hague, a residual workforce took over a few foreign orders, and the IvS remained under Techel and Blum's management until 1938. In 1936, the Bremen subsidiary was renamed "Ingenieurkontor für Schiffbau GmbH (IfS)" – i.e. the German translation of the Dutch name – and moved to Lübeck. The IvS shareholders again appointed Techel and Blum as directors, and thus, continuity was maintained. The new company's mission was to create offers for export submarines, which would be built in German shipyards for Chinese, Bulgarian and Turkish clients. A state-controlled export company was in charge of Romania and Yugoslavia. Furthermore, IfS designed hoisting finder and rod antennas for German submarines. The beginning of the war terminated IfS's export activities. A large number of staff was taken over by Deschimag, and the Germania shipyard. IfS's activities finally ended with the liquidation of the Germania shipyard after the Second World War, in 1946.

# The Type XXI Submarine – A Revolution at Sea

On 4 May 1945, Rear Admiral Karl Dönitz ordered his submarine captains to lay down their arms, return to their bases and surrender. The fight no longer made sense, and in a few days the Third Reich would surrender unconditionally. His radio message hit like a bomb on the boats which were still at sea, and many commanders thought it was a forgery of the Allies[1]. Only eight of them obeyed immediately.

Among them was the Knight's Cross recipient, Commander Captain Adalbert Schnee who was en route to the Panama Canal with his submarine U 2511. He had one of the few brand-new front-suitable "miracle" boats of the new Type XXI, which were to be tested extensively in the Caribbean under all conditions. Just a few hours after he had received the Grand Admiral's dispatch, he made a passive sonar contact with the British HMS NORFOLK cruiser, which was accompanied by some destroyers, to the north of the Faeroe Islands. He managed to break through the defensive shield dived and unnoticed and to approach within torpedo firing range of the cruiser. Mindful of Dönitz's order, however, Schnee left it with a feint and sailed away – again unnoticed. He returned to Bergen and turned over his boat to the British. When a few days later he met officers of HMS NORFOLK, he told them of his exploit and was met with embittered amazement. First of all, they did not want to believe that a submarine could venture so close to the Cruiser without being detected. In fact, today some historians doubt

*Three Type XXI submarines and other boats are handed over to the Royal Navy after the capitulation in the port of Bergen. U-2511 (middle), under Corvette Captain Adalbert Schnee, was the only type XXI submarine which was on patrol.* (Unknown English sailor)

the veracity of Schnee's report but, on the other hand, it is confirmed by crew members.

In any case, with the 1,600 tonne Type XXI submarine and its smaller brother, the 250 tonne XXIII Type boat, a genus of submarine emerged which was to revolutionise submarine travel. The construction of the new Type XXI became the model for all modern submarines and in particular for the first nuclear-powered submarines of the United States, England, Russia and France. In particular, the first nuclear submarine in the world, the USS NAUTILUS, was essentially an enlarged XXI. The German designers succeeded in constructing a submarine which actually deserved the name. Up to then, all submarines were nothing more

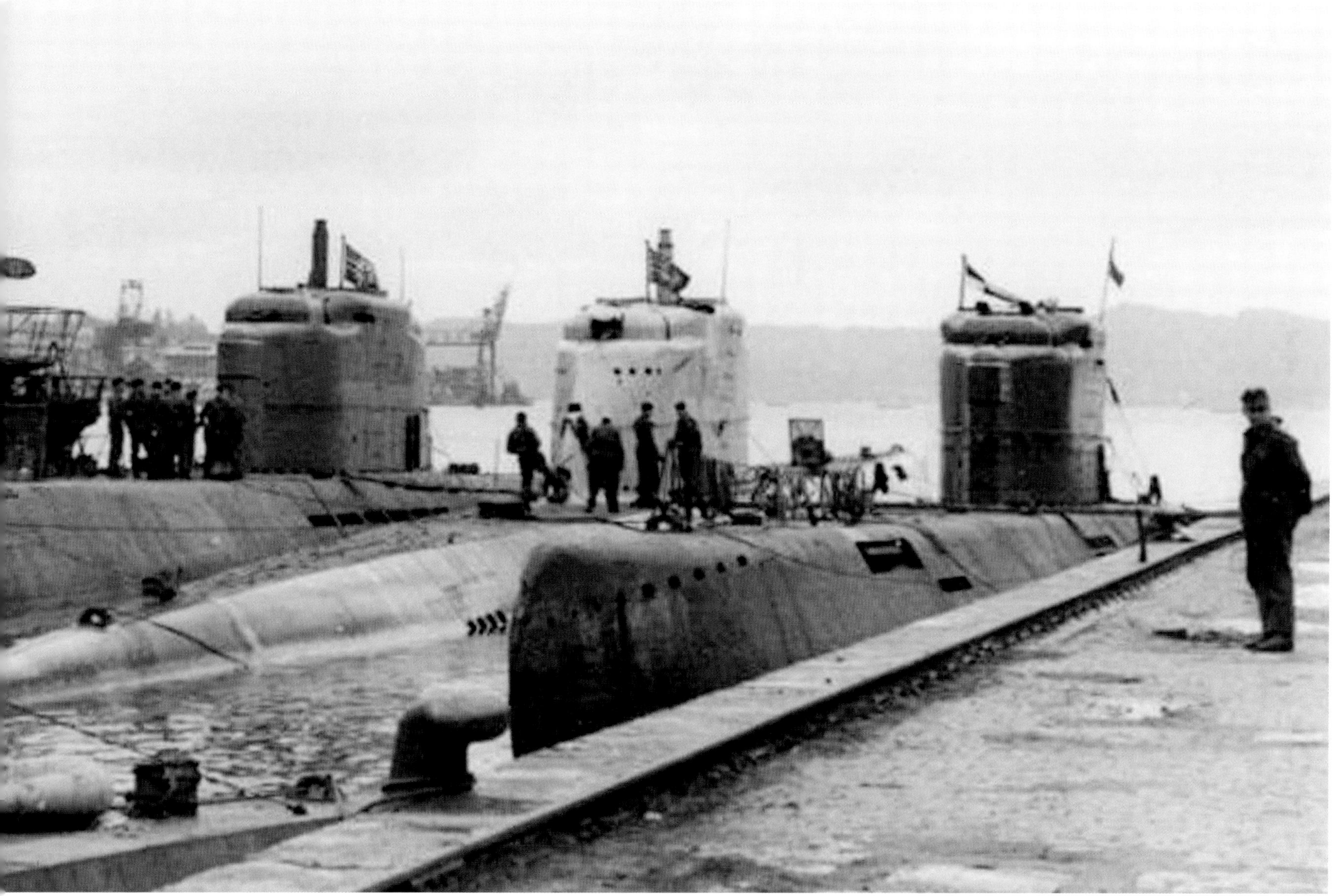

than submersible surface ships. The new type was completely geared to underwater travel and so effectively an underwater ship which was also able to surface – a milestone in the history of submarine building.

But in fact, this in itself revolutionary submarine type, which was still diesel-electric powered, was considered to be only a way point. The final destination of the Navy was an ocean-going Type XXVIII, which was also to be equipped with a diesel-electric drive for cruising, and with a Walter turbine for short sprints under water at speeds of up to 23 knots. The Walter turbine had however proven not ready for series production. Nevertheless, the ideas of the brilliant engineer Professor Hellmuth Walter for specially streamlined hull shapes were embodied in the new submarine type.

Walter had already experimented with a propulsion method in the 1930s in which with the aid of a catalyst, hydrogen peroxide was converted to superheated steam. Then, through a turbine and a generator, electricity was generated. The objective was not merely achieving high speeds under water, but rather the procedure also meant a drive that was not dependent under water on the external air. Today, this drive is known as an AIP drive (air independent propulsion).

In parallel to the development of his drive, Walter dealt with the construction of the hull. He realized that the submarines of his time had good handling characteristics when above the surface, but operated poorly under water. So he invented particularly streamlined submarine designs, from which he removed any disturbing tower constructions and facilities such as guns. He thereby greatly reduced the water resistance as well as wake noise, which created a superb boat for underwater operations. Also, his designs were significantly faster under water than above the surface. Prototypes of his designs – even with a sail – during trial runs in the Second World War achieved underwater speeds up to about 26 knots. For those times, these were unprecedented results.

The susceptibility of the still immature propulsion system to fault, the low availability of hydrogen peroxide, and last but not least the huge thirst of the drives meant, that Walter submarines could not be produced in series. That would have been beyond the capacities of the shipyards. The Navy's high command and the main office of warship building (K-Office) of the Navy had only reluctantly agreed to the prototypes anyway. Moreover, at the beginning of the war the conventional Type VIIC submarines were operating very successfully and there seemed to be little need to engage in experiments in such circumstances.

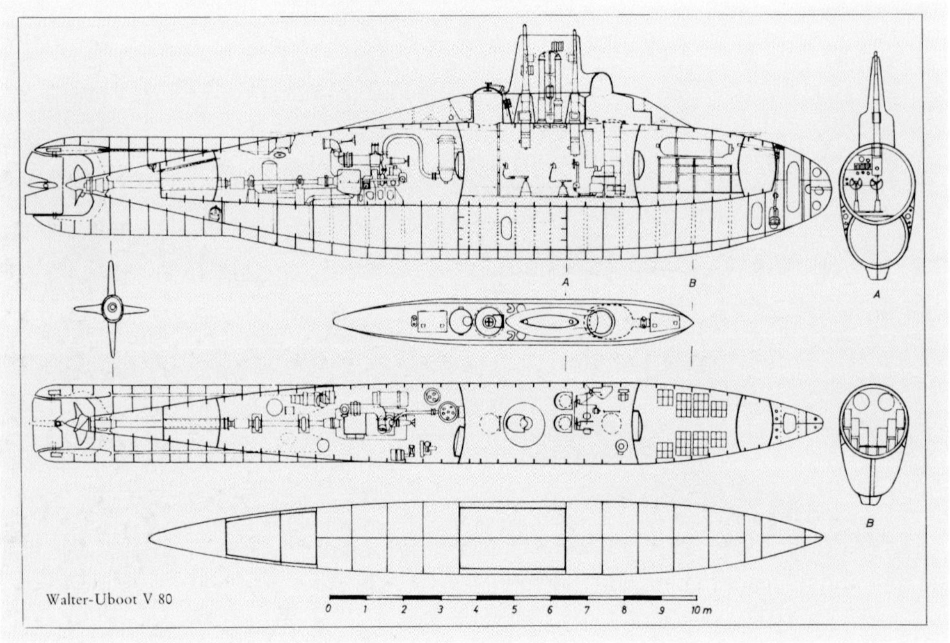
A
B
A
B
Walter-Uboot V 80
0 1 2 3 4 5 6 7 8 9 10 m

*Walter test boat V 80 of about 80 tonnes attained speeds up to 26 knots in 1940.* [2]

Dönitz, however, whom Walter had approached and who recognised the potential of the new types, would not let loose. He brought about that Hitler held a meeting in the Reich Chancellery in the autumn of 1942, which was attended among others by Dönitz as Commander of submarines, Admiral Werner Fuchs as head of the K-Office, Grand Admiral Raeder as Commander-in-Chief of the Navy and Dipl.-Ing. Christian Waas from K-Office. The meeting led to the breakthrough. Moreover, owing to the extremely high losses after "Black May" in 1943, the German submarine force was in big trouble because the Allied convoy system, their improved air reconnaissance and the radar made it incredibly difficult for German submarines to operate above the surface, as in the past. They were hardly up to their opponents. So it was urgent to create a new type in response to the crisis.

In the spring of 1943, a first draft was produced for the Type XXI submarine, which Dönitz accepted in June, and in November the order was given for the construction of 170 boats. The design was based on the hull shape of the Type XXVIII Walter design, but conventionally diesel-electric powered, because production of the Walter drive was impossible. The 1,600 tonne boat, in addition to its high underwater speed of up to 16 knots, was distinguished through the huge capacity of the batteries and high-performance electric motors – a good reason to call these boats "electric boats". It had a snorkel, with which it could travel submerged almost without limitation. Six torpedo tubes could be loaded hydraulically within 20 minutes, instead of the previous several hours. The range of the boats, which were designed to dive to 220 metres, was a maximum of 15,500 nautical miles (28,700 km) in surface mode, and 340 nautical miles (630 km) submerged. In addition, the boat was equipped with all technical innovations of the day: the new sonar made it possible to locate opponents and accurately fire torpedoes at 50 metres depth, and new radio monitoring and detection systems were able to better find enemy ships and warn against aircraft attacks. Special

*Type XXI submarine – the "electric boat".* (Archive HDW/TKMS)

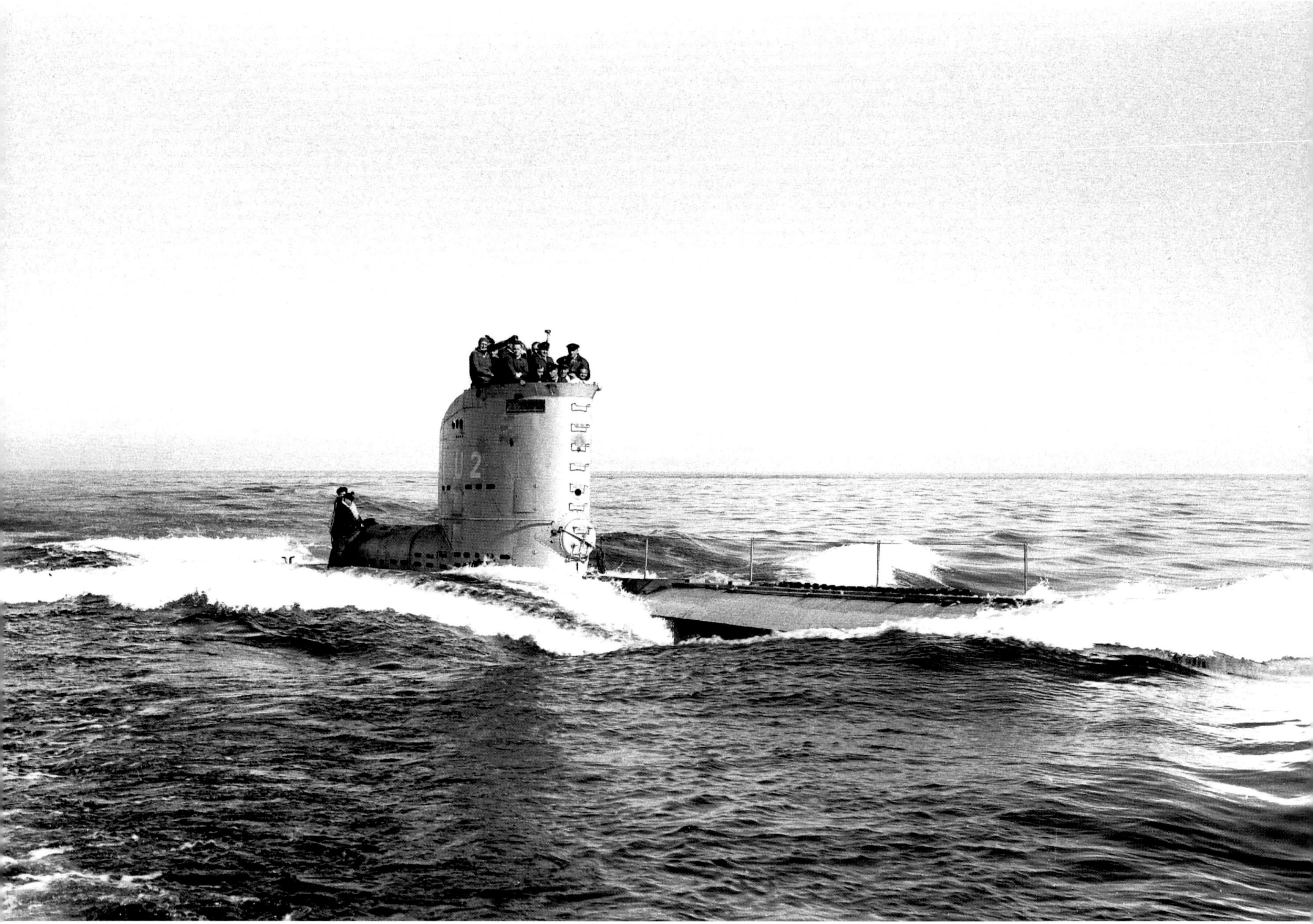
U 2

*Type XXIII submarine U 2365 was scuttled at the end of the Second World War in the Kattegat and salvaged in 1956, repaired at the Howaldtswerke in Kiel, and deployed as U-HAI by the German Navy as a training boat, here on sea trials on the 25 September 1957.* (Archive HDW/TKMS)

rubber cladding protected the boat better against radar detection, and false target decoys against sonar. And the boats were quiet. During test runs with captured Type XXI submarines, the Americans discovered that the German boats were much quieter than their quietest submarines.[3]

A "little brother" for the large submarine was built on the same design principles. The Type XXIII was also an electric boat, but intended for coastal operations. The 250 tonne boat was likely armed and equipped with comparatively small tracking devices. It had only two torpedo tubes and could not carry spare torpedoes, because the tubes could only be loaded from the outside. As the Type XXI they had an figure 8-shaped pressure hull, which, although it deviated from the ideal circular form for pressure hulls, allowed the installation of higher battery capacities. Surfaced it reached a speed of around 10 knots and could operate at a maximum of 12.5 knots under water. The range was 2,600 nautical miles (4.818 km) in surface travel and submerged 194 nautical miles (359 km). From June 1944 until the war's end, shipyards turned out 61 boats, of which six saw active service.

Also another submarine type, the XXVII "Seehund" midget submarine, had an unmistakable similarity in design. This submarine type displaced 17 tonnes and had a crew of two, and carried two torpedoes. It had a maximum range of about 150 nautical miles (280 km), which was increased in later types with additional tanks to approximately 300 nautical miles (556 km), and reached a speed above water of eight knots and submerged of six knots. 285 boats were completed in the short period from late 1944 until the end of the war. 60 of them were actually used.

Dönitz, who in late January 1943 became Navy Commander-In-Chief, put pressure on production: the Type XXI and XXIII boats now took precedence over the previous submarines. Valuable support came from the Armaments Minister Albert Speer, who also took over naval armaments.

*Type XXVII (Seehund) midget submarine. This unknown boat was restored by HDW apprentices during their training and is now in the International Maritime Museum Hamburg.* (Rothaug/HDW)

He hired an industrial manager, the Director-General of the Magirus works, Otto Merker, as head of the submarine-building programme, who transferred the production line system of vehicle construction to the construction of submarines. So, submarine sections were made in different companies located throughout Germany, and were welded together at the shipyards. It worked reasonably well. However, the air attacks disabled transport of the sections to the coast. In addition to other difficulties, the dimensional accuracy of the sections was not

1D 00 42 L

*Production on the assembly line: prefabricated aft section a Type XXI submarine in the Deutsche Werke shipyard in Kiel, 1945.* (Archive HDW/TKMS)

always ensured, so they had to be readjusted by the shipyards. Nevertheless, it was possible to reduce the number of production hours per boat. In total, up to the end of the war, out of the originally planned 750 boats, 143 Type XXI submarines were built, of which 119 boats were taken into service. In particular, due to the hastily launched construction programme defects had to be eliminated, and in addition the boats had to undergo shakedown cruises and have their crews trained. That cost valuable time. Therefore only a tiny number were battle ready. And only one was actually used: U 2511 under Adalbert Schnee.

U-Boottyp XXI
OKM-Typskizze
von Anfang 1944

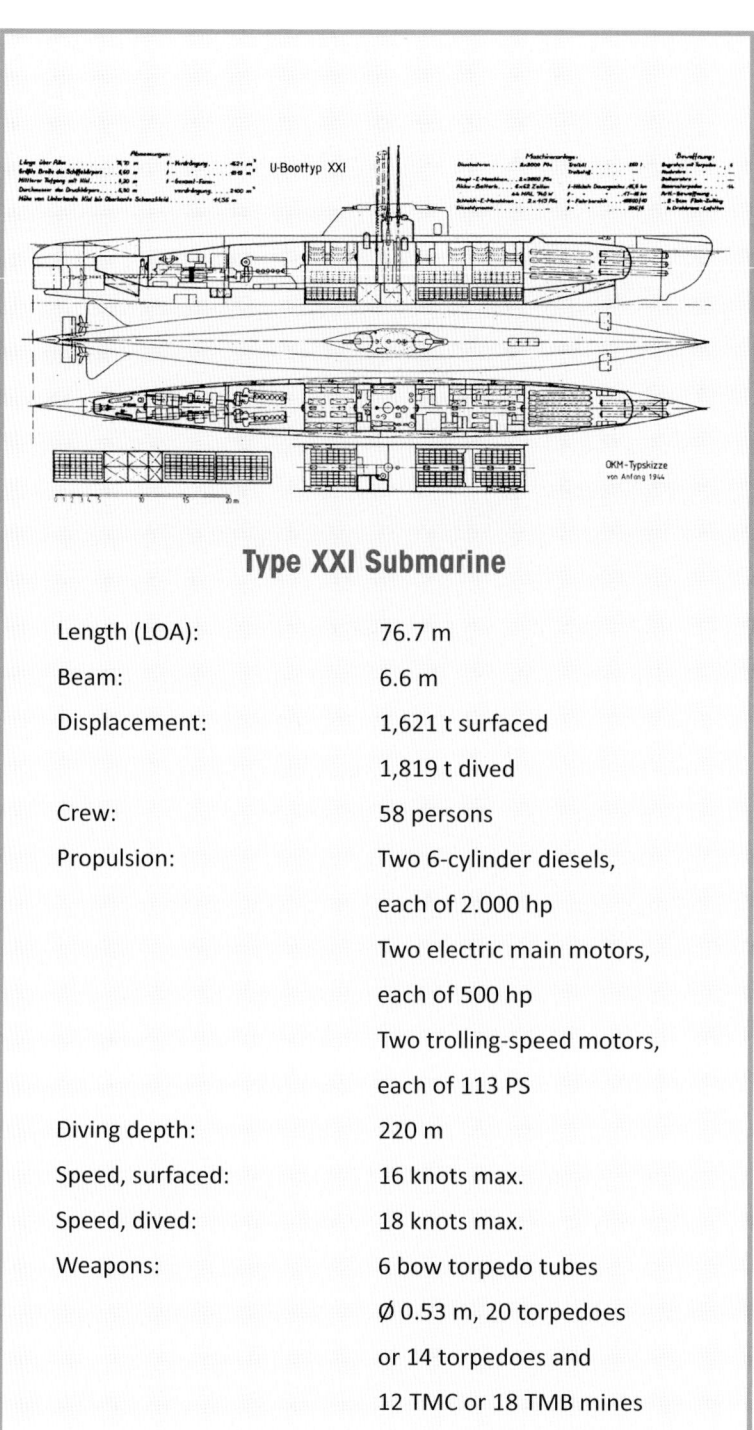

## Type XXI Submarine

| | |
|---|---|
| Length (LOA): | 76.7 m |
| Beam: | 6.6 m |
| Displacement: | 1,621 t surfaced<br>1,819 t dived |
| Crew: | 58 persons |
| Propulsion: | Two 6-cylinder diesels,<br>each of 2.000 hp<br>Two electric main motors,<br>each of 500 hp<br>Two trolling-speed motors,<br>each of 113 PS |
| Diving depth: | 220 m |
| Speed, surfaced: | 16 knots max. |
| Speed, dived: | 18 knots max. |
| Weapons: | 6 bow torpedo tubes<br>Ø 0.53 m, 20 torpedoes<br>or 14 torpedoes and<br>12 TMC or 18 TMB mines |

Plan nach Rössler, U-Boottyp XXIII, p 46
0 1 2 3 4 5 6 7 8 9 10 m

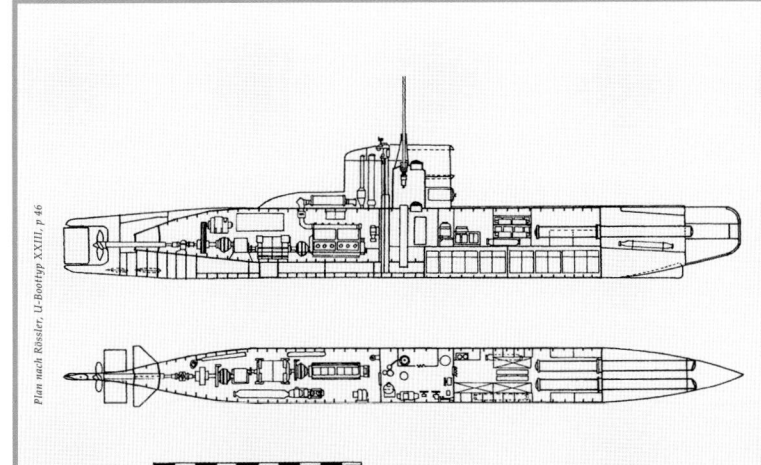

## Type XXIII Submarine

| | |
|---|---|
| Length (LOA): | 34.7 m |
| Beam: | 3.0 m |
| Draft: | 3.7 m |
| Displacement: | 234 t surfaced |
| | 258 t dived |
| Crew: | 14 - 18 persons |
| Propulsion: | Single 4-cylinder diesel, |
| | 576 hp |
| | Single electric main motor, |
| | 580 hp |
| | Single trolling-speed motor, |
| | 35 hp |
| Diving depth: | 150 m |
| Speed, surfaced: | 12.5 knots max. |
| Speed, dived: | 10.0 knots max. |
| Weapons: | 2 bow torpedo tubes |
| | Ø 0.53m, 2 torpedoes |

1 Dieselmotor
2 Dieselkupplg (vorl. elastisch)
3 E-Maschine
4 Tachometerantrieb
5 feste Kupplung (Bamag)
6 Drucklager
7 Wellenlager u. Stopfbuchse
8 Zuluftmast
9 Lichtbildkompaß
10 Sehrohr, fest, 2m lg., drehb.
11 Sauerstoffflaschen
12 Druckluftflasche
13 Batterietröge
14 Fahrtrichtungsschalter
15 Treiböl-Verbrauchsbehälter

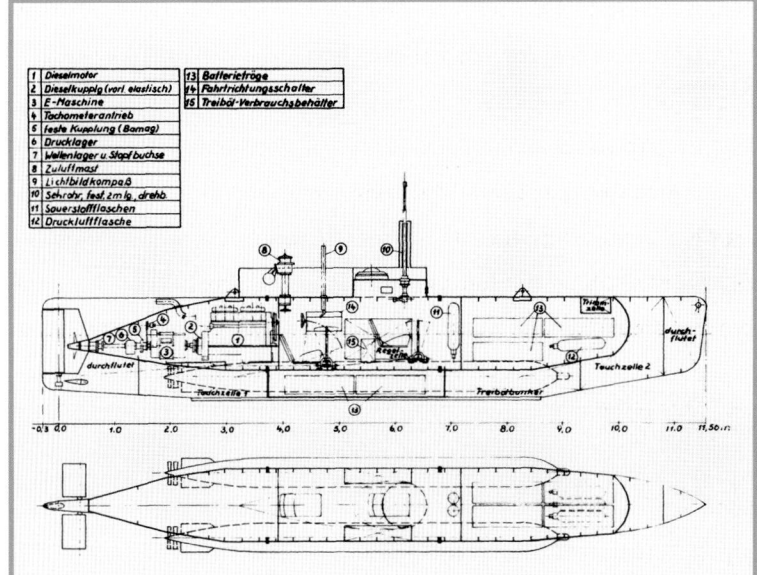

## Type XXVII Submarine

| | |
|---|---|
| Length (LOA): | 11.9 m |
| Beam: | 1.7 m |
| Displacement: | 17 t |
| Crew: | 2 |
| Propulsion: | Single 6-cylinder diesel, 60 hp |
| | Single electric motor, 28 hp |
| Diving depth: | 30 m |
| Speed, surfaced: | 6 knots max. |
| Speed, dived: | 8 knots max. |
| Weapons: | 2 G7e torpedoes, |
| | slung externally in recesses |

## END OF THE WAR: THE COVETED GERMAN SUBMARINES

The Allied intelligence services had been able to collect information about the German submarine developments even during the war. It is understandable that after Germany surrendered, they did everything possible to get hold of the construction plans of the world's most advanced submarine technology. The Potsdam Agreement of 2 August 1945 had stipulated that each of the three Allies, United States, Great Britain and Russia should get 10 German submarines for technical evaluation and testing. A Tripartite Naval Commission (TNC) was, however, to decide. Nevertheless, the Royal Navy, which had first access to the boats and their construction documents, did not even wait for the outcome of the deliberations within the Commission, but began the tests immediately, especially since almost all submarines which had surrendered in May were taken to Lisahally in Northern Ireland and to Loch Ryan in south-western Scotland, to be scuttled later in operation "Deadlight".

This was done with full knowledge of the American brothers in arms, but without informing the Russians. The incipient Cold War was already

*U 190 surrendered on 14 May 1945 in Newfoundland and was taken to Halifax.* (Archive SUBSIM Radb Room)

making itself felt, and distrust of the Western powers towards Stalin had grown to considerable proportions. They were well aware that submarines would play a crucial role in the naval combat in any war against Russia. Therefore they had the greatest interest in learning about the advanced German designs as fast as possible, especially the Walter designed XXI and XXIII type submarines – and to do everything to make sure that the Russians got as little information as possible. Hence also the relocation of the German submarines to British waters, without this being notified in advance to the Russians[4].

And they took advantage of the unique opportunity to submit the boats to a very intense scrutiny of their own.

The British were also the first to investigate the German submarine yards within their sphere of influence, with specially trained forces immediately after the war, and took extensive collections of construction plans and official documents back home. And they did everything to keep the Russians from information about advanced submarine technology. But they could not shut out their Eastern Allies completely. Furthermore, sections and half-finished Type XXI submarines, as well as many documents fell into the hands of the Russians in Danzig. From these, they developed their "Whisky" class boats end of the 1940s.

In June 1945, the Royal Navy had put together a force of about 500 officers and crews who were to examine the captured submarines and conduct test runs. The US Navy, which had not captured any boats, was to receive two Type XXI boats, which it was particularly interested in. So U 2513 and U 3008, behind the back of the Russians, were taken in all secrecy to the United States, also using German submarine crews who were prisoners of war.

Whilst the Royal Navy had little luck with testing the XXI and XXIII type

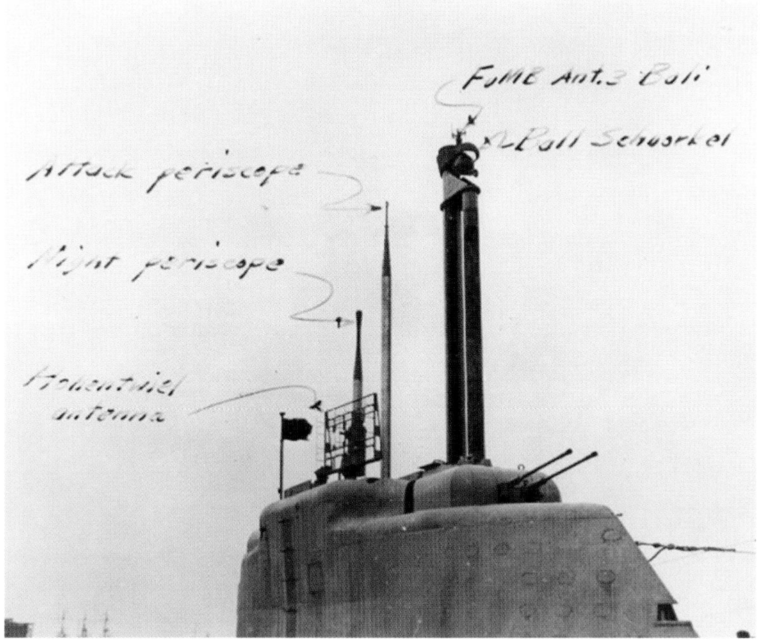

FuMB Ant. 3 Bali
Attack periscope
Night periscope
antenna


*Allied studies: hoisting masts on a Zype XXI boat* (submarine archives – netdesign studies)

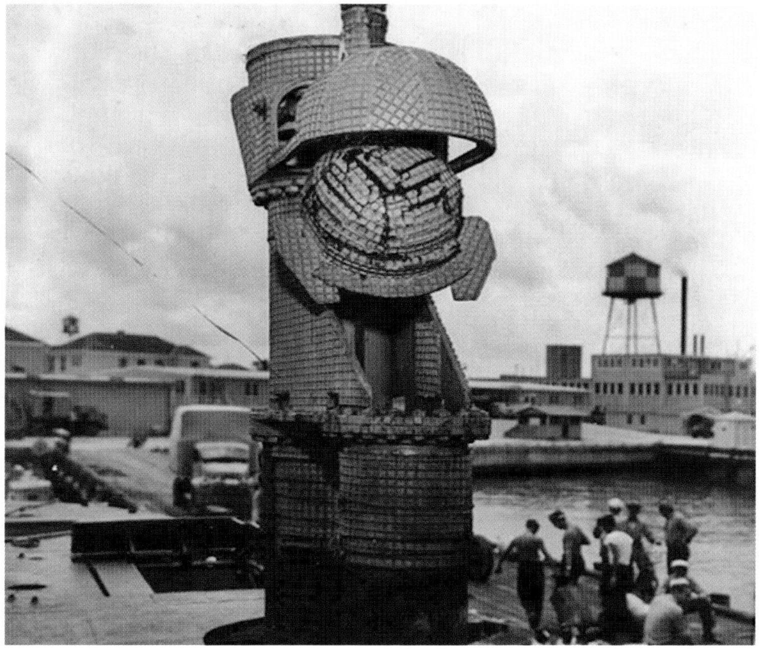

*Much admired by the Allies, a snorkel covered with radar deflecting material.*

(Submarine archive – netdesign studies)

boats, and therefore gave up, probably also due to lack of maintenance and repair capabilities, the testing of U 2513 and U 3008 in the United States was successful and brought the US Navy valuable insights. In addition to the deep insight into the most advanced submarine technology, they also served to test the development of new submarine tactics. As reported in February 1946 by Rear Admiral John Wilkes, Commander Submarine Force Atlantic Fleet to the Chief of Naval Operations (CNO): *"Investigations of the Type XXI submarine (U 2513) have already shown that this type represents remarkable progress in the characteristics which are significant for future combat submarines."*[5] And Captain J. P. Clay, the Acting Commander of the American Fleet Training Command, endorsed him: *"The superior qualities of this submarine show a boat that is superior in underwater speed and endurance to all those that our submarine defence has so far produced."* [6]

This meant that the submarine defence of the US Navy would be useless if an opponent of the United States could use such boats. And thus the strategists of the US Navy were quickly convinced that a Soviet Union, which also possessed such vessels, would constitute a serious threat to the their country.

A similar view was expressed by the Chief of Naval Operations, Chester Nimitz, in a letter to President Truman on 4 June 1946. As the leading U.S. Navy authority on submarines, Nimitz had thoroughly inspected the boat a month earlier, and pointed out that this particular type of submarine operating in deep water could almost without any risk, attack a convoy or a task groupprotected by the usual means, and was at the same time virtually immune to destruction by any ship or aircraft, or a combination of both.[7]

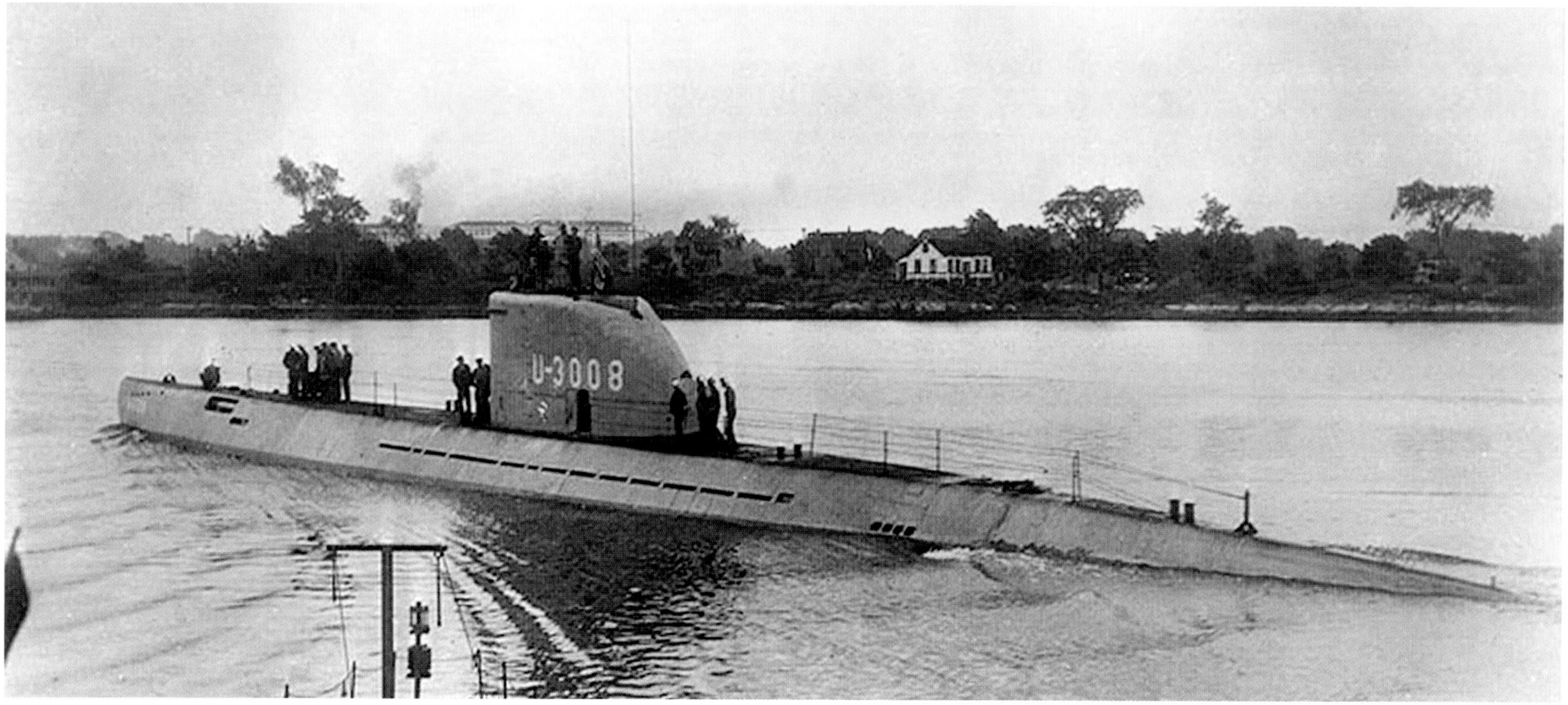
U-3008

*Testing and investigation of a Type XXI boat: U 3008 with a modified conning tower before the Portsmouth Navy Yard, Kittery, Maine (United States).*

*(Submarine archive – netdesign studies)*

So President Harry S. Truman insisted on seeing the boat for himself and visited U 2513 in Key West in November 1946, where he dived to 130 metres. He also witnessed the snorkel in action, as reported by "The Miami Herald" on 22 November, with a photo of the him on the sail . And a year later, Truman awarded the test team officers two gold and two bronze stars for merit.

The Royal Navy, which had little luck with the testing of the Type XXI boats, was pursued with more misfortune in testing Walter submarines for which it had a very particular interest – especially in the Type XXVI's sophisticated design. They tried to complete a partly finished new-build to which they had access at the Blohm & Voss shipyard in Hamburg, and into which Walter turbines were to fitted, but foundered because, for political reasons, the yard had been dismantled and any remains blown up.[8] Nevertheless, the British did not give up, and built two boats named EXPLORER and EXCALIBUR which entered service ten years later. However, the Royal Navy was not able to master the problems with power plants and drive systems, and suffered numerous accidents. Thus the boats were given the uncomplimentary nicknames "Exploder" and "Extruder" by their crews – and the programme was aborted without result.

But other submarines which could operate with long endurances, at high speeds and in great depths were successfully built on the basis the Type XXI which dovetailed into the American Greater Underwater Propulsion Power Program (GUPPY), which led to the design and construction of nuclear submarines such as the USS NAUTILUS and the SKIPJACK class boats.

The British diesel-electric OBERON class was developed from the German design, the Russian Navy built the WHISKY and the ZULU class with diesel-electric propulsion system, and the French Navy built its OBERON class based on the German template.

Only one Type XXI boat has survived, U 2540. It was scuttled in the wake of operation Rainbow on 4 May 1945 and salvaged in 1957 for refurbishing in Kiel at the Howaldtswerke. Renamed WILHELM BAUER, it was re-deployed by the German Navy, which was by then permitted to rebuild a submarine fleet. It served as a test platform and was finally decommissioned in 1982. Today, this sole survivor of a revolutionary concept is kept in good shape by the "Submarine Technology Museum Wilhelm Bauer e.V." and is on display at the German Maritime Museum in Bremerhaven.

*US President Harry S. Truman in November 1946 after sailing aboard the U 2513.*

(Submarine archive – netdesign studies)

# Germany Builds Submarines Again

After the end of the Second World War, the German submarine world was in tatters. Around 200 boats had been sunk in operation "Rainbow" in May 1945, or were destroyed by their crews, so they did not fall into the hands of the victors. The remaining over 150 boats had to be surrendered to the Allies and were transferred to the Scottish ports of Loch Ryan and Loch Eriboll and to Moville and Lisahally near Londonderry in Northern Ireland to the extent that they could still travel. From there, they were scuttled between November 1945 and February 1946 in operation "Deadlight", apart from about 40 boats, which were distributed among the victors. The victorious powers agreed at that time: Germany should not have or build submarines.

But never?

*June 1945: 52 surrendered German submarines berthed at Lisahally, Northern Ireland.*

(Collection of the Imperial War Museum)

In fact the relationship of the Western powers to Stalin dramatically worsened after the war. Suspicion arose from mutual dislike and the Cold War from suspicion. It culminated in a proxy war of West against East, which brought the world to the brink of a third world war and nuclear conflict in the Korean War, in the early 50s. Only the prudence of President Harry S. Truman prevented pressing of the red button to drop the atomic bomb, insistently requested by General Douglas MacArthur. Under the impact of the ideological and military confrontation between the West and the Soviet bloc, it was soon understood by the Western powers that West Germany had to play a role in their strategic considerations as a *cordon sanitaire* to contain Soviet expansion in Western Europe. Already in 1946 it is stated in a paper of the British Joint Chiefs of Staff, which deals with the future of the Kiel Canal, that: *"Now, however, we consider that we may have to build up N.W. Europe as a protective area against the possibility of Soviet aggression."*[1]

This led to the establishment of NATO and also of the Federal Republic of Germany in 1949 through the combination of the three Western zones of Germany. Shortly afterwards, the United States conducted secret negotiations on the establishment of German armed forces with the Federal Government of Konrad Adenauer. In 1951, the Federal border police was introduced as a paramilitary force, and in 1954, after the Paris agreements had given extensive sovereignty to Germany, the young state joined NATO in 1955 and, despite significant opposition from the war-weary German population, created the Bundeswehr. This was not without preparation: the Office Blank had existed since 1950, founded in preparation for a future Ministry of Defence and a future Bundeswehr and which, under Theodor Blank, dealt with the future equipment of future German forces. It is obvious that this office was not entirely in line with the provisions of the Potsdam Conference, that wanted to prevent any re-militarisation of Germany. But in the face of the increasingly intense Cold War, the Western powers were only too happy to tolerate the efforts of the office.

When the Office Blank was awarded on 8 March 1955 the contract to develop new submarines for the Federal Navy, which was still to be established, German submarine efforts did not have to start from scratch. The British had already assembled a team of German experts and former Wehrmacht members, and instructed them to examine what contributions the now allied Germany could make in sea defence.[2] The Office Blank also had its thoughts on the setting up of a German submarine fleet and entrusted two experienced submarine designers, Christoph Aschmoneit and Ulrich Gabler, with the task of drawing up proposals for a submarine force in the future Federal Navy. It was Germany's strategic position close to the entrances of the Baltic Sea, and to Eastern Block countries bordering the Baltic Sea, that made it desirable that a future German Navy should be equipped with submarines. And thus, German submarine expertise was once again in demand.

There were similar considerations in the neighbouring young German Democratic Republic. In consultation with the Soviet leadership, it planned to build its own submarine service, which until 1955 was to include 13 submarines with the associated infrastructure of bases and training facilities. But in fact it became nothing. A fitting port was soon found on the island Rügen and its expansion started. However, recruitment of the submarine-experienced officers and men proved to be incomparably more difficult, since they had to be free of a Nazi background. So, they barely managed to attract sufficiently qualified personnel. They did, however, establish a submarine school, whose operation was shut down in 1953 – and with it all submarine dreams were put on the shelf – ultimately owing to short funds for a far too ambitious submarine construction programme.[3]

*Removal of a Type XXIII boat from the Deutsche Werke shipyard in Kiel, 1945.*

*(Archive HDW/TKMS).*

Not so in West Germany. Here the decision had been made to build up a submarine force and the project was tackled with vigour. But the new NATO Allies were not yet ready to trust the German submariners only nine years after the Second World War had come to an end, and were only prepared to permit pocket sized boats not larger than 350 tonnes.

Thus, in March 1955 Senior Government Counsellor Christoph Aschmoneit and Dipl.-Ing. Ulrich Gabler, two submarine design experts, were asked by the Blank Office to produce an expertise over a proposed 350 tonne boat. Christoph Aschmoneit had studied shipbuilding, and was one of the people who had received submarine training in Finland in 1933, on the IvS boat CV 707. In 1935, he joined the German Navy's submarine testing committee as a marine surveyor. Next he was transferred to the Navy Board's design office in 1938, after which he succeeded Friedrich Schürer (who had been instrumental in submarine development at IvS) as head of the department of submarines (K I U), a sub-division of the main office for warship construction. The Type XXVII midget submarine Seehund had been developed on his watch, and he had been involved in testing the Type XXI boats. After the war he first worked in the waterways and shipping administration, and later at its directorate in Kiel. In 1957, he was appointed senior government official of the Federal Office of Defence Technology and Procurement (BWB), where together with the IKL, he created the Class 210 and 205 submarines. In the early 1960s, as the Norwegian Navy ordered 15 KOBBEN Class submarines from the Nordseewerke shipyard in Emden, and were lent the German Navy's U 3 for training purposes, Aschmoneit became the Royal Norwegian Navy's external counsellor tasked solve technical and contractual problems, which he did so quickly, thoroughly and without red tape, that Olav V, King of Norway, awarded him the Order of Saint Olav. After retiring in 1977, he continued to advise HDW in Kiel for eight years on contractual matters and turned his attention to the then-new Class 209.



Ulrich Gabler[4], studied mechanical engineering and ship-building, joined the Lübeck Engineering Office for Shipbuilding (IfS), the offshoot of IvS, in 1938. At the beginning of the war, he volunteered for the submarine force and continued to work on submarines as Chief Engineer until 1942.In the same year, he was sent to the Walter engine and turbine works in Kiel, where under the stewardship of the Naval Senior Civil Engineer Dr. Karl Fischer, he made decisive contributions to the new Walter Type XXII, XVIIA and XXVI submarine designs. In order to become fully acquainted with the boat's new drive technologies, Gabler took part in various trials and often helmed the small experimental boat V 80 with its top speed of 26 knots. Together with his colleague Heep, he furthermore refined the snorkel (a Dutch invention), and prepared for serial installation. Together with Dr. Karl Fischer, he was moved in 1944 to the Central Submarine design office "Glückauf" in Blankenburg, a town in the Harz mountains of Northern Germany which was much safer than Kiel from allied air raids. Here he headed the project office and completed the design and construction drawings for the Walter Type XXVI boat, as well as the "Seehund" and "Delphin" midget submarines. He himself tested the prototype of the latter in the Neustädter Bay of the Baltic.

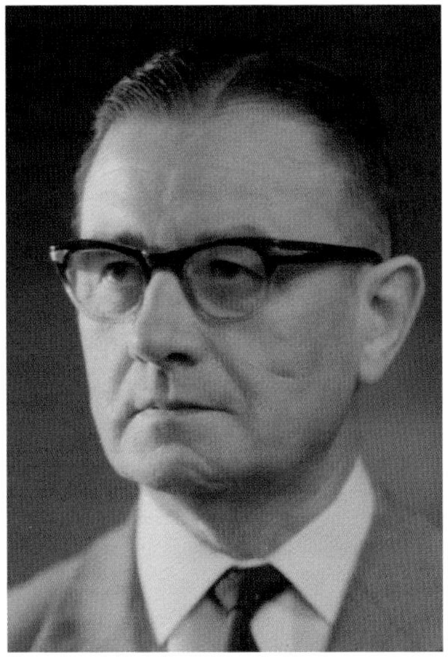
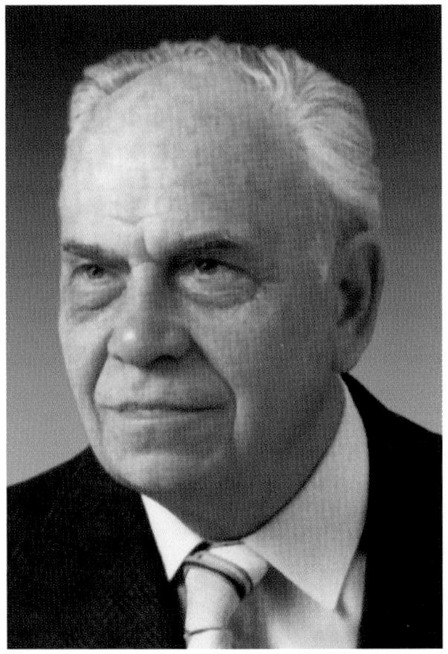

*Christoph Aschmoneit (left) and Ulrich Gabler (right).*

The end of the war saw him as a flotilla engineer in Wilhelmshaven, and in an irony of fate, shortly before it was captured by the British, he received orders to scuttle all submarines in port. In only three hours he sank 22 submarines with the help of two elderly submariners ...now, if that's not effective ...

In 1945, he received the news that his ex-employer, IfS in Lübeck, still existed and that he continue work there again. It had turned to new tasks and saw a future in designing machinery for the building, agriculture and forestry industries. However, as a subsidiary of Friedrich Krupp Germaniawerft shipyard, the IfS had to be shut down. Thus, in 1946 Gabler together with the director of the IfS, Fritz Ebschner, acting as a silent partner, founded a new company the Ingenieurkontor Lübeck (IKL) – the Engineering Office Lübeck. The young company's main business fields were in heavy steel construction, machinery for agriculture and radio antennae. An involvement in a small shipyard remained a mere episode. But Gabler, who had a reputation abroad as a designer of Second World War's most modern submarines, remained interested how submarine design would develop, and in 1949 the Swedish Navy invited him to inform them about the latest innovations. At around this time, two submarine designs had been created, the IK 1 at 560 tonnes and the IK 2 with about 300 tonnes. They were based on the German Navy's last submarine projects. In 1954, IKL received the contract for a submarine design for the Italian Navy and in 1955 another for Brazilian Navy submarine.

IKL in 1957 was awarded its first domestic development order for a small 58-tonne "attack submarine" by the Atlas Werken in Bremen, and a year later, IKL received the order for the construction of a 350 tonne submarine, based on the Type XXIII boat. It was to be a pure submarine, sail as quietly as possible and have as many torpedo tubes as possible. It became the Class 201 – the beginning of the setting up of a new German submarine fleet – and since then, all ensuing submarine classes for the Federal and German Navy have been created by the design office in Lübeck.

It was the tonnage limit that forced the Lübeck submarine designers to accommodate as much performance as they could in the smallest possible space, and in the process thus create exceptionally tough fighting submarines. Over the years, IKL had been behind the design of submarines for foreign navies, which include "best-sellers" such as the Class 209 boats, making this the most successful diesel-electric submarine class in the world. Tom Clancy, speaking from the high horse of nukes, called them "the people's submarine" in his book "Submarine". It might seem a bit derogatory, but the Volkswagen, the people's car, as we know, runs and runs and runs ...

IKL, to which the success of the German submarine industry is largely attributable, was taken over by Howaldtswerke-Deutsche Werft AG in Kiel in 1994.

The German Navy had also been working hard on the construction of the new German submarine force. It was first of all necessary to win sufficient personnel for the new submarines – and have boats on which they could be trained. The tonnage limit of 350 tonnes was a big problem, because none of the NATO navies had such small boats available. Thus the unceremonious plan to salvage scuttled Second World War boats from the bottom of the Baltic, which, as they sank, were the most advanced in the world. They would be repaired and put back into service for training. And so in 1956 the Hamburg-based salvage company Beckedorf raised the Type XXIII submarine U 2365 in the vicinity of Anholt in the Kattegat, and its sister ship U 2367, in the vicinity of Schleimünde. The boats were towed to Howaldtswerke in Kiel and lifted ashore. It turned out that the good state of preservation of both was beyond expectation. The last commander of U 2365, who accompanied the salvage of his command, had opened the lube tanks before scuttling, enabling a protective oil film to cover the boat's interior and systems. Both boats were repaired and modified within a short time, and as U HAI (S 170) and U HECHT (S 171) re-entered service as training submarines on 15 August 1957. IKL was in possession of the Type XXVIII construction drawings that Gabler had saved through the end of the war, and which now contributed to the rapid refittings. The news that Germany was re-deploying two of Grand Admiral Dönitz's dreaded wolf packs submarines hit the headlines. The New York Times of 16 August 1957 reported: *"Re-floated Nazi U-Boat put into operation at Kiel".*

With HAI and HECHT, the German Navy now had two suitable training boats. However, in 1957 John Beckedorf salvaged a third cutting edge Type XXI submarine U 2450. This boat had been scuttled in the Gelting Bay, and was in good condition too. But what next, as this boat did not in any way fit into the rules governing tonnage limits? Then the Howaldtswerke in Kiel purchased it at short notice, especially as the German Navy was interested in it. And finally, the Federal Ministry of Defence decided to use the boat as a training and experimental boat, and use it as a template for the new boats of the German Navy. In 1960, U 2450 re-entered service as WILHELM BAUER, and owing to its new streamlined conning tower shape, was affectionately renamed by its crew "Schnelltriebwagen" – express train engine. Until 1980 it served as an experimental platform crewed by civilians and after decommissioning, the WILHELM BAUER was returned to its original state, and is now on display in Bremerhaven as a museum ship.

*Rescue of a Type XXI boat sunk during bombing raids at Deutsche Werke AG in Kiel in 1945.* (Archive HDW/TKMS)

# THE RECONSTRUCTION OF THE GERMAN SUBMARINE INDUSTRY

Unlike in most countries, in which naval ships are built in state-owned shipyards, the construction in Germany is privately organised and operated by a number of shipyards. Amongst them, ThyssenKrupp Marine Systems GmbH (TKMS) – formerly HDW – is the only shipyard in Germany which still builds submarines today. The reconstruction of the German submarine industry began in Kiel.[5]

In 1956, when the two Type XXIII boats were towed to Howaldtswerke in Kiel, merchant shipbuilding was booming, and busy German shipyards had little interest in building a handful of submarines because, first of all it was not obvious that a business could be made out of them. Submarine building was a tiny niche in the shipbuilding industry, but one which also demanded investment. And secondly, so shortly after the war, preoccupation with naval ships was not exactly popular, and thus submarine construction at HDW was coyly known as "special shipbuilding" for many years. Yards were not prepared to use the word "submarine" with regard to critical public sentiments. However, at the beginning of the 60s it had become clear that the German Navy intended to order a large number of submarines, and when it was later allowed to export submarines, the German industry's interest in this sophisticated ship-building trade, which requires

*The Type XXIII submarine U 2365 after salvage in the Kattegat in 1956 at Howaldtswerke in Kiel.* (Archive HDW/TKMS)

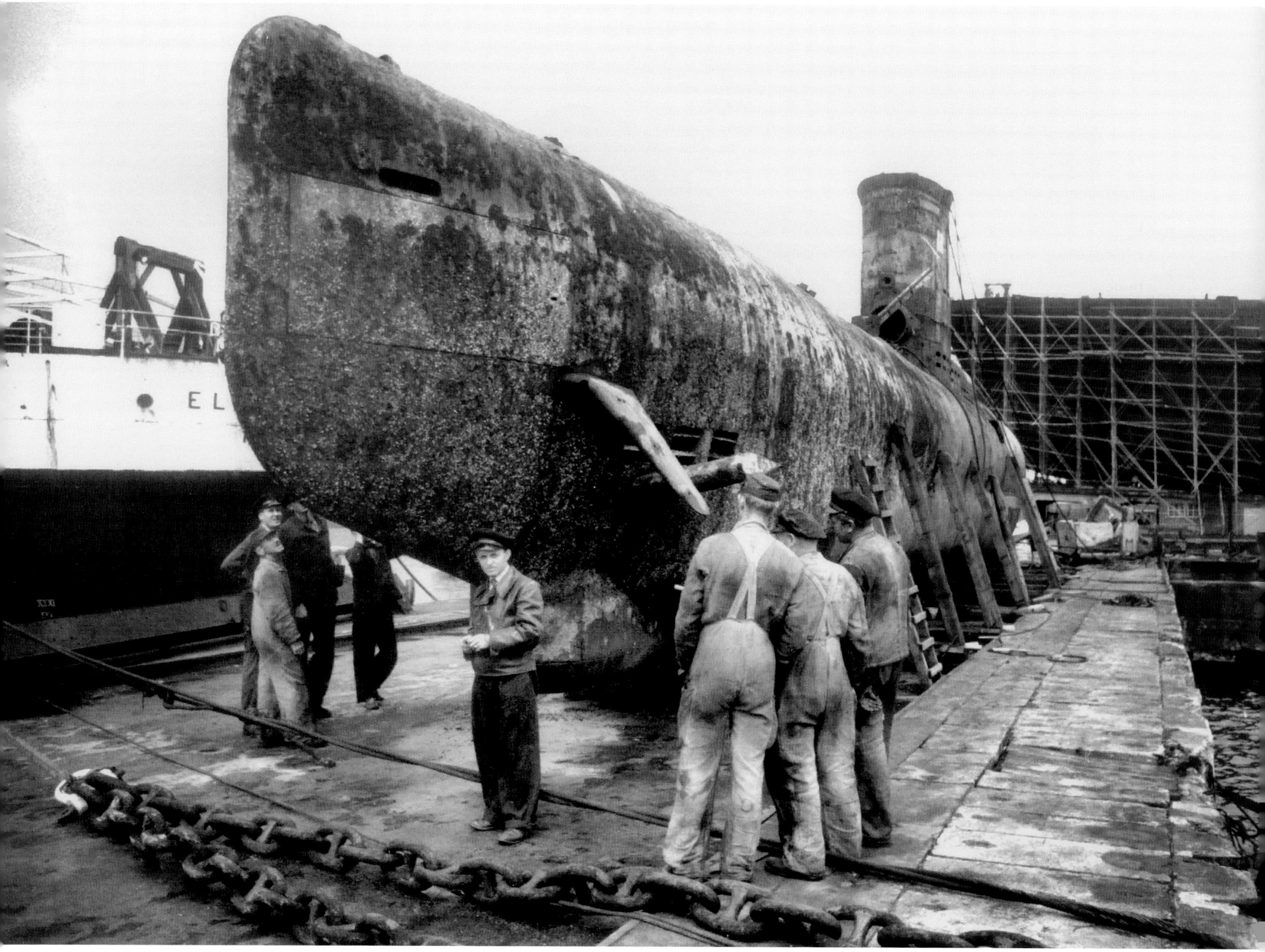
EL

technological excellence,finally awoke. This led to a powerful industry, and today comprises companies such as ATLAS ELECTRONIK with sensors and weapon command and control systems, Zeiss with state-of-the-art periscopes, SIEMENS with electronics and Fuel Cells, Raytheon Anschütz with navigation systems, L-3 ELAC nautical with underwater acoustics, MTU with submarine diesel engines, Gabler Maschinenbau with hoisting masts – as well as many more companies in the Federal Republic. This extremely powerful and innovative industrial base forms the basis for the world-wide success of German post-war submarine construction, which Professor Gabler and IKL initially kicked off. This also has its consequences on employment: today, one employee building a submarine at the shipyard generates work for about five people in the supply industry. In numbers, that means that around 10,000 families in Germany live off submarine building conducted on the coast, and of them, about half have their homes far inland.



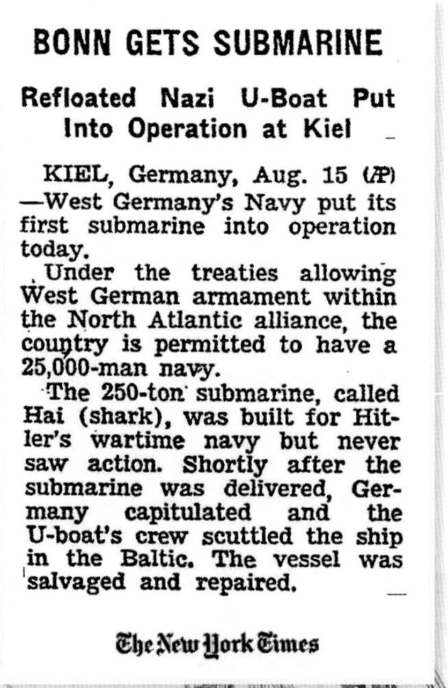

**BONN GETS SUBMARINE**

**Refloated Nazi U-Boat Put Into Operation at Kiel**

KIEL, Germany, Aug. 15 (AP) —West Germany's Navy put its first submarine into operation today.

Under the treaties allowing West German armament within the North Atlantic alliance, the country is permitted to have a 25,000-man navy.

The 250-ton submarine, called Hai (shark), was built for Hitler's wartime navy but never saw action. Shortly after the submarine was delivered, Germany capitulated and the U-boat's crew scuttled the ship in the Baltic. The vessel was salvaged and repaired.

The New York Times

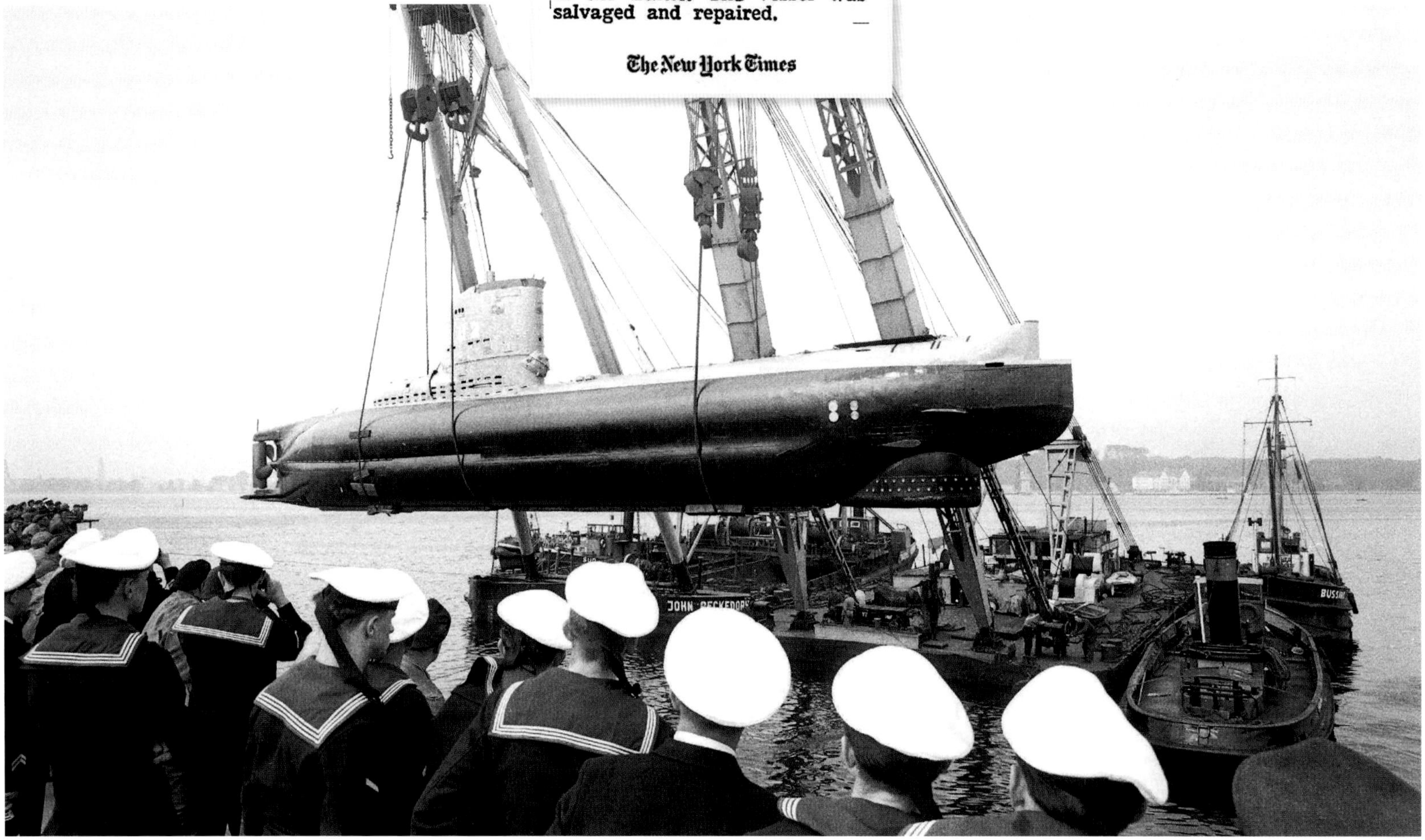
JOHN BECKEDORF
BUSSARD

*Above: 15 August 1957: the restored and modernised U 2367 is lowered into the water as U HAI at Howaldtswerke in Kiel.*

*Centre inset: the New York Times clipping from 16 August 1957.* (Archive HDW/TKMS)

The principle of general contractorship (GC) is critical for the success in Germany and later in export markets. It was introduced in 1969. Since then, and to this day, HDW/ThyssenKrupp Marine Systems is technically and economically solely responsible as general contractor for the overall system as well as the documentation of all contractual performance data of the submarines. This includes the full sea testing of boats under the responsibility of HDW/TKMS. The shipyard conducts trials with its own personnel, including own submarine crews, and provides two own escort vessels, PEGASUS II and HERCULES, for tests in the Baltic Sea, the Skagerrak and off the Norwegian coast. TKMS has a specially hired harbour in Kristiansand (Norway), from which HDW crews go out for deep water tests. Additionally, HDW/TKMS trains the crews of customer navies in the technical mastery of their boats at the shipyard's own training centre. And so HDW/TKMS delivers "turnkey" submarine solutions, which have been fully tested. This general contractor concept, already well established in Germany, has proven itself particularly in export, and is a unique competitive advantage. For at French and UK-based competitors, the responsibilities for the boats to be delivered are separated. The interaction of the Navy, government agencies and private companies does not lead to clear divisions of responsibility.

*Experimental submarine WILHELM BAUER, formerly the Type XXI submarine U 2450. (Archive HDW/TKMS)*

Thus unique identification and the responsibility for performance data laid down in the contract can be difficult to provide, and residual risks that are not negligible remain with the purchaser. Accordingly, many customer navies prefer the principle of the general contractor, who alone is fully responsible to them.

The German Navy as a "parent navy" plays an equally important role in export. A sign of confidence, which foreign customers appreciate, is the simple fact that it builds its boats in Germany and successfully operates them. The German Navy was also the first to order the new Class 212A Fuel Cell boats which have now proven to be a hugely successful development. In addition, German Navy gives foreign customer navies, especially if they have little submarine experience, assistance in learning to operate the boats and tactical training.

## NEW SUBMARINES FOR THE GERMAN AND SCANDINAVIAN NAVIES

On 16 March 1959, Howaldtswerke in Kiel received the order for the construction of 12 Class 201 submarines, and on 21 October 1961, the first 350 tonne boat U 1 was launched. U2 and U3 followed a year later. U 3 first went on loan to the Norwegian Navy in anticipation of the planned



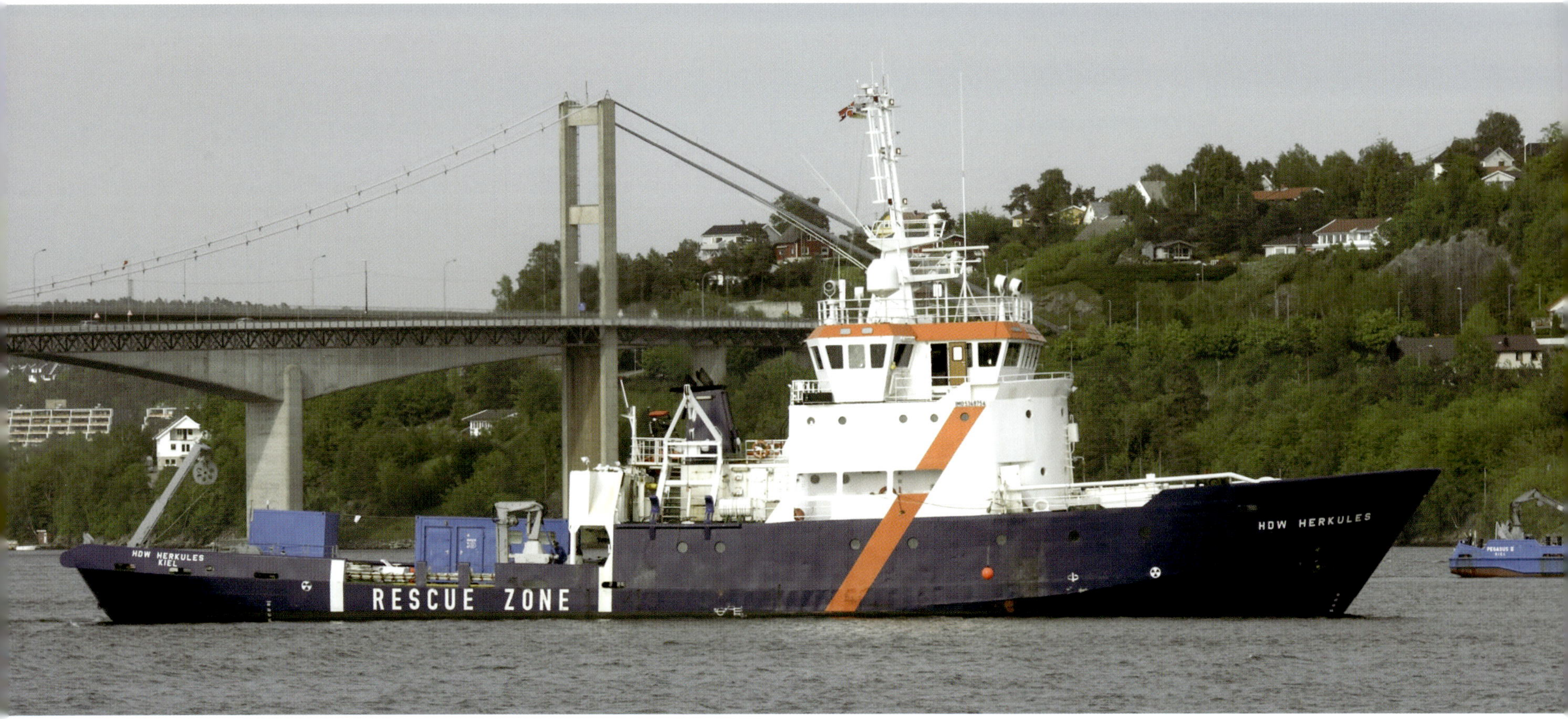
HDW HERKULES
RESCUE ZONE

*Left: submarine escorts PEGAGSUS II and HERCULES off Kristiansand.*

*Right: Kiel submarine construction: fitting out a torpedo tube.* (Peter Neumann/YPS)

15 Class 207 submarines, which the Norwegian Navy had ordered in 1961 from the Rheinstahl Nordseewerke shipyard in Emden. But the 201 boats were dogged by bad luck. They were to be built of anti-magnetic steel, but the selected steel however proved unsuitable. Unfortunately, two steel samples had been swapped during the material testing; the mistakenly selected steel cracked, and the submarines could hardly dive – Germany had its first arms scandal.

During the construction of the boats, the decision was made to equip subsequent boats with a new, but bulky, wide sonar system (WSS). This initiated a redesign by IKL, referred to as the Class 205, which however exceeded the tonnage limit of 350 tonnes by almost 50 tonnes. At the request of the Federal Government, the WEU raised the permitted tonnage in 1962 to 450 tonnes, and with an exceptional approval also gave permission for the construction of six Class 208 attack submarines of about 1,000 tonnes. But the Ministry of Defence pondered long and hard over the new boats, did not come to any decision – and thus they were never built.

Meanwhile, the Americans had taken notice of the young German submarine industry, and particularly of the small but powerful, robust attack submarines. They installed a "Military Assistance Advisory Group" in Hamburg, which "should observe" the construction during the building of the class 207. [6] Indeed, the Americans, faced with the threat to the

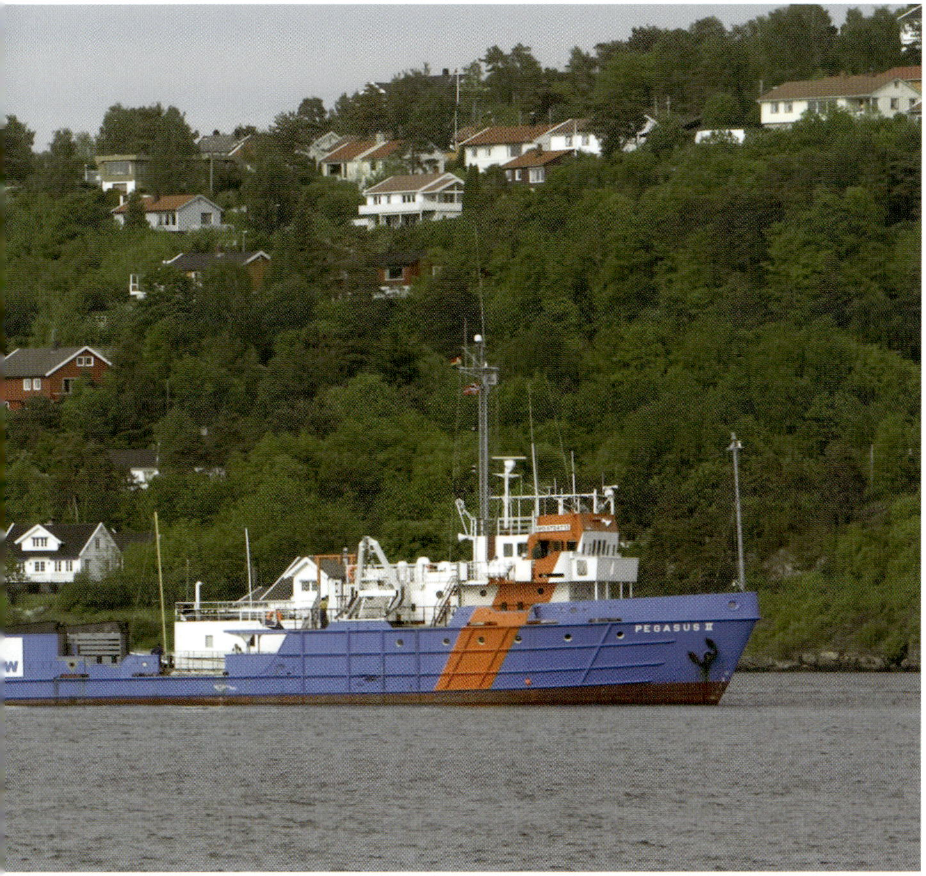
PEGASUS II

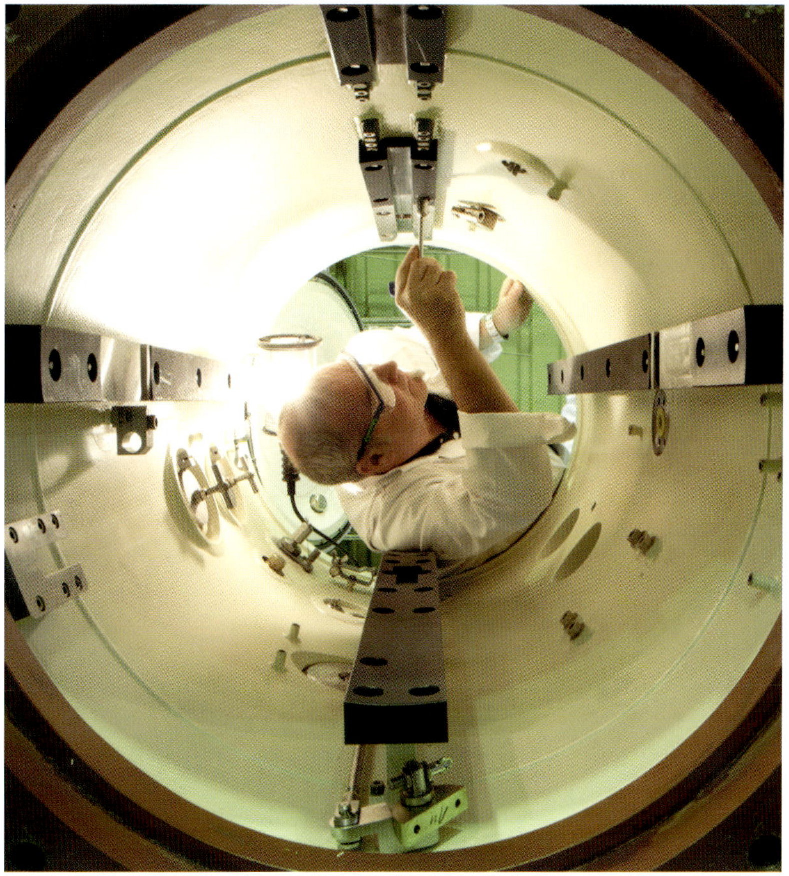

NATO northern flank during the Cold War, were willing to cover half of the costs of the Norwegian boats.[7] And they had a reason to show legitimate interest in construction work progress, and later on, in the boats' operational performances.

In the meantime, the construction of two Class 202 submarines – HANS TECHEL and FRIEDRICH SCHÜRER – remained a mere intermezzo. The 137 tonne small boats were intended to be test platforms for the Class 201 and 205 boats. HANS TECHEL and FRIEDRICH SCHÜRER were to be used for reconnaissance, but ultimately proved to be useless, and were thus scrapped almost immediately after entering service.



On 12 December 1960, Howaldtswerke in Kiel received the order for nine Class 205 submarines, which IKL had developed from the Class 201. The extent of the changes to the original Class 201 design was so large that the redesign now meant a new design. The first boats – U 4-U 8 – had been built with the wrong steel alloy, since its unsuitability had not been established until after construction began. Thus, the Navy placed the boats in service under restrictions for training purposes, and for the subsequent boats a freeze was imposed until a suitable steel alloy could be found. Various non-magnetic steels were tested before one proved to be particularly well suited – which, since then, has been used on all German submarines. At the same time, the Class 205 underwent further improvements and became the Class 205mod. Two further Class 205 boats were built on licence at the Copenhagen Orlogswerft and entered Danish Navy service in 1970 as NARVHALEN and NORDKAPEREN.

The 18 Class 206 boats, all of which entered service in the 70s, represented the German Navy's provisional termination of its submarine construction programme. With these boats, IKL had managed to make use of the total tonnage of 450 tonnes as approved by the WEU. The Class 201 and 205 boats utilized a high proportion of ballast in the assumption that it was

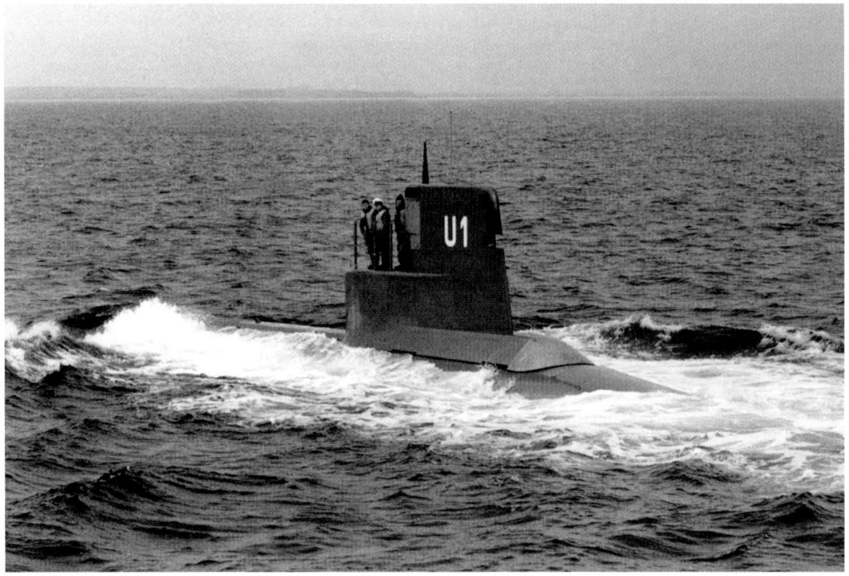
U1

*Class 201 submarine U 1.* (*Archiv HDW/TKMS*)

**CLASS 201 SUBMARINE (U 1 – U 3)**

| | |
|---|---|
| Displacement: | 350 t surfaced |
| | 450 t dived |
| Length (LOA): | 42 m |
| Beam: | 4.6 m |
| Crew: | 21 persons |
| Propulsion: | 1,200 hp diesel engine |
| | 1,200 hp electic motor |
| Speed, surfaced: | 10.7 knots |
| Speed, dived: | 17.0 knots |
| Range: | 3,800 nm surfaced |
| | 230 nm dived |
| Weapons: | 8 torpedo tubes, Ø 533 mm |
| | 8 torpedoes or 16 mines |

deductible from the total tonnage under the WEU rules.

Now a submarine was to be invented in which the ballast and other deductible weights were to be fully replaced by batteries required to feed the increasingly power-hungry electronics (sensors, communication, fire control systems etc.). At the same time, dived performances had to be maintained. Furthermore, the boats had to be able to fire wire-guided torpedoes, and in order to avoid limitation to the number of on-board torpedoes, the German Navy boats were to be fitted with belts holding 24 mines, attached to the hull exteriors.

HDW in Kiel and the Rheinstahl Nordseewerke in Emden received the building contract jointly in 1969, and for the first time, the principle of the general contractorship (GC) came into play. HDW took over the role of the general contractor with the overall responsibility for the project and Nordseewerke acted as subcontractor.

These submarines, with their distinctive bow sonar domes, some of which were rebuilt into Class 206A boats, have proven to be extremely useful over their service times. During the Cold War, they operated primarily in the Baltic Sea and its approaches. Then they were deployed to the Mediterranean where they successfully participated in operations and exercises. Between 1973 and 2011, these boats have demonstrated their superiorities over any other submarine in shallow and littoral water missions. But they have also proven themselves in deep water. They have taken part in Atlantic and Caribbean NATO manoeuvres, and even managed to scare the wits out of the US Navy when they managed to surface undetected, in a feint attack, inside the stiff protection zone of an American aircraft carrier. In other words – these boats were impossible to locate.



## GERMAN NUCLEAR SUBMARINES?

In older German submariner circles, a rumour regularly resurfaces, rather like Nessie, the Loch Ness monster, that Germany wanted to build nuclear-

### CLASS 205 SUBMARINE

| | |
|---|---|
| Displacement: | 450 t surfaced |
| | 500 t dived |
| Length / Beam | 45.7 m / 4.6 m |
| Crew: | 22 Persons |
| Propulsion: | Diesel-electric |
| | Two Diesel generators, 600 hp each |
| | 1,500 hp electric motor |
| Speed: | 10.0 knots surfaced, 17.0 knots dived |
| Range: | 4,200 nm surfaced |
| | abt. 230 nm dived |
| Nominal diving depth: | 100 m |
| Weapons: | 8 torpedo tubes, Ø 533 mm |
| | Mines |

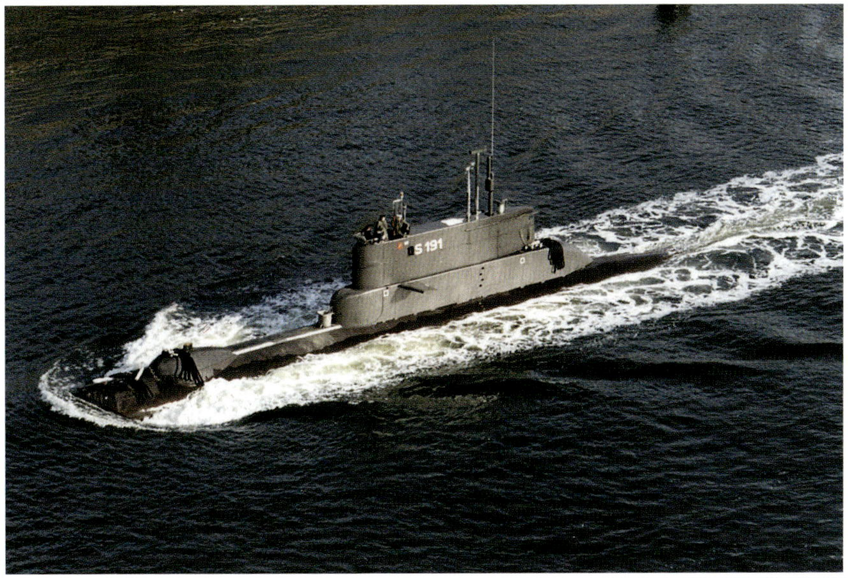
S 191
*Class 205 boat with an experimental bow.* (Archive HDW/TKMS)

powered submarines. But unlike the legendary Scottish sea monster, a German nuclear submarine was no chimera – not quite. In August 2008, under the headline "Desirous Dreams", the SPIEGEL reported[8] the findings of Alexander Lurz, a young historian, in the British national archives. He had uncovered the once-secret report of the British Ambassador to NATO, Frank Roberts, after a meeting with NATO's Supreme Commander in Europe, General Lauris Norstad. The SPIEGEL story indicated that the Adenauer Government and its Defence Minister, Franz Josef Strauß, wanted nuclear submarines for the Navy.

In the report dated 26 April 1960, Roberts cites an incensed Norstad, who was angered that Germany had been putting the pressure on Washington for more than two years for a nuclear submarine. Only recently had Germany's Foreign Minister Brentano followed up the issue again. According to Norstad, the Germans had to be given a firm "no". An ocean-going German nuclear submarine with unlimited endurance was the last thing NATO wanted from Germany. There was no military justification for it. The American State Department should have made that clear to the German Government a long time ago. The former had asked for his advice, and that he (Norstad) was tired of shifting the burden of policy decisions to his shoulders.

In Franz Josef Strauß, the Adenauer Government had a fervent supporter for the nuclear armament of the German Bundeswehr in its ranks. He had been Federal Minister for Nuclear Issues from 1955 to 1956, and from 1956 to 1962 Defence Minister. And, like Konrad Adenauer, he was convinced that peace would only be possible after winning the nuclear race with the Soviet Union. The strange thing about his insistence on nuclear boats, however, was that the NATO Allies had just agreed to permit

## CLASS 206 / 206A SUBMARINES

| | |
|---|---|
| Displacement: | 450 t surfaced |
| | 498 t dived |
| Length (LOA): | 48.6 m |
| Beam: | 4.6 m |
| Crew: | 27 persons |
| Antrieb: | Diesel-electric |
| | Two diesel generators, 600 hp each |
| | 1,500 hp electric motor |
| Speed, surfaced: | max. 10.0 knots |
| Speed, dived: | max. 17.0 knots |
| Range: | 4,500 nm surfaced |
| | approx. 230 nm dived |
| Nominal diving depth: | Over 200 m |
| Weapons: | 8 torpedo tubes, Ø 533 mm |
| | Belt for 24 mines |

*German Navy Class 206A submarine.* (Peter Neumann/YPS)

Germany the small 350 tonne boats – and only because the Cold War had forced them to do so. It was also ironic that in the Paris Treaty of 1954 Germany pledged to abandon warships *"that are driven otherwise than with steam engines, diesel or petrol engines, gas turbine or jet drives"*.[9] And this clearly excluded nuclear drives.

Strauß had a strong political supporter in Konrad Adenauer who now distrusted the protection of Americans. The launching of the Sputnik in 1957 seemed to be the final proof that Russia was now technologically so far ahead that America's era of nuclear superiority was past. In addition, Adenauer did not believe it to be correct that only two great powers should solely possess nuclear weapons, and thus determine the fate of the world. Accordingly he wanted to be independent and have nuclear weapons himself, [10] which the Paris Treaties ruled out. He got support from the French Government, which also no longer believed in American superiority, and made an amazing offer: Germany and France could develop nuclear weapons together with Italy, which had already expressed interest, and produce them – of course under strict secrecy. Adenauer tried to make this happen, deployed every means and every political trick, and ultimately together with the Americans under the keyword "nuclear sharing". He also pushed a bill for nuclear armament of the German Bundeswehr against all resistance through the Bundestag, the German parliament. But the atomic dreams came to nothing as France resigned its position as head partner of the group. It had become entangled with the Algerian crisis, the Indo-Chinese war, and had become leading negotiator for the European defence community – and was in the middle of a national crisis.

Against this background, Strauß, much to the dismay of the Foreign Office, tried to procure nuclear submarines for the Navy. Documents of the former reveal that the Ministry of Defence was involved in such plans, and "coast gossip" confirms this without possessing too many details – it was more a question of rumours. However, shipbuilding experts of the time agreed that there had not been a concrete submarine project, and that Germany was technically not in a position to build a nuclear submarine. HDW had just started on the planning and construction of the Class 201 submarines, and concentrated the Walter propulsion.[11] Prof. Dr. Fritz Abels, Managing Director of IKL, said his company *"never had a German nuclear submarine on the drawing board ... we couldn't do it"*. [12] And so, in the 1980s, IKL declined Brazil's request for the complete construction of a nuclear-powered submarine as *"we had no experience"*.

Wild speculations existed that the German nuclear freighter OTTO HAHN, which the Gesellschaft für Kernenergieverwertung in Schiffbau und Schiffahrt mbH (GKSS – the Society for the Utilisation of Atomic Energy in Shipbuilding and Shipping Ltd) had started to plan, and which was delivered by Howaldtswerke in Kiel in 1968, was intended not to be a research vessel for peaceful use, but a test bed for a reactor fitting for a large submarine. Supposedly this was the reason why the Type XXI submarine U 2450 had been salvaged from Baltic Sea and put into service of the Federal Navy as WILHELM BAUER. And the reactor was supposedly to have been for this boat. But, the claim looses validity once the height of the reactor (about 15 metres) is compared to the height of the submarine (just over 7 metres). And it's also speculation that a former submarine commander was OTTO HAHN's master, owing to the vessel's apparent secret purpose. It's worth pointing out that many former naval officers, including submarine commanders, entered post-war employment in merchant shipping.

IKL watched OTTO HAHN's development *"with interest"* according to Abels. The company occupied itself with comparative studies over nuclear powered submarines, on behalf of the German Defence Ministry[13] – it however, never created any designs for a build. As already stated, IKL lacked the experience. Accordingly, it is doubtful whether the OTTO HAHN was designed, built and operated as a test bed for a German Navy nuclear submarine. It should rather be seen in the light of other nuclear powered merchant ships such as the SAVANNAH (United States, 1962) and MUTSU (Japan, 1970). OTTO HAHN had first and fore-mostly been built to evaluate the civilian use of nuclear energy in the merchant shipping industry.

Western powers ensured that the German nuclear submarine remained a pipe-dream for the fireplaces of Bonn, Germany's then capital. The true fact is, seen from a shipbuilder's point of view, owing to lack of German experience, the development and construction of such boats would have taken too much time, cost far too much money, quite apart from the problems associated with radioactive waste disposal. German submarine builders re-focused in 1960 on the Walter propulsion, which cumulated some 20 years later in the Fuel Cell, which has become a global success.

*OTTO HAHN: Inserting the safety container with reactor in HDW 1967. (Archive HDW/TKMS)*

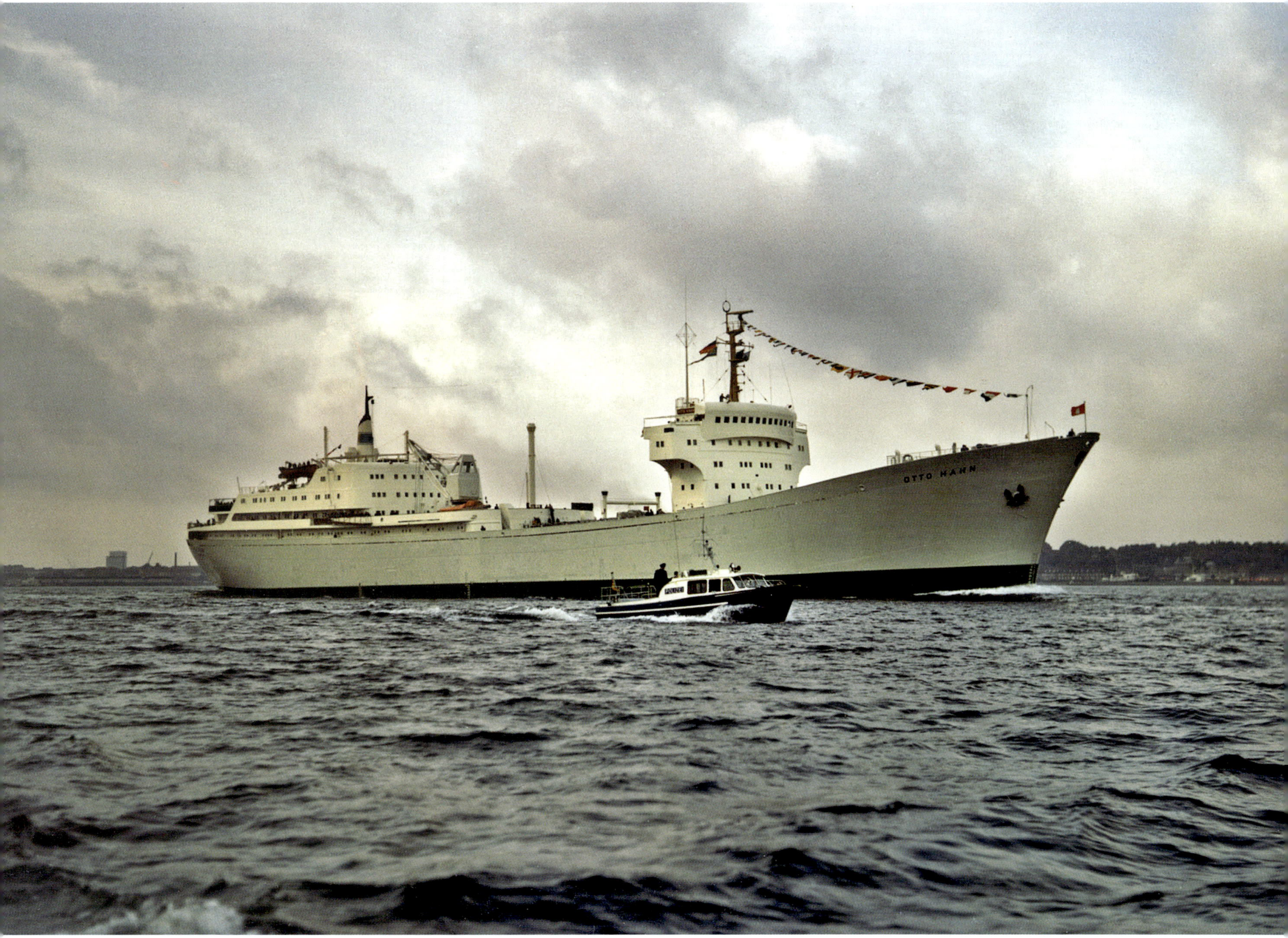
OTTO HAHN

*Nuclear cargo and research ship OTTO HAHN 1968* (*Archive HDW/TKMS*)

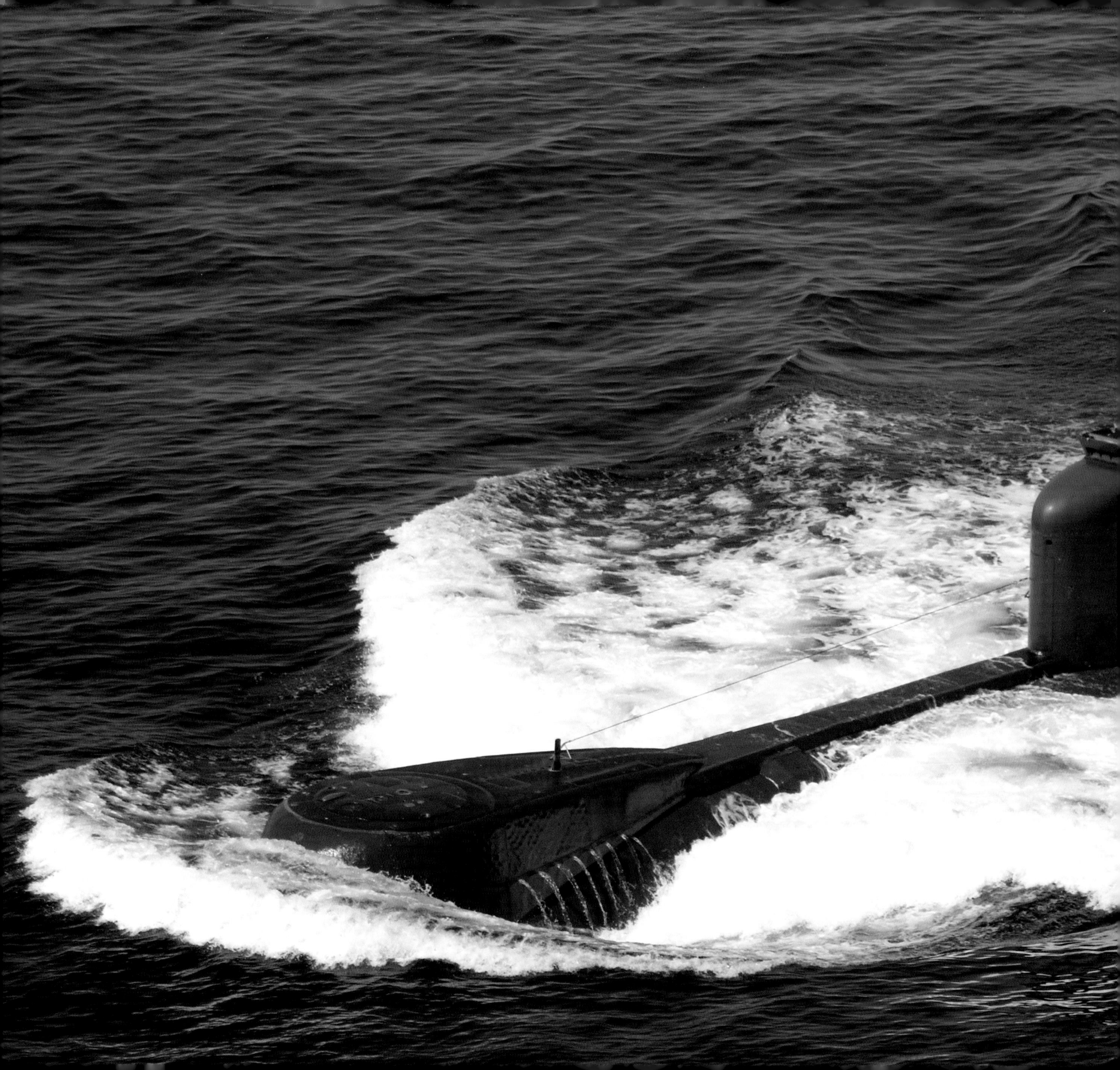

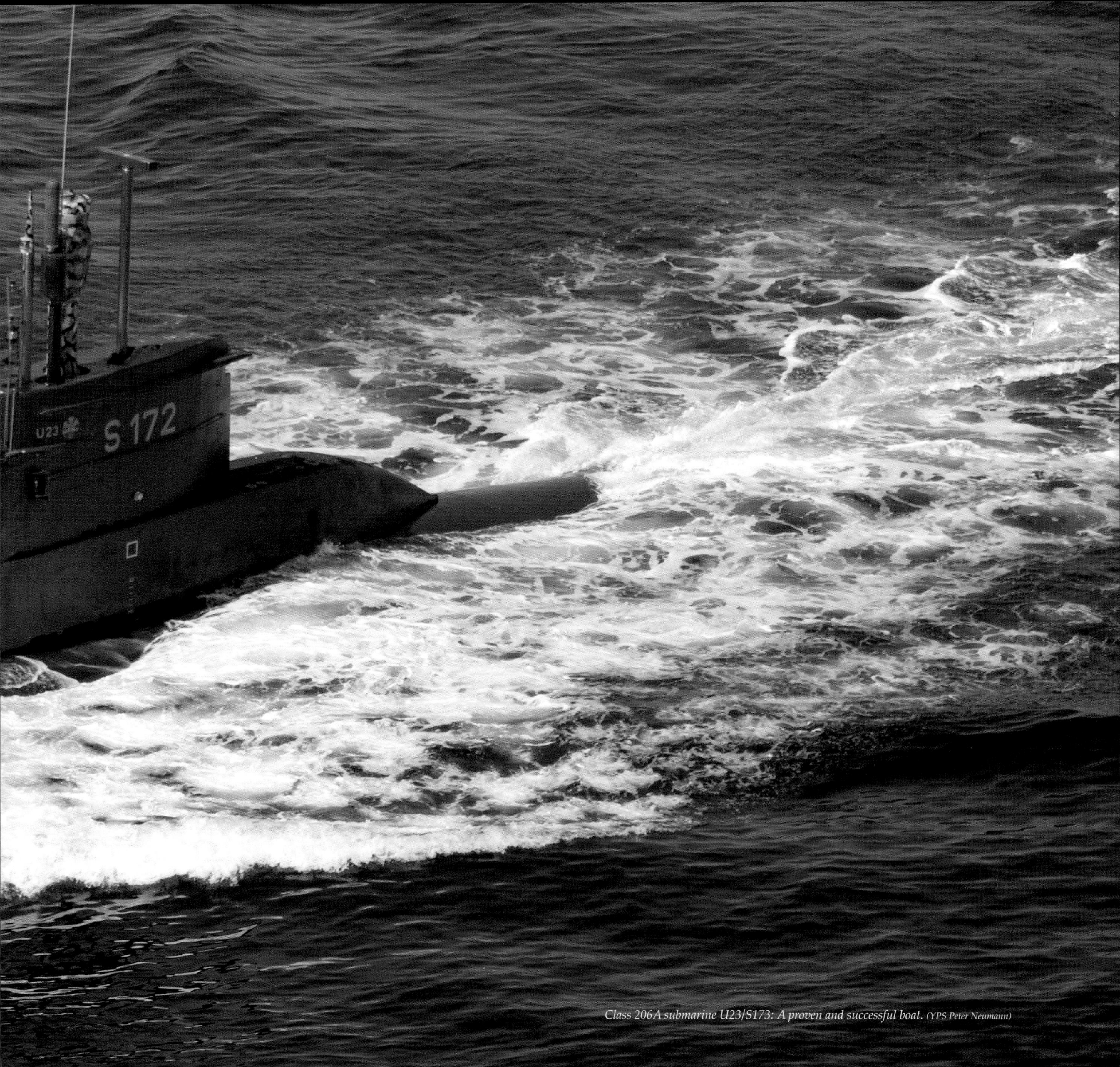
U23
S 172

*Class 206A submarine U23/S173: A proven and successful boat.* (YPS Peter Neumann)

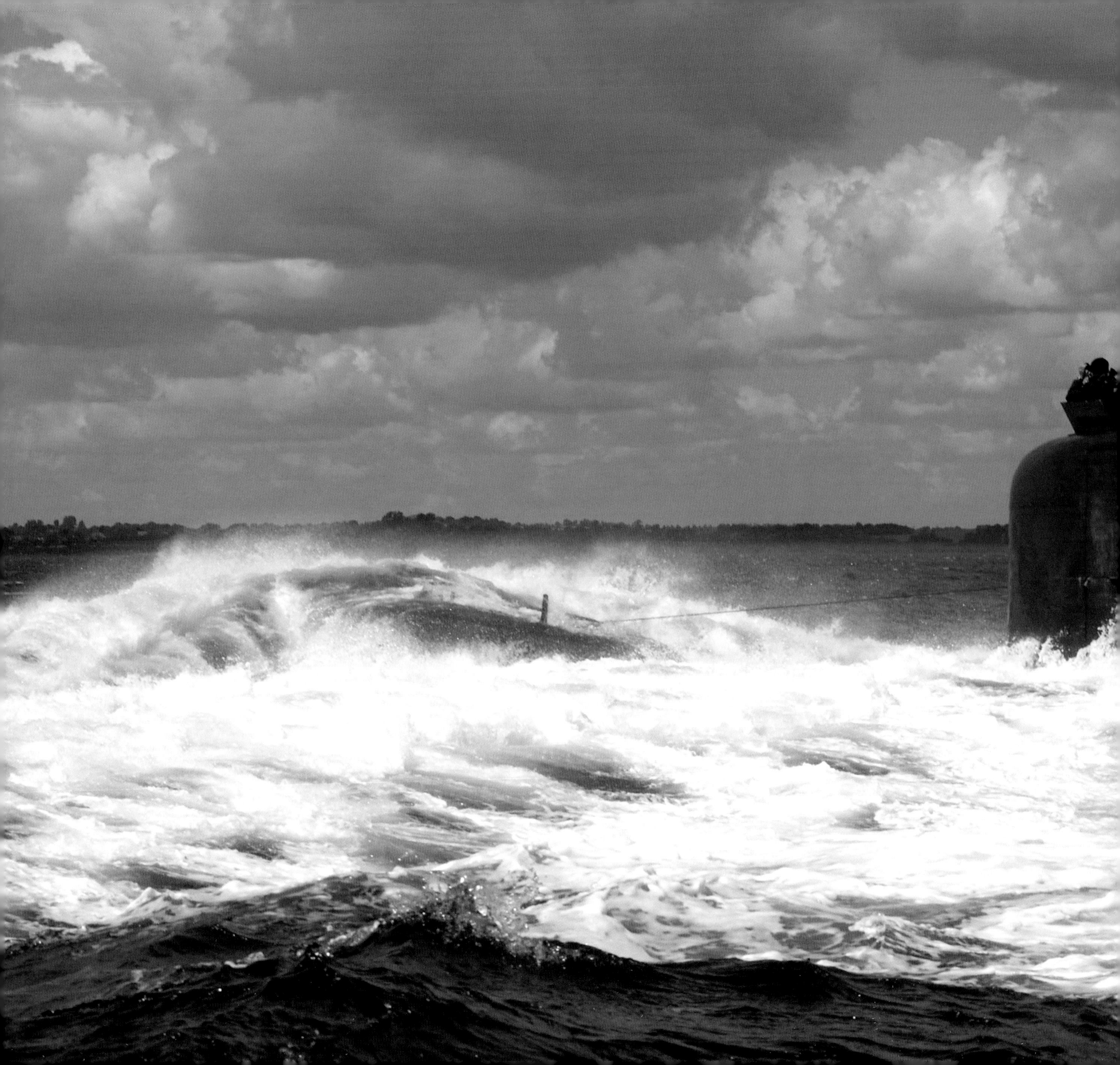

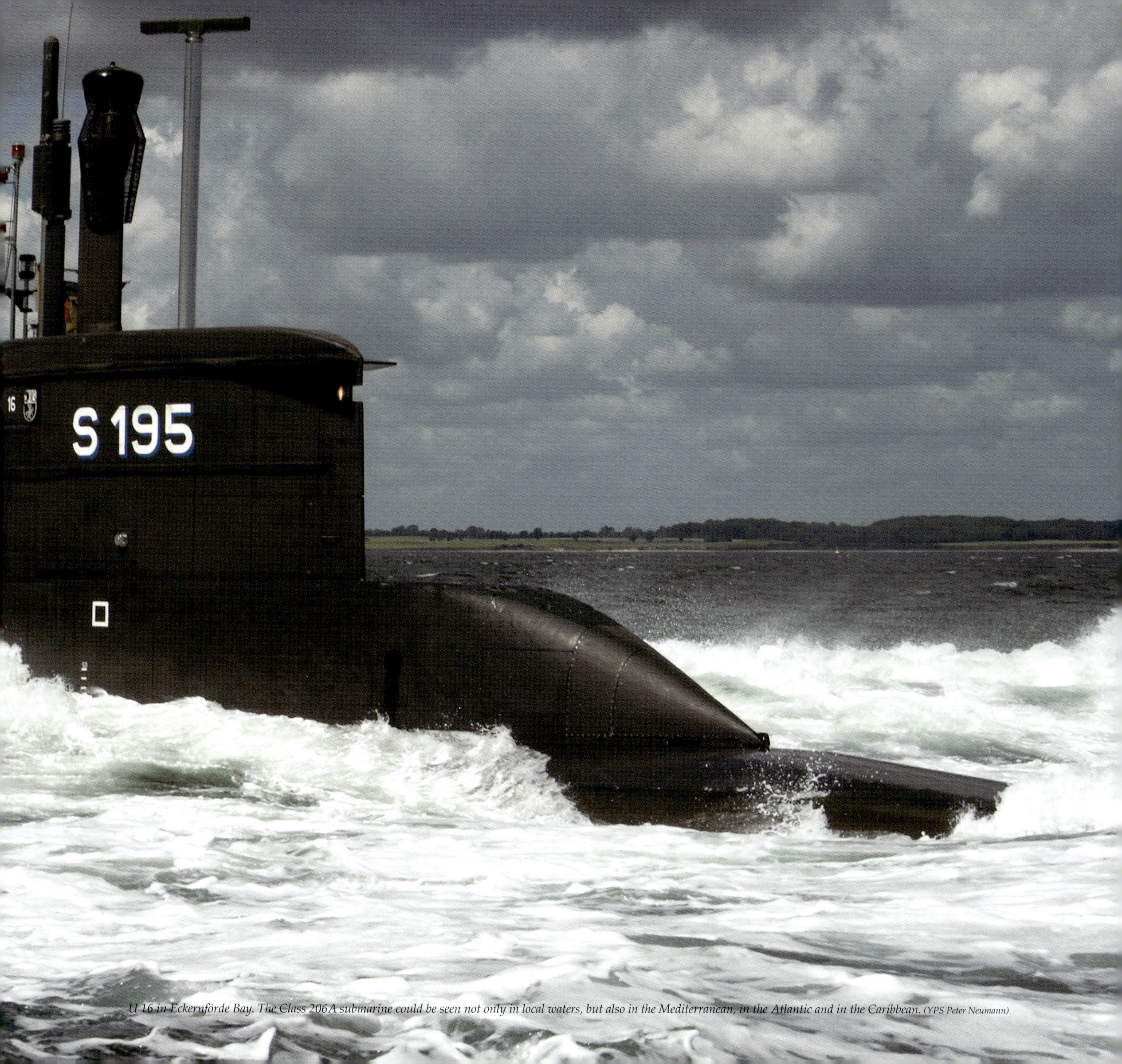
16
S 195

*U 16 in Eckernförde Bay. The Class 206A submarine could be seen not only in local waters, but also in the Mediterranean, in the Atlantic and in the Caribbean.* (YPS Peter Neumann)

# Submarines "Made in Germany"

**THE ROAD TO EXPORT: THE CLASS 209 SUBMARINE**

Today, 20 navies in four continents operate over 100 submarines designed in Germany, and built either in Germany, or built with German assistance in their home countries. The German submarine shipyards systematically pursued export markets, after completing the first submarine construction programme for the country's navy in the 60s.

In the absence of national orders, as the German Navy now had sufficient boats, significant problems with the utilisation of submarine building capacities arose, and especially at HDW in Kiel. The modern recently erected facilities needed continued employment. On the one hand, the shipyards had assembled a base of highly qualified employees, which they did not want to lose. And on the other hand, the German Navy knew it need national shipyards in which its boats could be maintained, modernized and kept in operational condition. Thus the Federal Government had no objections against the export of German submarines, especially as it served German Navy interests. However, the German government has always retained the rights of consent to any export business. Even today, not every country can order a German submarine.

A partner was quickly found for foreign business affairs. The trading house Ferrostaal in Essen had the experience for the acquiring orders, had a worldwide distribution network, and thus was able to coordinate and support ministries and competent authorities in negotiations with foreign navies. In passing, its worth pointing out that Ferrostaal had worked for IvS in the 1920s.

The German yards discovered a favourable market. As the US Navy had quit deploying conventional diesel-electric submarines, and now relied entirely on nuclear submarines, hardly any competition existed for German designs except the British OBERON and French DAPHNE class boats. Both were further developments of Second World War submarines, which were inferior to the new modern designs of IKL.

The restrictions laid down by the WEU for Germany's new boats forced IKL accommodate maximum performances in minimum space, which resulted in submarines that were characterised with high fighting capabilities, eight torpedo tubes that could simultaneously launch their torpedoes, small crews, long underwater endurances and high speeds. Yet another telling argument was that the purchase price and operating costs were low compared to those of the competition[1].

The first major export success were the Class 207 submarines for the Norwegian Navy. They were a further development of the IKL's Class 205 boat. Norway had to maintain a small but task-ready submarine fleet assigned with the defence of the important NATO North flank. At the end of the 1950s, it consisted of a colourful mixture of obsolete English and German Second World War boats, that had to be replaced with new constructions. The United States took over half of the cost.[2] Norway opted for IKL its designers, because the small new German submarines were particularly powerful in relation to their size, and superior to any comparable boats. Rheinstahl Nordseewerke in Emden were awarded the order for 15 boats.

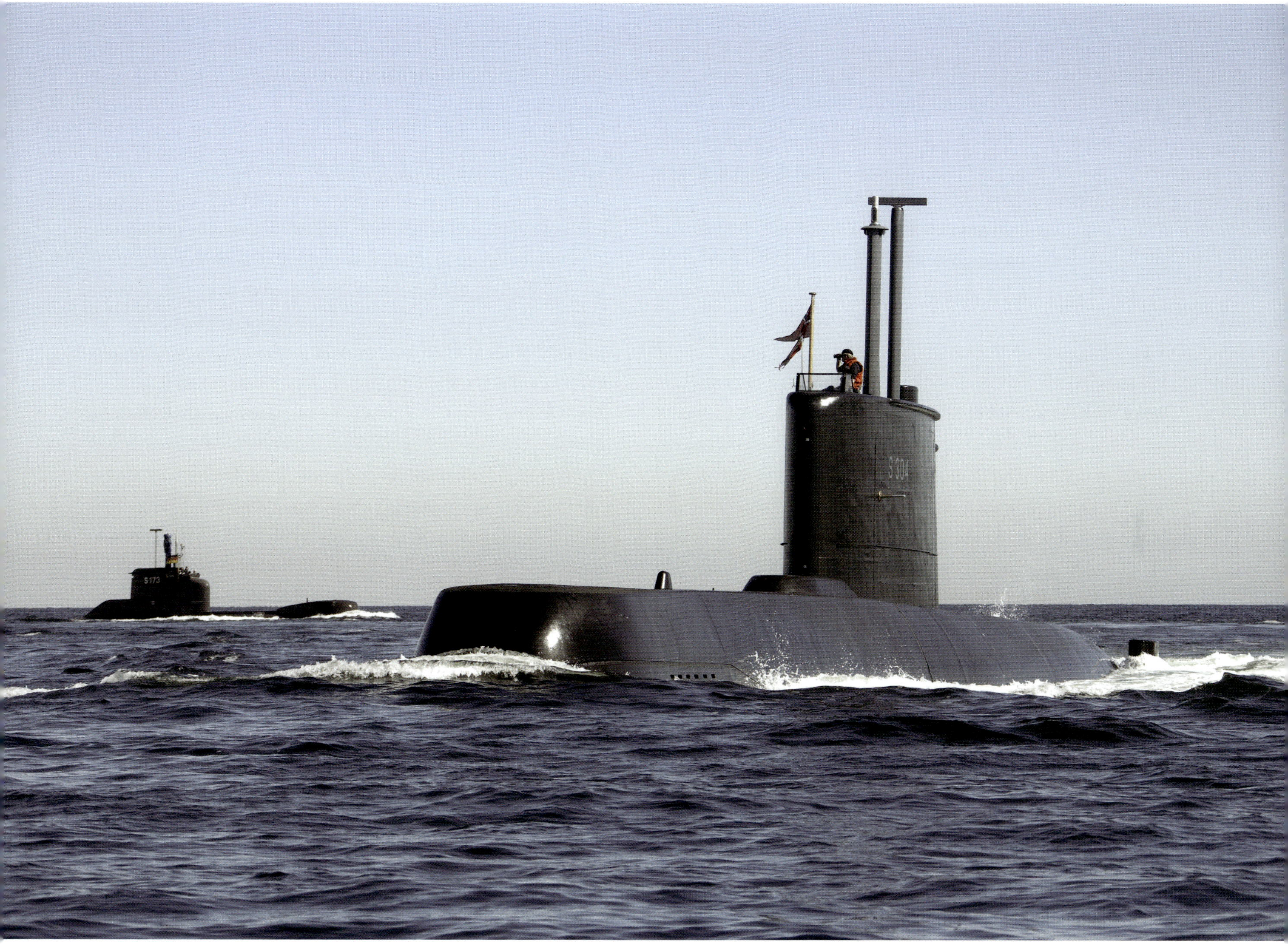
S173
S 304

*"German Design": U-24, a German Navy Class 206A boat (left) and UTHAUG, a Royal Norwegian Navy ULA Class boat.* (YPS Peter Neumann)

The Norwegian boats were designed for the specific operational conditions off the Norwegian coast. The 500 tonne KOBBEN class boats, were thus not built of anti-magnetic steel, but of a special high-tensile steel – HY 80 – which is more suitable for large depths. The boats could, as Wikipedia asserts[3], dive up to 180 metres beneath the surface, and on 8 April 1964, the Norwegian Navy took the first boat, KINN (S 316), into service. The 15 boats in service between 1964 and 1967 proved their value in the difficult weather conditions of the North Atlantic so well, that in 1982, the Norwegian Navy ordered as a replacement for the Class 207 units, six ULA Class boats (a design variant similar to the German Class 210 submarines) from Nordseewerke in Emden.

A special episode is the construction of submarines for Israel. The Israeli Navy, after the establishment of the State of Israel, was out to obtain submarines in Western Europe, and here Germany became the first choice. Contacts with the German Navy, and particularly with its experienced submariners, had started since the early 1950s. However, Israel was not in the position to order any submarines in Germany at this time, owing to the latter's dark past. Thus, in 1958 the Israeli Navy acquired two English S and T class 800 tonne submarines, which had been built in 1944 and 1946, and since then slightly modernised. But given the serious threats to which Israel was exposed, the Israeli Navy pushed for modern submarines, especially those from Germany.

Thus, IKL developed the GAL Class (type 540) boats with a 500 tonne displacement, and that were based on the Class 205 and 207 boats. These deep-diving submarines were made of magnetic steel and equipped with modern weapons and command and control systems. As construction was still not possible in Germany (for political reasons), Israel, the Federal Government and the United Kingdom agreed that a contract to build them would be awarded to the British shipyard Vickers in Barrow-in-Furness. In 1971 Vickers, HDW and IKL closed a contract regulating the export of conventional submarines, and the resulting three boats were named GAL, TANIN and RAHAV, and entered Israeli Navy service in 1976-1977. The boats were decommissioned between 1997 and 2002 and replaced by the modern DOLPHIN class boats. The first of the former boats, the GAL, has found its final home in Haifa's Naval Museum.

*The German Navy's Class 206A submarine was template to the GAL class submarines.*

## THE CLASS 209 SUBMARINE

The Class 209 submarine has evolved into a phenomenal success. Today, over 60 boats operate in 14 navies. These submarines have been in production for more than 40 years, and in this period, boats have changed. Each Navy ordering boats always had its own special requirements, and technologies have changed over time. Accordingly, very differently equipped boats have been built, and on delivery each of them represented the most modern state-of-the-art vessel of its age.

There has been no change to the basic brief of submarine design: high battery and engine performances, low probability of discovery, high underwater speeds, strong armament with eight torpedo tubes, diving depths of up to 500 metres, extremely low signatures and great endurance at sea. The different requirements of client navies have led to various subclasses featuring different displacements, resulting in the Classes 209/1100, 209/1200, 209,1300, 209/1400, 209/1400mod and 209/1500. and the corresponding building list is impressive:

- Argentina 2 (209/1200)
- Brazil 5 (209/1400),
- Chile 2 (209/1400)
- Ecuador 2 (209/1300)
- Greece 8 (209/1100 and 209/1200),
- India 4 (209/1500),
- Indonesia 2 (209/1300)
- Colombia 2 (209/1200)
- Peru 6 (209/1200),
- Portugal 2 (209PN),
- South Africa 3 (209/1400 mod),
- South Korea 9 options (209/1200).
- Turkey 14 (209/1200 and 209/1400),
- Venezuela 2 (209/1300).



But the start was difficult. The stimulus for developing a new class of submarines was the request from the Peruvian Navy for boats with a displacement of at least 800 tonnes. In cooperation with Howaldtswerke in Kiel, IKL came up with a design for a boat of 900-1,000 tonnes. It represented the ultimate in fighting power and underwater endurance at the time for a non-nuclear powered boat of this size. 25 per cent of the boat's displacement was planned for high-performance batteries, which in conjunction with a new large Siemens motor, delivered the sensational

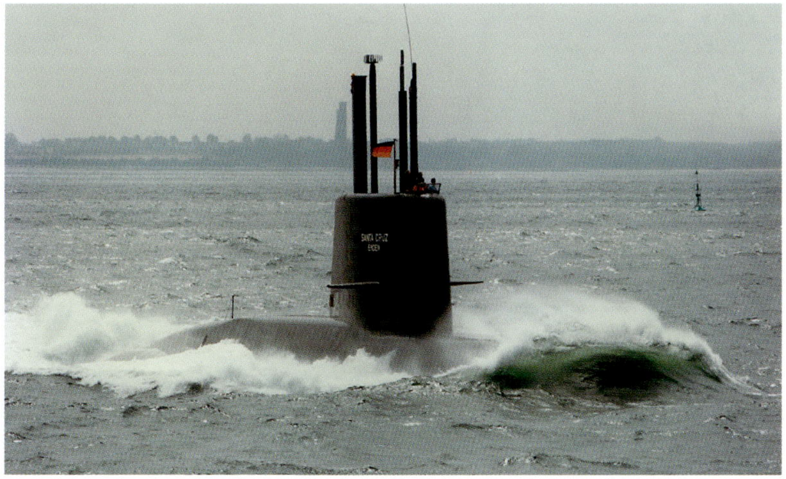

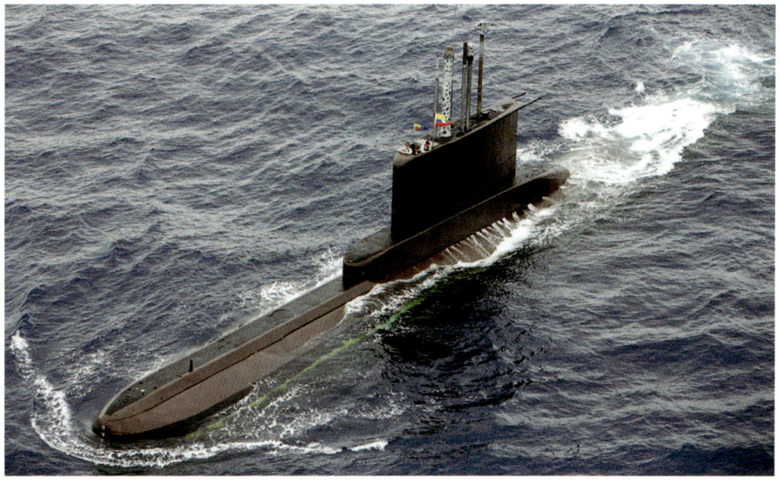

*Successful HDW Class 209 submarines: 1,200 tonne boats for Argentina (left) and Columbia (right).* *(Argentine Submarine Force/Colombian Flotilla)*

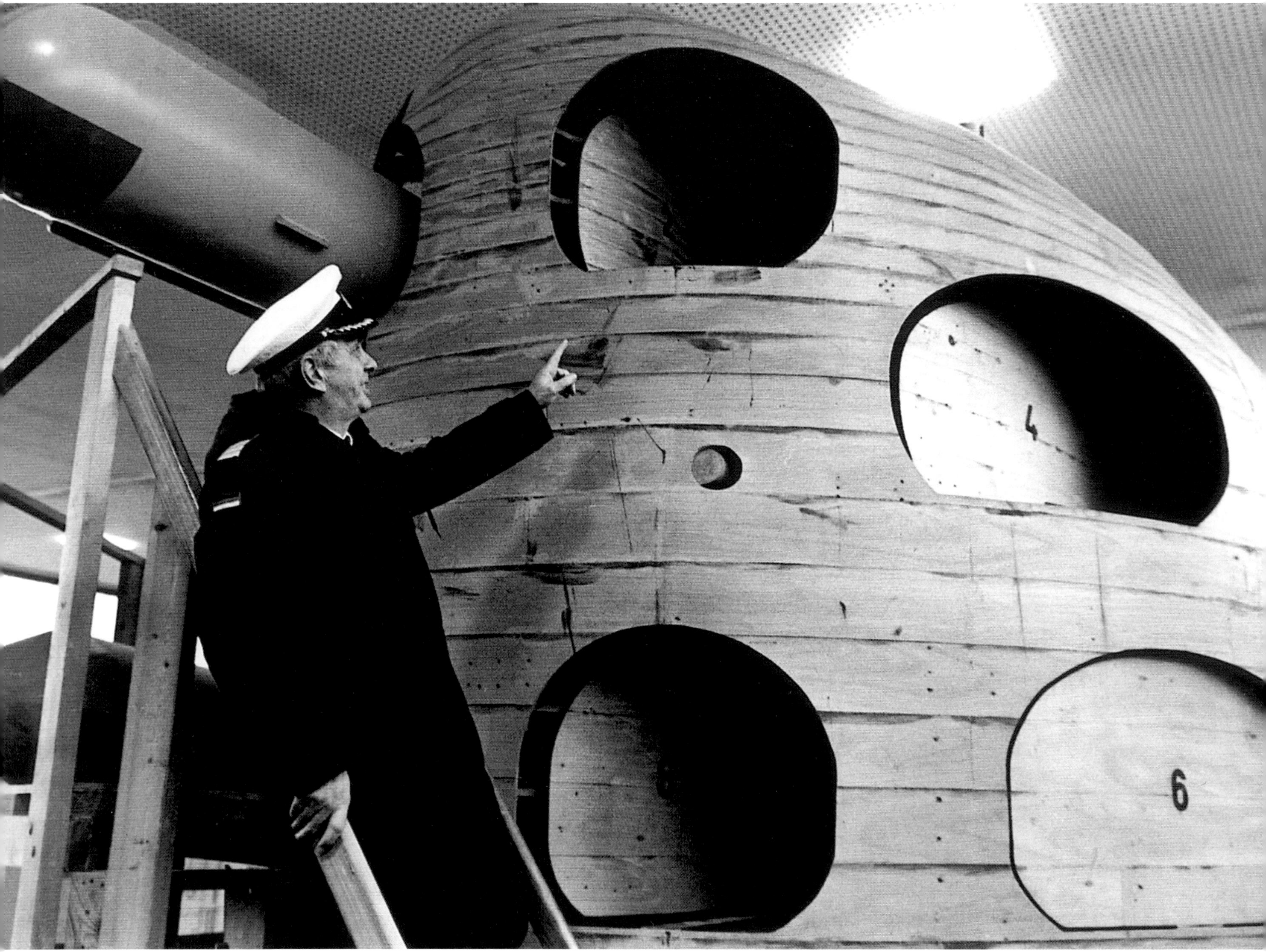
4
6

*The Hellenic Navy was the first to place an order for a batch of Class 209 submarines at HDW. A German naval officer explains the boat with a mock up.* (Photo: Archive HDW)

underwater speed of 22 knots over a relatively long distance – a speed that had previously only been achieved by nuclear submarines. In addition, the design offered the noise reduction measures implemented in recent German Navy submarines, which was far superior to anything the foreign competition had to offer.

The Class 209 design was targeted at the interesting South American market. South American navies had been operating American FLEET Class since the end of the Second World War, and these boats had become antiquated and needed replacement. The United States were ruled out as suppliers, as the American submarine industry was now entirely focussed on nuclear-powered submarines, and had abandoned conventional submarine building. The only remaining competitors were the UK and France with their OBERON and DAPHNE Class boats, against which the German shipyards had to prevail. IKL and Kiel's Howaldtswerke presented the new design to Venezuela, Peru, Chile, Argentina and Brazil in a large scale road-show, however in-coming orders remained slow.

The first customer was the Greek Navy – which also needed to replace its vintage FLEET class boats, and after lengthy and tough negotiations, ordered the first German export submarines. On 22 October 1967, Howaldtswerke in Kiel and the Greek Government signed the contract for the building of four Class 209/1100 submarines, and in 1971 the Hellenic Navy commissioned the first boat named GLAFKOS after the Kiel shipyard learnt some tough lessons the hard way in terms of weapon integration and the sea trials of this new boat. Nevertheless, this boat cemented the shipyard's excellent reputation not only with the Hellenic Navy, which had ordered a further four of the same classed boats in 1975, but also with other navies. And then at last the orders started to come in from South America: Argentina kicked the process off in early 1969. And further countries followed suit on four of the world's five continents.

The number of modifications grew with the number of clients. For example: the Chilean Navy THOMSON Class (209/1300) submarines were fitted with emergency escape hatches in the torpedo and engine rooms, as well midships on deck. In addition, they were equipped with taller periscopes, snorkels etc. for operations in severe sea conditions. The five Brazilian TIKUNA class boats were modified Class 209/1400 submarines and had been lengthened with an additional 0.85 m. They had improved diesel engines, other generators and batteries, and improved sensors and electronics. The four Indian Naval Submarine Arm's SHISHUMAR Class (209/1500) boats were fitted with a novel rescue sphere.

Over the years, numerous improvements have been done to the boats and cover, for example, platform technology, the command and weapon control systems, as well as sensor and weapon configurations. Furthermore, suction diesels have been replaced by turbo-charged diesel engines, and the piston compressors have been replaced by quieter screw compressors. These measures have significantly reduced the already very low noise signatures of the boats. However, the designers have never been allowed to rest on their laurels. Rather they see it as a constant and central task to reduce boat signatures. They have achieved amazing results: today the boats emit less energy into the water, in the form of noise, heat or water pressure than a tiny LED. These submarines are the perfect stealth ships.

Whilst the older Class 209 models still used stand-alone apparatuses for the weapon and sensor systems, the modern boats have completely integrated Command and Weapon Control Systems (CWCS) operated from sophisticated multifunction consoles (Multifunction Common Consoles – MFCC). They allow users to see desired tactical scenarios on their screens. Digital images can also be shown on the MFCC, provided by advanced periscopes and the Zeiss optronic mast. In addition, the optronic mast (which does not penetrate the pressure hull, and thus permits greater freedom in the design of the Combat Information Centre – CIC), reduces the risk of discovery.

Meanwhile new acoustic sensors, such as a side sonar (flank array sonar) has been developed. They, together with optimised sensors such as the range finding sonar and the cylindrical hydrophone, have made it possible to substantially increase the range at which objects can be detected and classified. Today sensors benefit from optimised, streamlined outer hull claddings components of reinforced carbon fibre, which have replaced the pressure hull cladding structures once made of steel. Opposed to its predecessors, current Class 209 boats are equipped with the latest generation fibre-optic guided heavyweight torpedoes, the boats can also launch submarine-to-surface missiles. And finally, yet another advantageous feature is containerised torpedo defence systems integrated into the hull claddings. Developed by HDW, the systems provide boats with new instruments of self-protection against torpedo attacks.

*Class 209 pressure hull and bow sections under construction at HDW for the South African Navy. (YPS Peter Neumann)*

## THE CLASS 209/1400MOD SOUTH AFRICAN NAVY SUBMARINES

HDW made headlines in the "Blueprints Affair" at the end of the 80ies. It was involved the illicit export of submarine plans to South Africa, which was ostracised owing to its apartheid policies, and in consequence, subject to an arms embargo imposed by the United Nations. Actually, far earlier, in the beginning of the 80ies, HDW and IKL had closed contract with the South African Navy, after the German Chancellor's Office had informed them that the CDU-led Federal Government had given its approval to the deal. This led to a political scandal with a correspondingly large media fallout as the opposition did their best to discredit the Federal Government with the matter. It used HDW and IKL as the stick with which the dog was to be beaten, and both companies were dragged over the cobblestones of politics. At the start of 1990s the case came under jurisdiction at Kiel's Higher Regional Court where HDW and IKL were acquitted, and the affair ended.

Ten years later, in 2000, the South African Navy, under new leadership, ordered three Class 209 submarines, which would be built by HDW (as consortium leader) and the Thyssen Nordseewerke shipyard. The first boat, SAS MANTHATISI – S101, was handed over to the South African Navy in Kiel on 11 November 2005, in brilliant sunshine, and on 18 February 2006, after the successful completion of all tests and training of the crew, the boat started on its way to South Africa. The South African Navy's diesel-electric boats are the latest Class 209 versions, and a detailed description was penned by the highly respected expert Hans Karr. He described the boats as follows in 2005 in "Marine Forum" (a German navy news magazine) [4]:

### VESSEL CHARACTERISTICS AND TECHNICAL DATA

*The Class 209/1400mod single hull boats have a length of 62 metres, a pressure body diameter of 6.2 metres and a displacement of 1,454 tonnes surfaced, and 1,586 tonnes submerged. Their diving depth is more than 200 metres. As all Class 209 boats, everything has been done to keep signatures extremely low and to make the chance of discovery as hard as possible. All noise-generating equipment and aggregates are mounted on vibration absorbers. The boat's exterior cladding is of fibreglass, which enables a particularly swirl-free, flow-optimised form that and makes it even more difficult to detect. The size of the crew is small – only 30 persons with additional accommodations for five more. This figure is 21 persons* less than the French DAPHNE class boats, which are half as big, for the reason that the German boats operate largely automated because of their modern technologies and electronics. The boats have a sea endurance of up to 50 days.

Four type 12V 396 SE84 MTU diesel engines provide on-board power generation with a maximum power of 1,250 kW each through generators. The Siemens electric motor draws its power from batteries located in two battery rooms, one forward, under the crew compartment and the second in the lower aft body underneath the diesel engines. The high skew propeller with seven scimitar-like blades ensures low noise emissions. Dived, the boat is capable of over 20 knots, and surfaced or in snorkel mode 10 knots. These boats have a maximum range of 11,000 nautical miles.

**ARMAMENT AND EQUIPMENT**

Eight 533 mm bow torpedo tubes form the main armament of the boat. In total, 14 torpedoes can be shipped board, the six spare torpedoes are stored in the bow area. Alternatively, the boat can deploy mines or mixed loads. Missiles are not currently planned, but can be easily fitted during a retrofit.

CIRCE (Containerised Integrated Reaction Countermeasures Effectors), an anti-torpedo self-defence system for submarines has been installed in the bow area between the cladding and pressure hull. This system is a joint development of HDW and Whitehead Alenia Sistemi Subacquei (WASS) of Italy.

It comprises four fold-out starting containers with 10 effectors each, which after launching, distract approaching torpedoes from the actual target with jammers and target emulators (the soft-kill principle). The attacked submarine's sonar detect in-coming torpedoes and activate the system.

Atlas Elektronik is supplier of the ISUS 90 (Integrated Sensor Underwater System) submarine combat system which is an advanced fully integrated sensor, command and control, and weapon engagement system. It integrates the acoustical sensors with optical and electronic sensors via a high data bus with the central computers. The collected data is recorded, classified and evaluated on multi-purpose consoles. From here, the weapons, and external and internal communications are deployed.

The CSU 90 (Compact Sonar for Submarines) hooks up the sonar systems which operate between 10 Hz to 100 kHz. This system comprises a cylindrical hull array in the bow, passive ranging, interception and flank array sonars, as well as a self-made-noise signature monitoring system. The suite can be expanded with a towed array and mine detection sonars.

The South African submarines are the first Class 209 boats to be equipped with an optronic mast, and in their cases, it is an OMS-100 (optronic mast system) supplied by Zeiss. The main advantages of this sensor are the fast 360° viewing, its video recording and an infrared sensor, which is of particular benefit in poor visibility conditions. Furthermore, an integrated ESM antenna saves the installation of further hoisting mast. When the mast is in deployment, the probability of detection is reduced as it only has to pierce the surface for short extremely periods. Zeiss is also supplier of the attack periscope SERO 400 featuring an optical range finder, residual light amplifier, TV camera and an ESM warning receiver.

The Class 209/1400 mod is equipped with reliable and precise navigation systems which include a Thomson Scanter navigation radar, a Doppler log and three GPS antennas, which can be used at periscope depth. All internal and external navigation data is processed in an integrated data management system.

External communications consist of HF, VHF, UHF, INMARSAT-C, UHF-SAT-COM gear, and a data link system.

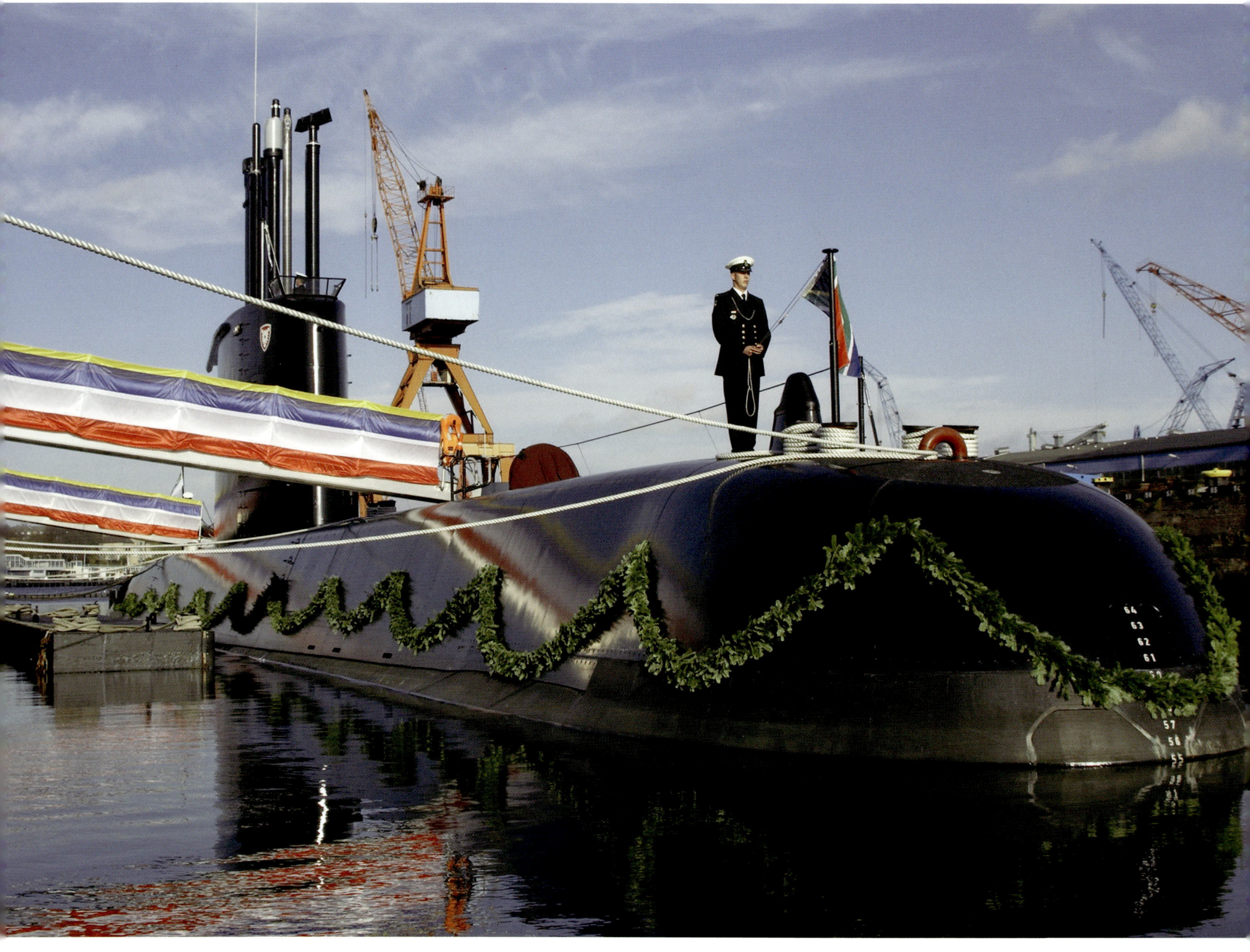

*A proud moment for the South African Navy. The country's flag is raised at the commissioning of the SAS MANATHATSI on 11 November 2005 at HDW.* (YPS Peter Neumann)

# HDW-CLASS 209/1400 MOD SUBMARINE

*The second 209 for South Africa: QUEEN MODJADJI – S103/HDW class 209/1400mod. (YPS Peter Neumann)*

| | | | | | |
|---|---|---|---|---|---|
| Length (LOA): | approx. 62.0 m | Max surface speed: | approx. 10 knots | **INTEGRATED RADIO** | |
| Height including sail | approx. 12.5 m | Max dived speed: | approx. 20 knots | **COMMUNICATIONS SYSTEM** | |
| Pressure hull Ø | approx. 6.2 m | Range, surfaced: | 11,000 nm | HF, VHF, UHF, VFL | |
| Draft: | approx. 5,5 m | Range, dived: | 400 nm | INMARSAT-C | |
| Displ. surfaced. | 1,454 t | | | UHF-SATCOM | |
| Displ. dived | 1,586 t | **WEAPONS** | | GMDSS | |
| Pressure hull: | ferromagnetic steel | 8 torpedo tubes | | | |
| Diving depth: | over 200 m | Heavy weight torpedoes | | **NAVIGATION SYSTEM** | |
| Crew: | 30 + 5 | | | Inertial navigation system | |
| Endurance: | 50 days | **INTEGRATED SONAR SYSTEM** | | Attitude and heading reference system (AHRS) | |
| | | Cylindrical hull array | | | |
| **PROPULSION** | | Passive ranging sonar | | Electromagnetic log | |
| 4 Diesel generators | | Interception and flank array sonars | | Navigation radar | |
| DC drive motor | | Towed sonar | | Echo sounder | |
| | | Mine hunting sonar | | GPS | |

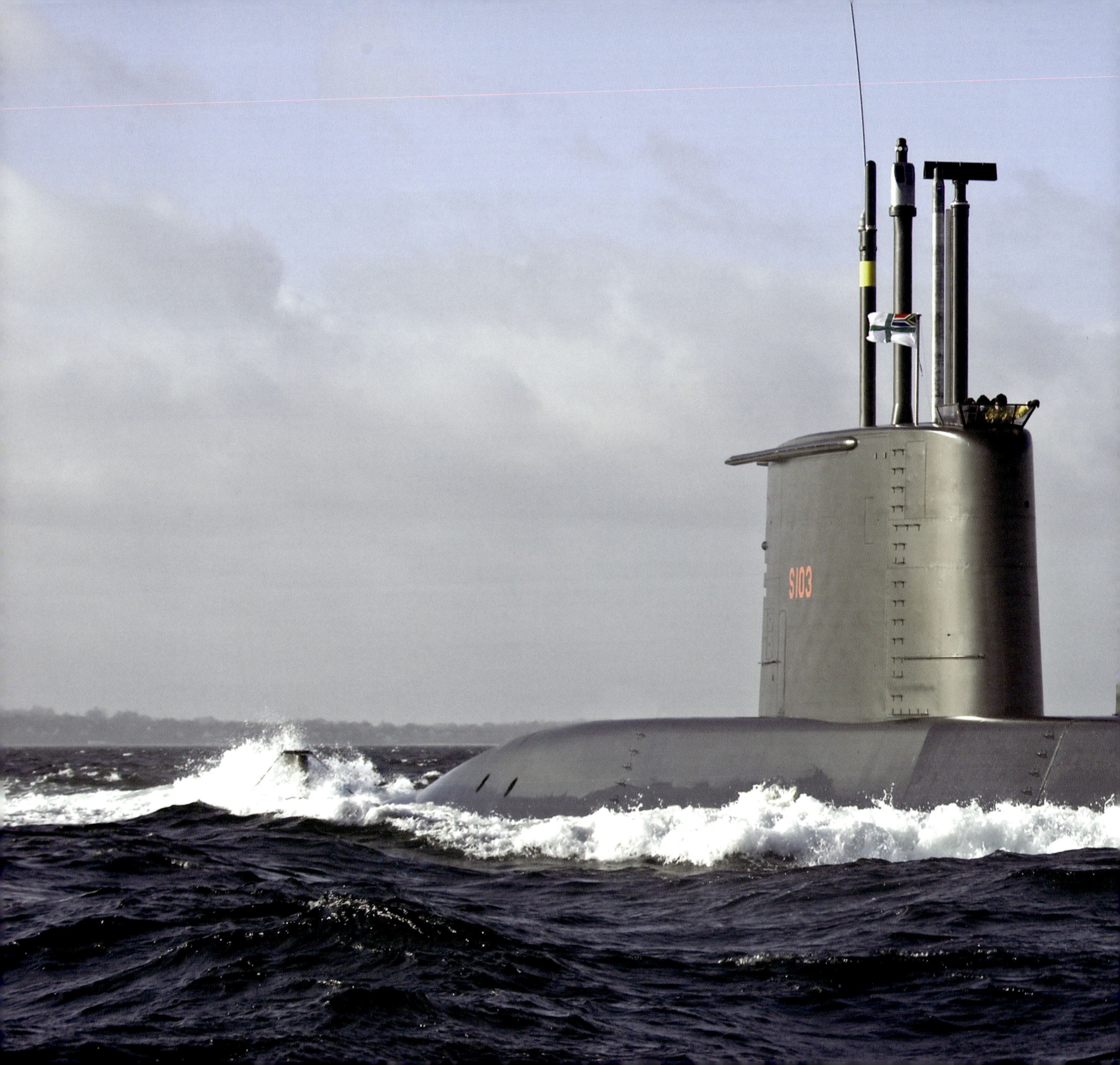
S103

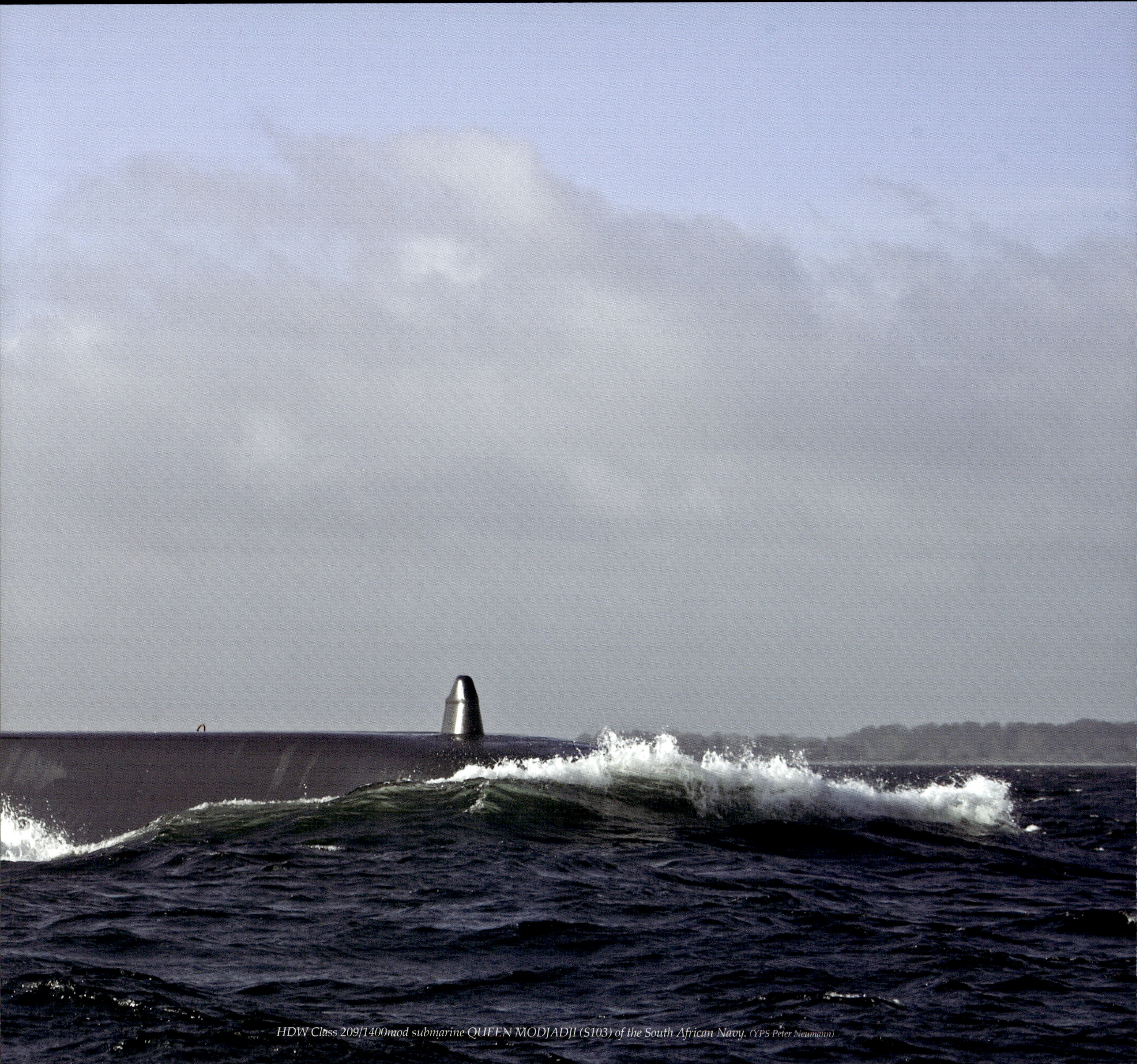

*HDW Class 209/1400mod submarine QUEEN MODJADJI (S103) of the South African Navy.* (YPS Peter Neumann)

## THE FUEL CELL PLUG IN:
## UPGRADING CLASS 209 SUBMARINES WITH AIP

The first AIP (air independent propulsion) system to be installed in a Class 212A submarine was a game-changing revolution, and enabled the propulsion unit to become truly independent of external air supplies. Obviously the desire to retrofit earlier generation boats now arose, and HDW responded to the demand with a Fuel Cell plug-in for past Class 209 boats. The plug-in unit contains the entire Fuel Cell system as well as the storage tank for liquid oxygen. The hydrogen storage cylinders are fitted beneath the keel, outside of the pressure hull, and as ballast, counter-balance the Fuel Cell unit and positively influence the boat's stability.

Submarines are designed and built in sections. A pressure hull can be cut and its LOA lengthened up to the equivalent of the hull's diameter. The procedure is unproblematic owing to the modular structures of the boats and the Fuel Cell's handy dimensions. After fitting, boats retain their characteristics, and sub-systems do not loose significant performances or need to be changed. As the Fuel Cell operates fully automatically, crew sizes stay the same.[5]

A Fuel Cell unit increases underwater travel distances four to five fold, and again, the Hellenic Navy was the first in the world opt for this technology. In 2002, within the framework of the NEPTUNE II programme, HDW equipped the Greek Class 209/1200 boats with fuel cells.[6] Four have since been upgraded, further retrofits have been removed from the agenda owing to the Greek financial crisis.

## CLASS 209 OFFSHOOTS
## THE ISRAELI NAVY CLASS 800 DOLPHIN SUBMARINES

When it became clear that the GAL, TANIN and RAHAV were approaching the end of their service lives, the Israeli Navy looked around for successors. And once again, at the end of the 1980s, the choice fell on Germany. HDW and Thyssen Nordsee Werke formed a working group under the leadership of the former, to build the boats together. They were originally to be funded with American military aid, which came to a halt in 1990. However, after the second Gulf war, it became increasingly apparent that Israel was suffering under Scud missiles that had benefited from German assistance. Therefore in 1991 the Federal Republic decided to cover the costs of two new submarines, quasi as reparation. A third boat was ordered in 1994, its costs were shared by Israel and Germany. The new boats, DOLPHIN, LEVIATHAN and TEKUMA were built in Kiel and Emden, feature conventional diesel-electric drives, and entered service between 1999 and 2000.

In 2011 Israel ordered a further three German co-financed boats. They are the largest ThyssenKrupp Marine Systems have ever built, and are a further Fuel Cell powered development based on the previous DOLPHIN submarines. Of these, the first boat – TANIN – entered service in June 2014, the second – RAHAV – was to be delivered to the Israeli Navy in 2015. The third, yet to be named boat is still under construction and is expected to enter service in 2017.

The first three diesel-electric DOLPHINs have Class 209 DNA, but the design and engineering mission was

*Left: HDW converted a Class 205 submarine (U1) to test – and demonstrate – the Fuel Cell system's performance. The hydrogen storage cylinders are clearly visible outside the pressure hull.*

(Photo: Archive HDW)

pushed to incorporate the wishes and requirements of the Israeli Navy, thus the "Class 800 Dolphin" classing. In comparison to a Class 206 boat, they have been greatly modified and have much higher displacements of 1,604 tonnes.

The second batch boats have many similarities to the Class 212A and Class 214 boats, but with 2,050 tonnes displacement and bigger crews, are a lot larger. Submarine experts consider the boats to be amongst the technically most demanding, most powerful non-nuclear submarines in the world.

Their technical data and outfitting is top secret. However, a number of claims have been made in the specialist naval press, of which some are speculative, or at least have not been confirmed either by the Israeli Navy or the shipyard. Nevertheless, the guesses do give an indication to how the boats are equipped. The first three diesel-electric powered boats have surfaced displacements of 1,640 tonnes on lengths of about 57 metres. For the first batch conventional diesel-electric boats, the specialist media works the following information[7]: The diameter of the pressure body is thought to be 6.8 metres and the draft 6.2 metres.

The boats have three MTU 16V 84 396 SE diesel engines and three generators, each with a capacity of 750 kW. The Siemens electric motor driving the propeller has a 2.85 MW output for 20+ knot speeds dived. The boats have ranges of about 8,000 nautical miles at 8 knots surfaced, and dived of over 400 nautical miles, also at 8 knots. Guesses on the maximum diving depth ranges between 300 and 350 metres, and the boat, it is said, can stay at sea for over 30 days.

The batch one boats have Atlas Elektronik ISUS 90 command and weapon control systems, electronics such as the sonar systems are manufactured in

*The namesake of der HDW-Class 800 submarine, DOLPHIN, during sea trials on the Baltic.* (YPS Peter Neumann)

Bremen. The ELTA surface search radar, however, is made in Israel. The submarines are exceptionally well armed. They even have ten torpedo tubes in the bow, six of which have a diameter of 533 mm, and four of 650 mm. According to official information, the tubes can launch various types of modern torpedoes and lay mines. They can carry 16 torpedoes – or missiles as they have launchers for Harpoon ship-ship missiles. These boats have the assignment to fend off attacks, monitor deployment areas and conduct special operations.

The second Dolphin batch of submarines, as previously mentioned, are considerably larger, and represent virtually a complete re- or new design, which almost has only its name in common with the previous boats. They have Fuel Cell propulsion systems, their dimensions have grown significantly in comparison to their predecessors with a surfaced displacement of 2,050 tonnes and 2,400 tonnes dived. As with their predecessors, the diameter of the pressure body is 6.8 metres and the draft is over 6.2 metres. As the first generation DOLPHINs, the second also have 10 torpedo tubes – six with 533 mm and four with 650 mm diameters. Thus their armament of torpedoes and cruise missiles is the same as that of batch one. The boats are crewed by 35 persons, 10 further can be shipped aboard for special tasks. Various Internet sources allege speeds under water to be at least 25 knots, and the diving depth is reputed to be at least 350 m. As to be expected, the shipyard and Israeli Navy are tight lipped over these issues.

The four 650 mm diameter torpedo tubes have ignited discussions over the DOLPHIN Class boats' armament, and broad debates have been fought the international, specialist and daily press, which will not be repeated in detail here. The majority of professionals assume Israel has developed missiles that can carry nuclear warheads. The boats have allegedly been converted in Israel for this weapon, which can be fired from the large torpedo tubes. This possibility, according to speculations, would give Israel the option of a nuclear second strike aimed to deter potential aggressors, in particular Iran.

Israel has offered neither an official denial, nor a confirmation. Up to now, nobody has been able to present tangible evidence for the assumptions. But there is evidence that Israel's politicians and military have deliberately spread rumours of supposed capacities of the new Israeli submarines in order scare enemies.

In summer 1999 the first announcement claiming that the DOLPHINs could fire Harpoon missiles with nuclear warheads out of the large torpedo tubes was released to the Israeli press by the Peace Institute in Haifa, Israel. One can presume the Israeli secret service had leaked the information to the peace researchers. Soon after, the Los Angeles Times cited unnamed eyewitnesses that reported seeing a DOLPHIN boat in the Indian Ocean conducting cruise missile test launches. However, at the time of the allegation, the boats were berthed in Haifa, as other eyewitnesses reported.

Professor Joachim Krause, Director of the Institute for Security Policy at the University of Kiel, concludes that "the idea that these submarines, in a sideline, can be used as a strategic nuclear attack force against a possible Iranian nuclear threat is completely insane and belongs in the realm of fantasy."[8] Because the DOLPHIN boats are indeed designed to light launch cruise missiles with low reaches that are suitable for combating sea or land targets from the littorals. In fact, Israel has far a better deterrent with the land-based Jericho missile.

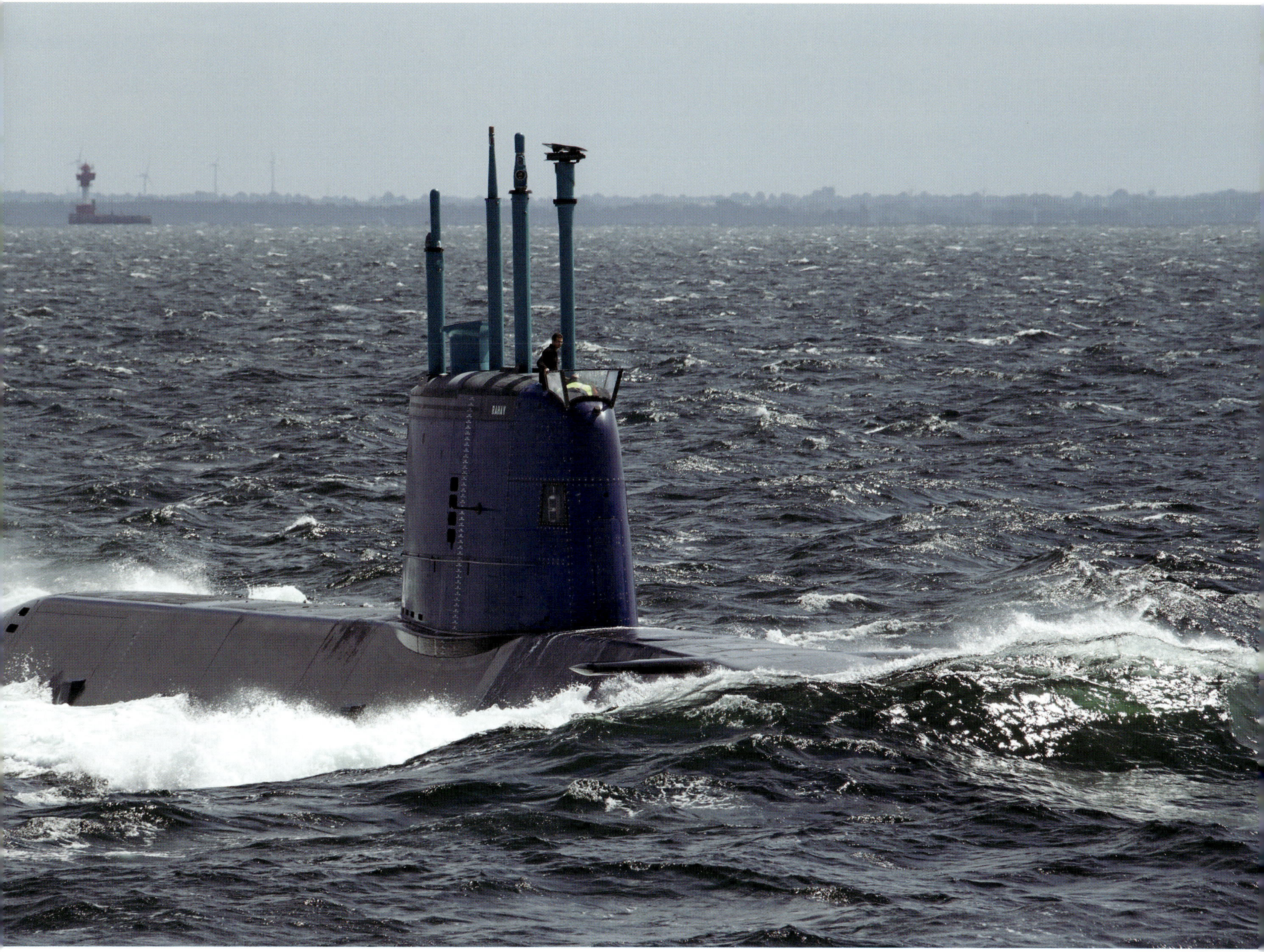
RAHAV

*RAHAV – a 2nd batch DOLPHIN AIP class submarine. These boats with Fuel Cells are larger than the first three DOLPHIN boats.* (YPS Peter Neumann)

# The Second German Revolution in Submarine Construction: The Fuel Cell

The 7th of April 2003 was a day with fabulous weather. The Western Baltic's shipping forecast promised brisk East to Southeast force 5-6 winds, and excellent visibility. The sun shone from a deep blue sky over Kiel, and early in the morning, a large crowd of guests milled around the pier in front HDW's submarine tender PEGASUS. They were going to witness U 31's first sea trial run in the Baltic Sea's outer Kiel Bay – the world's first submarine to be fitted with a Fuel Cell. The media interest was huge – the HDW class 212A submarine was a national and international sensation. Back in 1994, when the Germany's Federal Office for Defence Technology and Procurement approved the order to build four boats by the ARGE U212, a cooperative led by HDW, the announcement attracted global interest – and not only in professional circles. The New York Times reported the news with the headline *"The Boat Is Back Again"*.[1]

But the road to the first sea trials had been long, and started in the 1960s with debates on how to provide future German Navy submarines with a propulsion system that did not need to rely on an external air supply. The issue was a simple must for the future. The current conventional diesel-electric propulsion that permitted relatively small diving periods of a few days, was in the face of modern submarine operations, no longer sufficient.

The Kriegsmarine had already conducted experiments with the Walter turbine and the closed cycle diesel engines, but both systems had not reached maturity. For their time, experimental boats reached astonishing submerged speeds with the ingenious Walter drive, but suffered numerous mechanical problems and thus failed trouble-free continuous operations.

The Royal Navy also foundered to master the technology played into its hands at the end of the Second World War. It experienced nothing but bad luck with the Walter submarines, and as already mentioned, built in the mid-50ies two submarines fitted with the Walter turbine technology. After a plague of mechanical problems and explosions, the frustrated Royal Navy shelved the program. The Soviet Navy had a similar story to tell of its boat, and thus the experimental boats vanished without much ado.

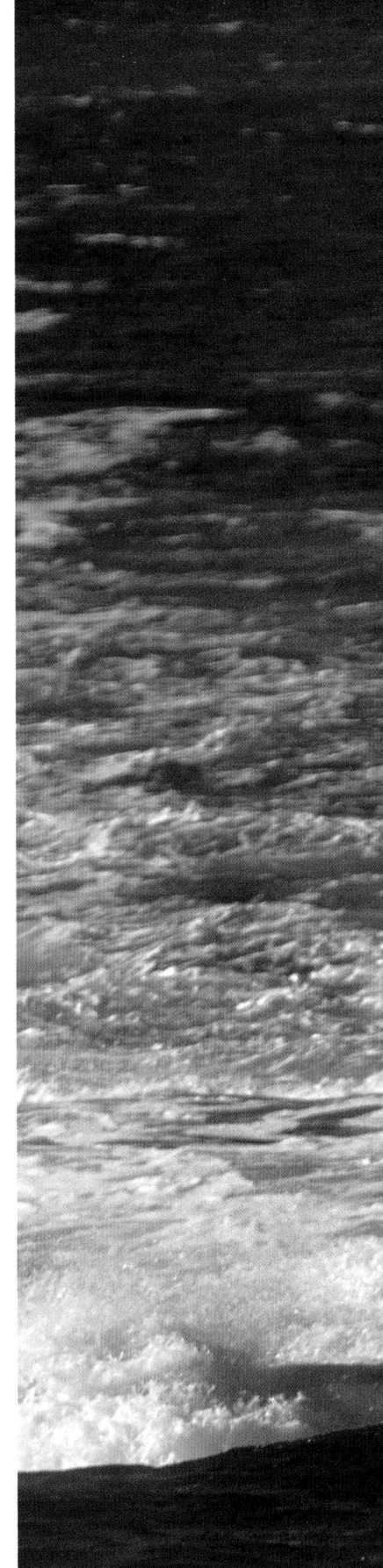

*A sensation: U31 sailing down the Kiel Bay on 7 April 2003 for its first sea trials.* (YPS Peter Neumann)

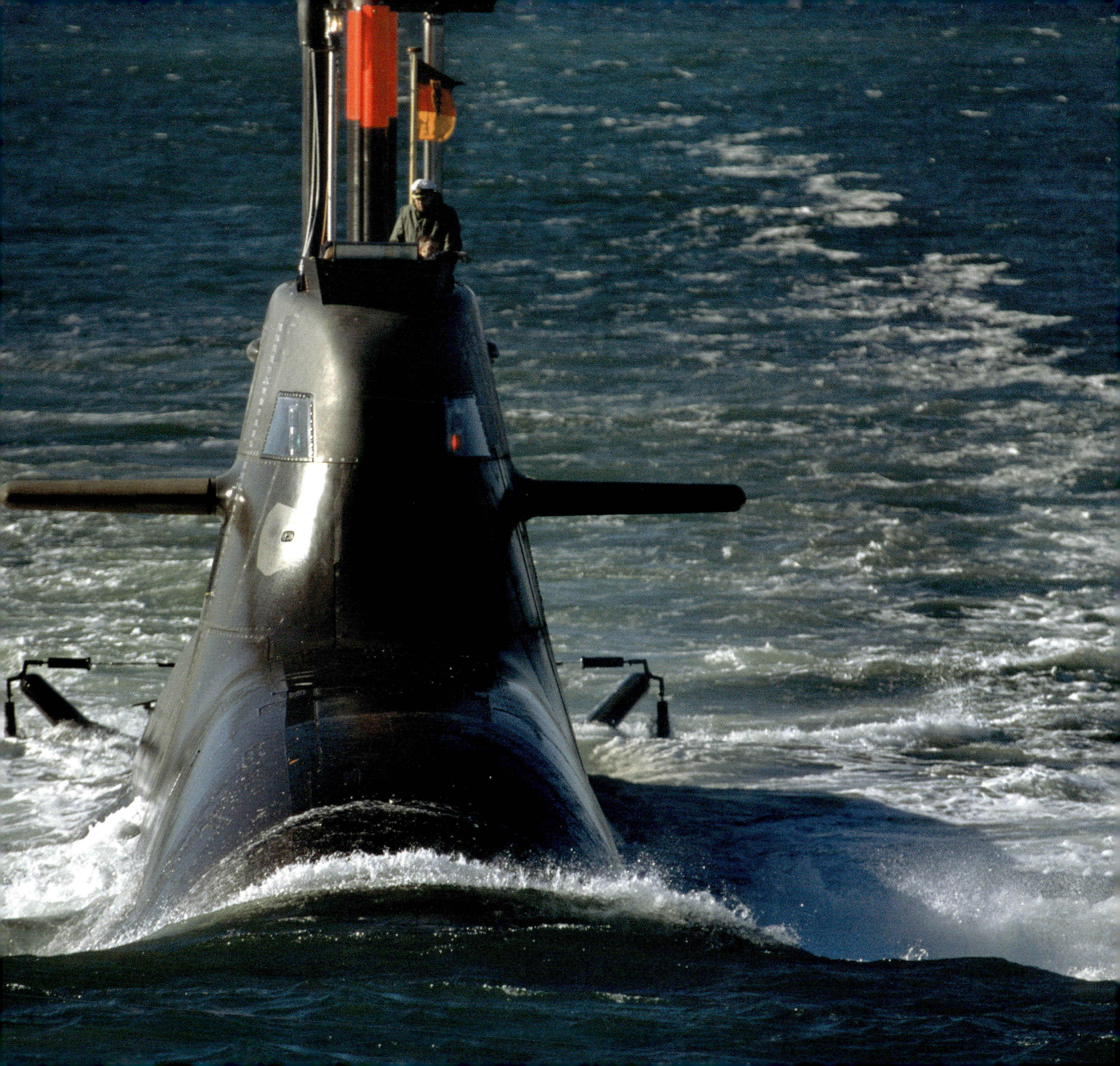

The closed cycle diesel suffered a similar fate. As only large submarines can accommodate a bulky nuclear drive chain, Sweden pushed to further develop the closed cycle diesel technology, and its 1,500 HP test facility was so successful that its Navy decided to install the system into six boats. But in the early 1960s, with the Fuel Cell becoming increasingly viable[2], it back-tracked and returned to conventional propulsion solutions, although the boats had been cut and prepared for installation.

Despite the Fuel Cell's better long term prospects – at that time it was an idea far from maturity, and even further away from any realistic deployment in a submarine – Sweden put its cards on the Stirling Engine, which it also had in development.

And thus the Fuel Cell faced an uncertain future as the power plant for a future next generation German submarine. The only issue that was really certain, was that an external, air-independent propulsion had become essential.

Even a future submarine type was open to discussion, and in the early 1960s, the Navy talked about six attack submarines, capable of high underwater speeds and with sufficiently radiuses of action. It was planned for them to operate in the North Sea and North Atlantic. Of course the question of the future propulsion was a big issue. IKL was commissioned to compare the Walter turbine and the closed cycle diesel systems, and to think about deploying a nuclear reactor. The IK20 and IK 24 project investigations proposed either a Babcock or a MAN-Wahodag reactor.[3] But these were only pipe dreams as a real submarine building project, let alone, a finished design, was never made by IKL.[4] The Western NATO Allies, as previously mentioned, would never have give their permissions, quite apart from the fact that it was forbidden for Germany to build such boats at the time. Furthermore, according to shipbuilders, the development and building of a German nuclear submarine would have taken far too long.

But technically speaking, a nuclear powerplant would have been unsuitable in the German Navy's small boats operating in shallow seas. Ulrich Gabler wrote, from that point of view, that the sheer weight of an atomic system made it more suitable for submarines displacing several thousand tonnes for blue water operations. Furthermore, the noise level generated by nuclear boats posed a particular problem as hulls and propellers make a lot of noise at high speed, as do the reactor with its pumps and generators.

The Walter turbine experienced a renaissance, even if only a short one. Its namesake Hellmuth Walter had proposed to the Ministry of Defence an improved version of his system, now called the "Walter exchange process", and had been commissioned 1960 to build and test a 3,000 hp system, and in 1965/66 he presented the results which also thrilled German submarine builders. The following quote is taken from a Howaldtswerke brochure of 1965:

*"Kieler Howaldtswerke AG are able to offer an extensive choice, beginning with the 90 t small boat and ending with the 1,000 t submarine. Besides the highly developed Diesel electric propulsion common today, we would like to refer to the most interesting solution of the "Walterpropulsion", which was developed during the Second World War for boats with an extreme high underwater performance. This concerns a propulsion plant working without atmospheric oxyden by using high concentrate hydrogen peroxide, a gas steam mixture for driving the turbines."* [6]

But things remained at the trial phase. In parallel to Walter's research, he and IKL had made designs (IK 13) for a Class 204 experimental boat. In the design process, it became apparent that the Walter Drive was not quiet enough at low speed – as the German Navy had little interest in high underwater speeds, [7] the boat was never built and work on the drive terminated. In 1965 IKL now concentrated on investigating air-independent drives for six attack submarines, designated as "Class 208" boats, and the fact-finding concentrated on the Walter Drive, the closed cycle diesel engine, the Stirling engine and the fuel cell.

## EXCURSUS:
## AIR-INDEPENDENT DRIVES – THE WALTER METHOD[8]

The basis of the system is a gas turbine with diesel as fuel and hydrogen peroxide ($H_2O_2$) as oxygen carrier. Walter began the first research in the early 1930s, and in 1935 founded his own engineering office. In 1936, a test facility on the Krupp Germania shipyard showed that his basic ideas were right – the turbine generated 4,000 hp, a result that led to the construction of the first V 80 experimental boat, which reached speeds of up to 28 knots in the Baltic Sea.

Walter's first research centred around the so-called "cold process" in which hydrogen peroxide is sprayed from a fine nozzle onto a catalytic converter which broke the hydrogen peroxide into hydrogen and oxygen, in the process producing his pressure steam and oxygen at a very high temperature of 6,500°C. The creation of the steam used up both of the hydrogen atoms and one of the oxygen, leaving a free oxygen atom in the mixture, which was discarded overboard, albeit to leave a tell-tale bubble trail, meaning that the boat could be detected.

Further research conducted in 1936 led to the so-called "hot procedure". Here the system consists of a decomposer or reactor, a subsequent combustion chamber, a separator and a steam turbine. The decomposer contains the catalyst of potassium permanganate or manganese oxide (Braunstein), through which multiple nozzles squirt hydrogen peroxide, which breaks down into its components of water vapour and oxygen. This mixture is fed into the combustion chamber and ignited, together with finely atomised diesel fuel, to a hot flame to about 2,000°C.

In order to prevent the combustion chamber from burning through, it is cooled by water, which is added into the hot gas flow with fine nozzles, and in the process generates enormous pressures, which account for the turbine's high performance.

As the catalyst caused abrasion damage to the turbine blades, a separator was fitted between the combustion chamber and turbine. Finally, the steam leaving the turbine was connected to a capacitor, which increased the turbine's efficiency and simultaneously recovered precious distilled water. The remaining $CO_2$ was expelled overboard, utilizing a compressor which dissolved the gas into the sea water without leaving a bubble trace.

In addition to this principle, Walter developed the "indirect method", which had a closed secondary steam cycle for the turbine. It produced steam through a heat exchanger and hot gas from the combustion chamber. This system's fuel consumption was more economical compared to the "hot" procedure, but required more space – and was much heavier.

### MESMA TURBINE

The Module D'Energie Autonome Sous-Marin (MESMA), a steam turbine powered by ethanol and liquid oxygen is a French development. The systems high temperatures cause

*Walter propulsion test facility at HDW in 1965. (Archive HDW*

signature problems, thus this AIP solution is still in research labs. Its development started in the early 1980s, and France, which only operates nuclear submarines, has not deployed it. The Pakistani Navy tested a trial version in one of the French Agosta Class submarines. The MESMA system is offered as the power plant for the Scorpene class submarines, jointly developed by France and Spain. The Indian Navy, which has ordered six Scorpene class boats is thinking about using MESMA turbines in the last three vessels.

### THE CLOSED CYCLE DIESEL [9, 10]

This power generating technology works with a normal turbo-diesel, which, when surfaced, burns unmodified diesel. When dived, the engine is supplied with liquid or gaseous oxygen is stored in tanks aboard. When submerged in snorkelling mode, the diesel uses atmospheric, external air. Dived deeper, the system switches into the closed cycle operation. Carbon dioxide from the exhaust is used replace the atmosphere's natural nitrogen content, and oxygen is drawn from the on-board supplies.

The Kriegsmarine had research projects running for closed cycle power plants for submarines and torpedoes, albeit they were abandoned in favour of the Walter drive. Nevertheless, in 1940 the Stuttgart University was tasked to developed a 53 and 1,400 HP closed cycle diesel power plant. The smaller engine was ready for installation in a submarine 1944; but the course of the war prevented on-board testing.

After the war, several countries continued to invest research into the closed cycle system, and approached the critical question how to handle the exhaust's carbon dioxide at different depths, before feeding it back into the engine, from different angles.

In Japan, Mitsui built a shore-based test facility in Japan. Italy built a number small civilian submarines for the offshore industry, in Germany Bruker Meerestechnik launched an experimental diving vessel in 1990. In their new start into building submarines in the early 1980ies, Thyssen Nordsee Werke cast around for an AIP drive that could continuously provide the power for a naval / civilian boat to remain submerged for at least 14 days. Their research culminated in the installation of a plug-in closed cycle plant in a Class 205 submarine that had been previously used to demonstrate a Fuel Cell's efficiency.

In March 1993 the boat successfully completed its sea trials in the Baltic Sea, and not only had its realistic diving time increased five fold in comparison to that of a conventional diesel electric submarine, it also showed it had a low noise signature. Further development was not pursued as the Fuel Cell, which was already ready for serial production, had proven to be superior.

### THE STIRLING ENGINE

The principle of the Stirling engine is nothing new. It is, in mechanical terms, relatively simple a heat-power machine, in which an enclosed working medium such as air, helium or hydrogen is heated by any external heat source in a closed chamber in one area, and then cooled in another area. The working gas is moved by a piston back and forth between the permanently heated and cooled areas. In the heated cylinder chamber, the working gas expands and in the cold cylinder it looses volume and shrinks, causing the internal energy of the gas to convert into deployable mechanical movement.[11]

Robert Stirling, a Scottish clergyman discovered the principle in 1816 and registered it as a patent. He wanted to create and engine that would be a counterpart to the high pressure steam engines, then prevalent in Britain, and which claimed many lives as they exploded.

The Stirling engine is a safe piece of machinery, and as easily manufactured, quickly spread into private homes and the cottage industry, where it was used as the small motor to drive fans, water pumps, sewing machines etc. At the beginning of the 20th century, over 250,000 Stirling engines were thought operate around the world. Ultimately, it was replaced by the more sophisticated petrol, diesel and electric engines.

But the engine was not entirely forgotten. Philips started to experiment with it in 1936, and in 1954 introduced a 200 kW Stirling generator in small series. Further US, Dutch, Swedish and German research labs and companies studied the Stirling motor in last century's fifties, sixties and seventies. In 1967 MAN, a manufacturer of large diesel engines, also started to test the Stirling engine, and in 1984 presented a study of the of its suitability to power ships.

The Stirling engine is an extremely noiseless and vibration-free device, making it an interesting choice as an AIP plant for submarines, providing oxygen can be carried on board for the combustion of the fuel. Sweden took this path with success, and refined the Stirling principle for use in its boats and for export. However, compared with other systems, the engine's efficiency is significantly lower and fuel consumption correspondingly high. This is the most probable reason why most of the countries experimenting with the Stirling engine have abandoned it at the end.[12]

*Inventor C. F. Schönbein.* (wikipedia commons)

## THE FUEL CELL DRIVE

In his 1874 novel "The Mysterious Island", Jules Verne's engineer Cyrus Smith said about future energy sources:

*"I think that water will one day be used as fuel. It is made of hydrogen and oxygen, which will be an inexhaustible source of heat and light, alone or together. And with an intensity that coal cannot match."*

The progress-believing visionary Jules Verne must have known the Fuel Cell. Already in 1838 had the chemist and physicist Christian Friedrich Schönbein linked two platinum wires with hydrogen and oxygen, and discovered electric current flowing between the wires – the first simple fuel cell. A year later, Schönbein published the results of his research. His English colleague Sir William Grove took up the thread and conducted further experiment. He and Schönbein recognized that the process was a reversal of electrolysis, by which – popular in physics classes – explosive gas is created as $H_2O$ separates into hydrogen and oxygen. At first, however, The fuel cell technology was first destined to fall into oblivion, not least because Werner von Siemens' generator and battery technology provided easy to make, cheap electricity. The Fuel Cell experienced its big revival in the 1950s and 1960s as the US aerospace industry used the technology on Apollo and Gemini missions as a reliable power source.

The Fuel Cell has evolved into an electrochemical device producing electricity without combustion. The electro-chemical reactions between a fuel and an oxidant, which lead to the direct production of electricity, have been researched in detail, and the greatest progress has been made with the reaction between hydrogen and oxygen. A modern Fuel Cell generates more electricity from its fuel than any conventional combustion device. It emits no harmful exhausts into the environment – only water vapour. Its efficiency is extremely high, because as an electro-chemical energy converter, it provides electricity through the free enthalpy G of a chemical reaction. In theory, this principle could permit a 100% conversion of the chemical to electrical energy –whatever, the fuel used German submarines can reach the very high efficiency of about 70% per cent.

The various types of fuel cells differ by the deployed electrolyte, operating temperatures, fuel and oxidants, and the following types are marketed:[13]

▶ **ALKALINE FUEL CELL (AFC)**
Uses two different types of electrolytes: a liquid caustic potash solution and electrolytes contained in a matrix. Due to their low weight and comparatively low operating temperatures, alkaline fuel cells have been first used in the aerospace industry and for portable, silent DC generators.

▶ **PHOSPHORIC ACID FUEL CELLS (PAFC)**
Highly concentrated phosphoric acid is used as an electrolyte. The robust fuel cell works with atmospheric air or hydrogen and is relatively insensitive to impurities of the gases. As a result of the aggressive electrolyte, however, their useful life is short and their efficiency is low. This Fuel Cell was developed for use in stationary systems for decentralised power generation. At operating temperatures up to 200°C, combined heat and power (CHP) generation is possible.

▶ **MOLTEN CARBONATE FUEL CELLS (MCFC)**
This fuel cell uses molten carbonates as electrolytes. Its operation is carried out at high temperatures of over 600 degrees Celsius to melt the carbonates (potassium/lithium carbonate). This allows the use of different hydrocarbon-containing fuels, such as earth, carbon, bio or landfill gas. They are suitable for both central and decentralised energy production but only in base load, and here also combined heat and power is possible.

▶ **SOLID OXYCERAMIC FUEL CELLS (SOFC)**
Here, the fuel cell uses solid zirconium as electrolytes that work at temperatures between 850 to 1,000°C. The same energy carriers as in the MCFC can be used as fuel, but there are some problems with its use. The life of the fuel cell stacks is considerably restricted by the instability of the cathode (resolution), the corrosion of the separator between the stack and the deformation of the electrolyte matrix. Applications could be centralised and decentralised electricity generation with co-generation in the base-load.

▶ **PROTON EXCHANGE MEMBRANE FUEL CELL (PEM)**
The PEM fuel cell contains an ion exchange membrane with electrodes placed on carbon as a solid polymer electrolyte. This membrane electrode is located between the liquid flow field and cooling units. A reaction with oxygen forms anions occurs at the cathode. They react with the hydrogen ions which have crossed the membrane and form water as a reaction product. The electric energy produced is intended for consumption.

PEM fuel cells operate at low operating temperatures of less than 80°C. They are absolutely silent, have high efficiencies, long lives, low maintenance requirements and fast to boot when cold. Due to its internal construction, a PEM can be designed as a simple modular construction delivering a few watts or several kilowatts. It is however not exactly cheap as precious metals, particularly platinum, are required for the catalyst, but as development continues, required platinum quantities are sinking.

## THE DEVELOPMENT OF THE HDW FUEL CELL SYSTEM

IKL's research into the Class 208 submarine's future AIP plants gave best marks to a Fuel Cell plant which existed only on paper. Also in the investigation team were the Bundesamt für Wehrtechnik und Beschaffung (BWB) – the Equipment Procurement Department of the Ministry of Defence – the Navy office and the German Submarine Flotilla. But progress suffered regular slow-downs and delays. For one, the building and re-building of the Class 205 boats fabricated with unsuitable steel cost considerable funds, leaving little money for experiments with new power plants. Then, owing to the trying economic situation at the beginning of the 1970s, which also brought the Federal Republic the first energy crisis, the business world had little inclination for financial adventures.

Thus the decision was made in 1971, to shelf further Class 209 developments until a suitable AIP propulsion was ready. Furthermore, the German Navy was in no special hurry as the new Class 206 boats had certainly proven themselves.

At the end of the 1960s, Norway, who wanted larger boats, was looking for a replacement for its KOBBEN class submarines, and their search led to the Class 210 (ULA class) boats. They had initially been planned as a joint project between Norwegian and German Navies, however they could not agree on details – the Germans wanted non-magnetic steel for their boats, and the Norwegians preferred a ferric high-strength steel alloy. Furthermore, the Norwegians had other ideas about the use of their boats than the German Navy, causing the latter to withdraw. Norway built the ULA Class boats at the Thyssen Nordsee works (TNSW) for itself.

In the meantime, the German Ministry of Defence awarded a number individual research contracts for AIP plants to various companies; Philips and later MAN worked with on Stirling engines and a joint task force developed a Fuel Cell at Siemens and VARTA.

However the Class 208 was far from consummation, nor were there any German follow-up projects on the horizon, Siemens, now alone, offered the Fuel Cell to German shipyards for export. TNSW declined the offer, but not so Howaldtswerke-Deutsche Werft AG together Ferrostaal and IKL. They had accumulated extensive submarine export expertise, and for them, it was clear that in the long run, export contacts could only be successfully acquired if they could manage to beat foreign competition with technological leadership.

This was especially true for the propulsion plants. An external air-independent propulsion unit filling the gap between a conventional diesel-electric and nuclear-powered boat, has long been a scale-tipping desideratum. Moreover, the Swedish competition's Stirling engine threatened to gain a head start in AIP systems.

In 1979, IKL re-evaluated the qualities of external air-independent drives and came to the conclusion that the Fuel Cell took a clear first place, and the Stirling engine second, especially in the light of new, safer storage technologies on board a submarine. Daimler-Benz had also cottoned on to which implications the Fuel Cell technology would have on eco-friendly cars and launched its own research programme. The Federal Ministry for Research and Technology was of great assistance to the Stuttgart based company in finding a hydrogen storage solution in which the volatile gas is stored in metal hydrides. The solution also turned out to be extremely suitable for submarines, they might have been heavy, the oxygen would be stored in its liquid state, but both could be well used for stabilisation and trim. Furthermore, space problem issues were reduced as the new boats were to grow to house extensive electronics and provide better accommodations for the crew.

In the same year, HDW, Ferrostaal and IKL formed a consortium to integrate the Fuel Cell with own resources. The target was a hybrid drive in which surface and snorkelling operations would be diesel-electrically powered, and submerged operations run with the Fuel Cell. From the outset the consortium focused on exports. Plans were drawn up to offer the system as a new technology plug-in for retrofitting older diesel-electric submarines – and especially Class 209 boats.

Originally, the consortium assumed that all parts were readily available: the Fuel cell from Siemens, and the Daimler Benz' metal hydride storage components.[14] But in truth, the project proved to be more complicated than originally imagined. Follow up studies at Siemens, for the Fuel Cell, and at IKL and Gabler Maschinenbau for storage, were necessary. Above all, a functioning system of all components had to be created, and a whole series of individual solutions developed. HDW, IKL, Siemens and Daimler-Benz worked together closely with the goal to produce a prototype system and test it. In 1980 the consortium decided to build a functional model – a land test system at HDW – to get the whole system and its peripheral devices running within a fixed time frame and at a fixed budget.[15]

And it was of vital necessity to dispel doubts. The German Navy was worried about the safe storage of hydrogen. Accordingly, the TÜV Rheinland (an international service group that tests and documents the safety and quality of new and existing products, systems and services) was involved, and in the course their recommendations, a number of solutions were implemented. As a matter of fact, existing submarines have always had to live with the danger of batteries degassing hydrogen into battery rooms and living areas, with ensuing gas explosions. The storage of hydrogen in metal hydrides, promised an improvement of safety, since it would now be contained in a small secure system.[16]

The land test system was built mid-1983 to mid-1984 in Kiel and was designed from the outset to be incorporated directly in a submarine after successful test results. It comprised the hybrid system together with original parts of a traditional submarine drive chain. The new system provided the power for a DC motor that could be slowed down with a water friction brake. An original submarine battery was chosen for parallel drive simulations.

In addition, comprehensive research and engineering work of IKL and other firms went into the production of large quantities of metal hydride blocks for the safe storage of hydrogen. HDW manufactured air-tight, welded steel cylinders into which circular aluminium cassettes holding the metal hydride cakes are inserted. The hydrogen is filled via a central filler valve into the cylinder, and on the first filling, the metal hydride decomposes into a fine powder, creating a very large surface on to which the hydrogen can accumulate. The metal hydrides have free spaces in their metal lattice structure that are filled in a reversible process with hydrogen atoms. Thus they can accommodate large amounts of hydrogen in a small volume. A controlled release of hydrogen from the storage cylinders is achieved in utilizing waste heat from the Fuel Cell. But what functions well today initially caused its developers headaches as the heat of the first test cells of alkaline was enough, as a participant recalls, "to arch the cylinders like bananas".

From the outset, the developers laid maximum emphasis on the safe operation of the hydrogen and the oxygen systems, and were grateful for TÜV Rhineland's support and advice, which also ensured no significant and costly changes would be needed for the later operation of the system.

In autumn 1984, the land test system was taken into operation after the test crew comprising HDW, IKL and Siemens staff had put all subsystems such as hydrogen, water and monitoring systems through their paces. To test the system, two separate computer systems were installed, one of which supervised the security of the system and automatically shut it down on any serious loss of water or oxygen. The second computer took readings and saved data.

In January 1985, HDW and IKL presented the system to the German Navy's Chief of Staff and admirals. A year later, after a successful 350 hour test run which convinced the BWB of the plant's reliable efficiency, the procurement office decided to integrate it into U I, a Class 205 submarine, for on-board testing. In 1987 trials and the training of the first Navy crew to operate a non-nuclear external air independent system on a conventional submarine started, with U 1 moored to the shipyards fitting out quay.

## U 1 ON TRIALS

In summer 1988 the nine-month sea trials in North and Baltic Sea could at last begin and started with relatively long submerged trips in which individual subsystems were subjected to extensive testing. During trials, U 1 also sailed to friendly nation ports where it was easily refuelled with hydrogen and oxygen. Transit journeys were carried out in constantly submerged conditions, utilizing only the Fuel Cell plant, and not the snorkel.

U 1's most impressive trip was in August when it sailed from the Helgoland, an island in the North Sea, to Kristiansand (Norway) in 44 hours, covering a distance of 240 miles. In his report dated 18 August 1988, U 1's Commander Dirk Uhde reported [17][18] doing the whole voyage submerged and dived deep. U 1 drew most of its power from the Fuel Cell plant, albeit a small amount of additional power was taken from the batteries, which at the start of the voyage had a capacity of 85%, and on arrival 70%. In comparison, a conventional submarine – according to Uhde – would have had to use its snorkel at various intervals every day for a total of about four hours. He also added that snorkel travel always involved increased risks – even in times of peace. On the way to Kristiansand he occasionally left his cruising depth and rose to periscope depth in order to confirm the boat's position. At sea level, dense fog – and yachts with navigation lights turned off by negligent skippers – often prevailed. He also became aware of the fact that, owing to long diving periods in the depths of the North Sea, that there urgent need had arisen for a navigation system that worked independently of the periscope depth. In all, however, Dirk Uhde reported his complete satisfaction, and said the trip was "quiet and deep" in the true sense. He noted the strain put on the crew was also less than operating in snorkel mode, as the Fuel Cell required little monitoring, which left the greater part of the crew free to concentrate on the actual deployment and its tactical issues.

Uhde gave the tactical perspectives of the new technology best marks and said his boat and the new system would be extremely suitable for operations in areas under threat, and the possibility to remain east of Bornholm with the utmost discretion (remember, this was in time of the Cold War) and complete the return voyage through dangerous waters with success, as not only would U1 have the advantage of being extremely quiet, but would have to use its hoisting masts less – further benefits linked to the Fuel Cell.

Uhde came to the conclusion that the Fuel Cell technology would enhance the total effectiveness of submarines, and said "Sea trials with U 1 proved that the Fuel Cell system on board a submarine would function without a problem". He also added a small, wry anecdote from the trials and said *"A few engine room staff came to me to complain that it was boring, there was no action, and there was nothing for them to do – but I'm sure they didn't really mean it."*

## THE MODERN FUEL CELL PLANT

### THE FUEL CELL SYSTEM

As U 1's trials had well demonstrated the efficiency of the Fuel Cell, HDW and Siemens went about making the system ready for serial production. After studying various Fuel Cell types, the developers opted the PEM fuel cell to be the best for submarines. It had a high degree of efficiency, generally requires little maintenance and none in operation. It works with pure oxygen and hydrogen and pure water is the only product left over after the chemical reaction, and it is used to the cool the Fuel Cell, and for consumption on board.

Single Fuel Cells are arranged together with the necessary additional paraphernalia and electronics into Fuel Cell modules and inserted into a pressure resistant steel container, in the flow of low pressure hydrogen. The Fuel Cell modules based on the know-how gathered from U 1 had outputs of 30-40 kilowatt-hours DC, and were installed on the first German Navy Class 212A boats. Progress has continued, and modules installed in the Class 214, 209PN, DOLPHIN AIP and in the 209 plug-ins, now have capacities of 120 kilowatt-hours. As many modules as desired can be connected together in series for higher performances.

The Fuel Cell's liquid oxygen is stored in specially insulated tanks, which, on the Class 212A boats, are located outside of the pressure hull, on its top, beneath a hatch. Other classes, including boats with plug-ins, have their oxygen tanks inside the pressure hull. The oxygen supply system consists of the oxygen tank, the evaporator, gauges and safety devices. The evaporator runs on waste heat supplied by the Fuel Cell. In dived modus, the oxygen tank also supplies the crew with breathing air. The system is absolutely safe, even in extreme situations. Shock tests have proved that.

Hydrogen, the highly reactive energy carrier for the chemical process of the Fuel Cell, is stored at neutral pressure in metal hydride cylinders attached to the pressure hull's exterior. Waste heat of the Fuel Cell is bled into the cylinder, dehydrates the hydrogen, and in the process, forces it out through double-wall pipes filled with inert nitrogen that enter the pressure hull. Storing hydrogen in metal hydride cylinders is safe. They have no impact on the environment, the hydride contains no gas and the amount of released hydrogen is limited by the amount of thermal energy fed into the cylinder.

The Fuel Cell system has two switchboards. One governs the electronics installed in the Fuel Cell modules, and the other regulates the plant and safety controls. The system runs on the central submarine systems control console, and does not require additional crew members. In the event of an emergency, the Fuel Cell system can be operated directly from its on-site control panel. A Fuel Cell's working conduct is based on the requested electrical output, thus its operation is inherently self-monitoring.

A Fuel Cell's auxiliary units comprise the cooling system, the nitrogen system and the tanks holding the reaction's water. Most of waste heat generated by the Fuel Cell is eliminated in the dual cooling system as it supplies the metal hydride cylinders with the thermal energy necessary to dehydrate hydrogen, and on its return, supplies the evaporator with its energy. Thus, only a minimum of residual waste heat is left over when it is discharged overboard, and thus the Fuel Cell delivers a minimal infrared signature far superior to any other air independent power plant.

Nitrogen keeps the Fuel Cell inactive over long periods of non-activity, and fills the double-wall pipes and gauges. A Fuel Cell needs no ballasting compensation as the reaction water is stored aboard, in a compensation tank, and it is required for the needs of the crew. Thus, boat's balance is guaranteed.

As previously said, plans were made from the very first for upgrades to existing boats, and particularly the Class 209 boats with an additional section containing the whole Fuel Fell system. HDW submarines are designed and built in sections, which makes cutting a pressure hull at a pre-defined point for insertion of a new section, complete with a Fuel Cell plant and oxygen tanks, a relatively easy task; the hydride cylinders are attached the boat's keel, outboards where they are beneficial as ballast.

Retrofitted submarines can roughly quadruple dive times and underwater ranges – i.e. up to about two weeks. Diving times on boats initially fitted with Fuel Cell systems (the HDW Class 212A, 214, 209 PN and Dolphin AIP boats) can remain submerged for several weeks but precise data is unknown as navies and the shipyard maintain stony silences. Internet rumour mills and submarine tittle-tattle speak of up to 60 days. One thing is certain: the Fuel Cell out-performs other non-nuclear AIP systems two-fold – after all, about 60 per cent of the carried hydrogen/oxygen energy is available for propulsion and on-board consumption.

The HDW Class 212A submarine U 32 proved the point when in March 2013 it travelled the longest distance and spent more time dived than any other German Navy submarine before. Of its 20 day delivery trip

*A technician works on a black metal hydride cylinder of a HDW Class 212A submarine.* (YPS Peter Neumann)

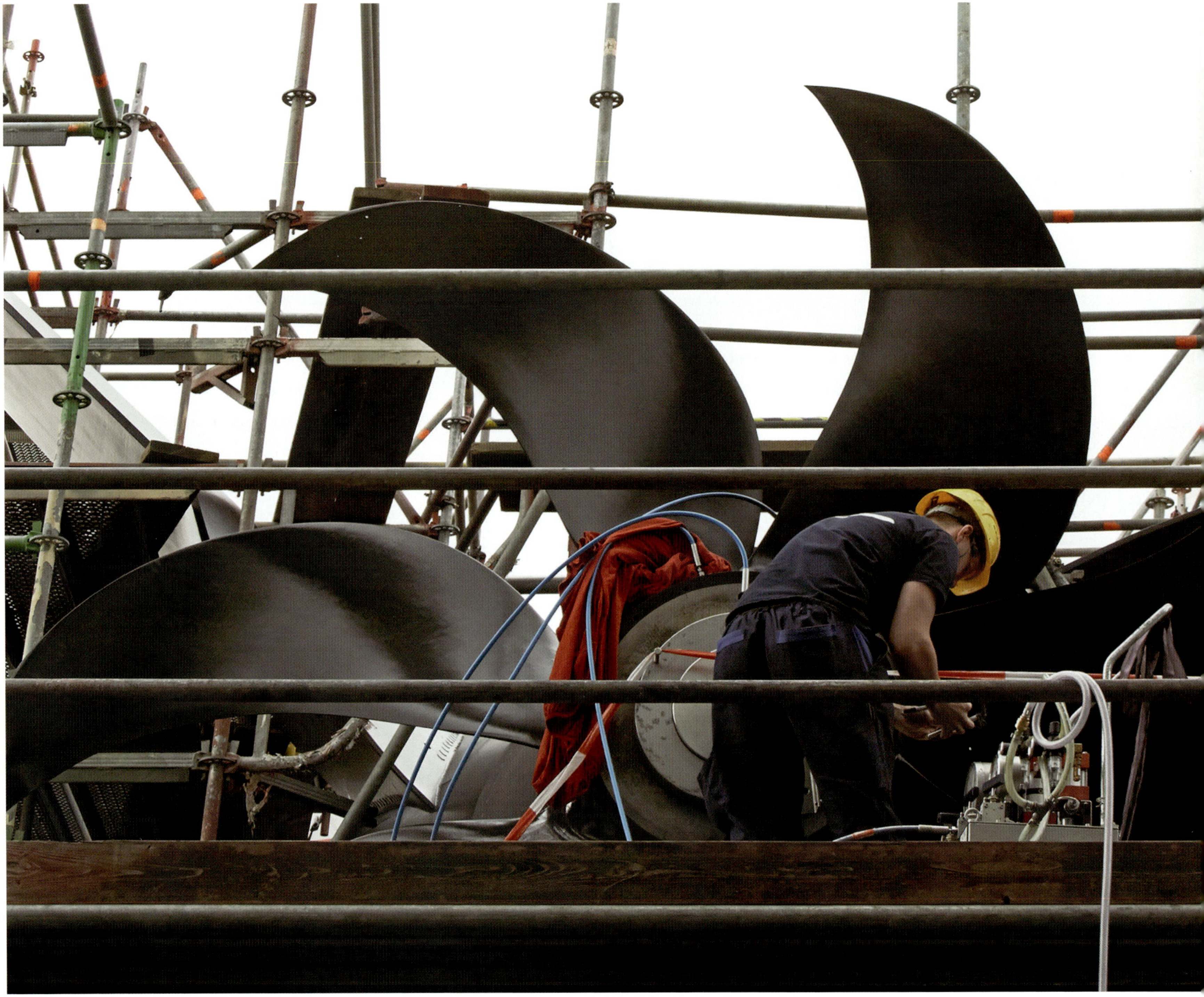

*The high skew submarine propeller – today of carbon fibre – on an HDW Class 212A submarine.* (YPS Peter Neumann)

from the Azores to Florida, for joint exercises with the US Navy, it spent 18 days dived, operating with its Fuel Cell. Stormy weather churned the Atlantic into wild water and eight meter waves forced the submarine's accompanying tender vessel MAIN to run south whilst U 32 sought shelter in the calm depths of the ocean. Apparently the only crew members which suffered were the smokers.

## THE SIEMENS PERMASYN® MOTOR

In order to meet the propulsion requirements of the new submarines, Siemens re-engineered its existing DC engines to make them even better, and the result, the Siemens-Permasyn® motor, is more efficient, smaller, lighter and quieter than its predecessor, which makes it particularly suitable for the HDW's new submarines. Meanwhile, they have been built into 31 boats, first the Class 212A German boats, then those for Greece, South Korea, Portugal, Israel and Turkey.

In the Permasyn motor®, excitation is achieved with permanent magnets and thus requires no exciter power. Furthermore, the poles and coils are designed for minimal power loss. Energy loses and noise minimization have been further increased as the electric power curve, pulse frequency and speed-dependent phase regulation have been optimized. The shaft, a part of the drive chain, is an integral part of the Permasyn® motor. Switching gears between different drive speed ranges is not necessary – with the aid of electronic speed regulation, torque-free shift intervals, gear switching noise and high current peaks are things of the past. In comparison to traditional drive chains, the Permasyn® achieves higher torque at low speeds when compared to conventional drive solutions. The high available torque across the entire speed range means that larger and more efficient propellers can be utilised. [19] [20]

The Permasyn® motor has extremely low signature values, it is well shielded, has particularly low vibrations and emits little heat and noise, which together further contribute to a submarine's undetectability. A highly efficient seven bladed "skew-back" propeller, another recent HDW development, is further component which counters noise. It has relatively small blade surfaces that reduce cavitation, a phenomenon in which low pressure vapour cavities implode with a loud, intense shock wave. Furthermore, the propellers have been engineered with balanced blade geometries and mass distributions to ensure minimum vibrations and low noise levels, even at high speeds.

## THE HYBRID POWER SYSTEM

In general, an electric motor drives a submarine's propeller, and the former can draw its current from different sources. In surface travel, it uses electrical energy drawn from batteries that the diesel generator re-charges. When dived, it can either draw power from the batteries, or from the Fuel Cell. On reconnaissance missions and longer transits, the submarine mostly runs on Fuel Cell power at four to six knots, and is absolutely silent and therefore undetectable. At high under water speeds, for exampe during a re-positioning sprint over a short distance, additional power drawn from the batteries boosts that of the Fuel Cell, making this type of boat extremely flexible – and fast.

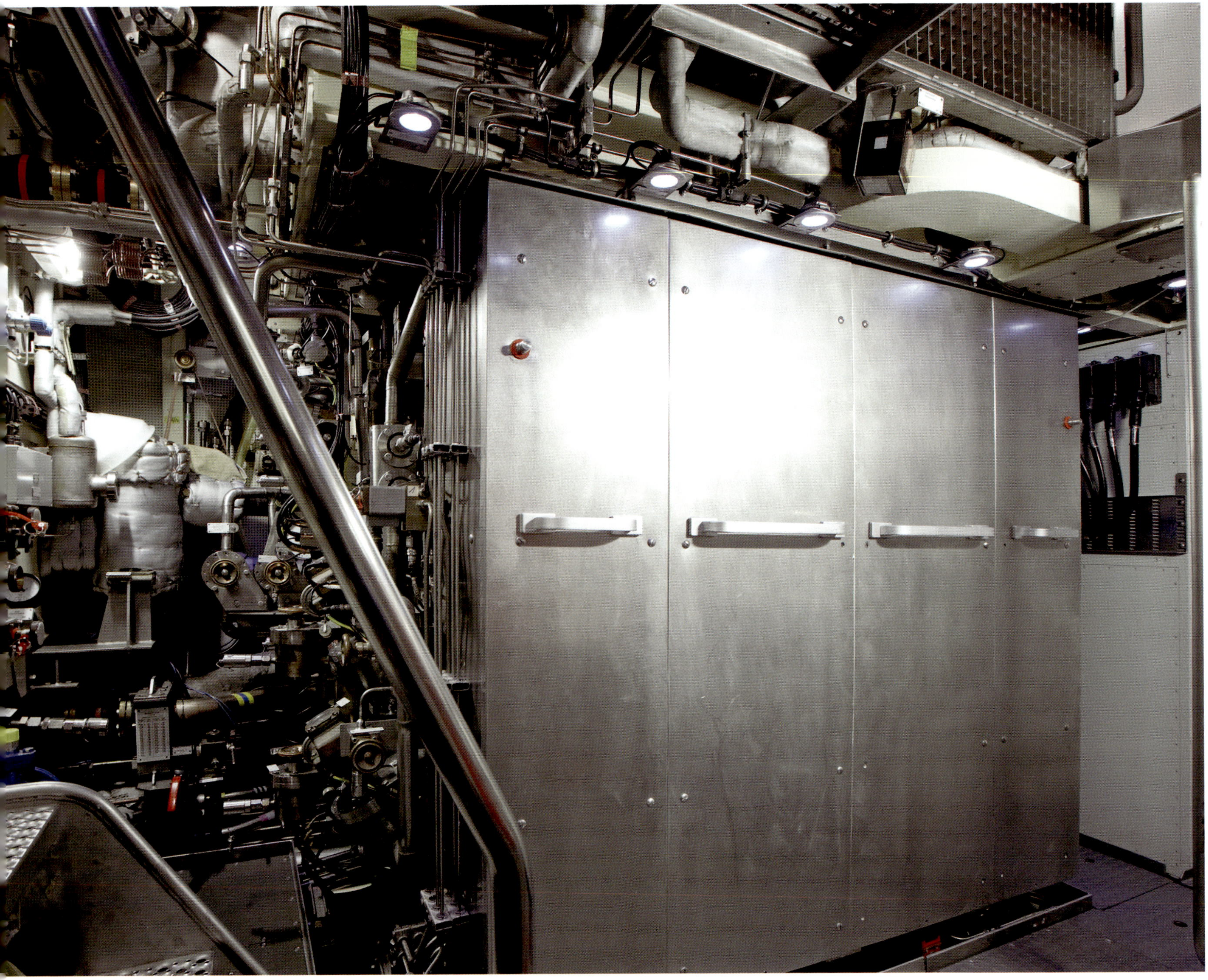

*The Fuel Cell on board a HDW Class 212A submarine – high-tech, but housed in a rather nondescript stainless steel container.* (YPS Peter Neumann)

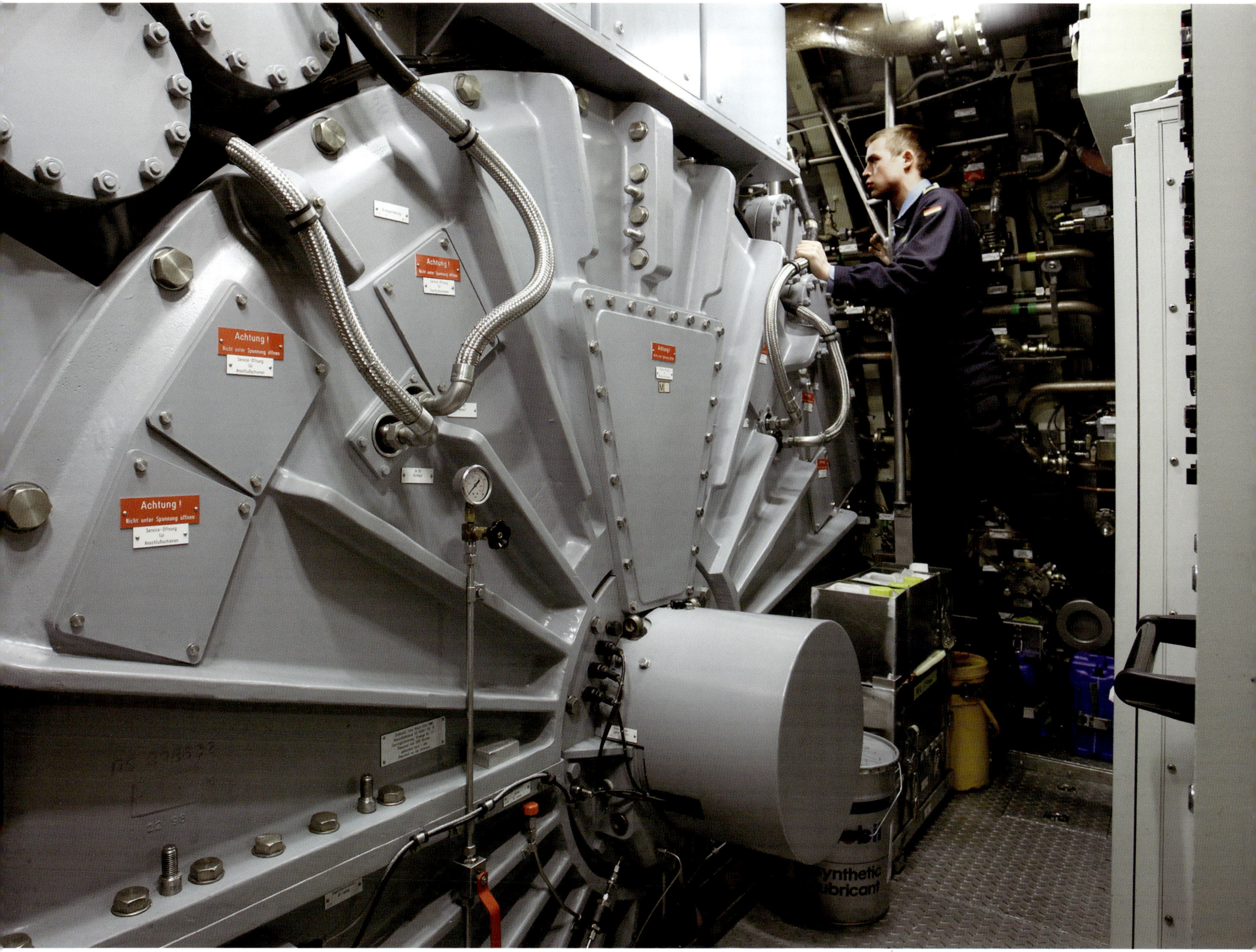
Achtung !
Nicht unter Spannung öffnen
Achtung !
Nicht unter Spannung öffnen

*High torque, even at low revs: the Siemens Permasyn® engine on board a submarine.* (YPS Peter Neumann)

# The Fuel Cell Embarks

**DETOUR: THE CLASS 212 DESIGN PROCESS**

In 1977, after the German Navy sent the Class 210 submarines into retirement, plans for a Class 208 boat were resurrected, albeit not for long, as in the early 1980s, no mature air-independent propulsion was yet in sight. In 1982 the Ministry of Defence finally buried the Class 208 in preference of two new design proposals: the Classes 211 and 212, the former for deployment in the North Sea, and the latter for the Baltic.[1] The Class 211 a conventional diesel-electric attack submarine would be missioned to defend the NATO alliance's North Sea northern flank. The boats were to operate from German ports without having to replenish in either Denmark or Norway, a size and equipment defining factor. The German Navy hoped to award a building contract of six boats in 1988, and commission them in 1992.

But it didn't work out. On behalf of the BWB, IKL made several designs and incorporated every wish of the German Navy and the purchasing office, with the result that the final design proved to be far too expensive. They next tried to delete various systems with the option of later implementation. But this was not enough make them affordable and fit into a tight budget having to also allow for the costs of an eight frigate new building programme. The Navy finally pulled the plug and stopped the project in 1987 as the frigates had priority within NATO.

All efforts now turned to the Class 212, which had been planned to replace the Class 206 boats, and fitted with an external air-independent fuel cell plant whose on-going development had been forced by HDW, Ferrostaal and Siemens, and which was regarded by the Navy to be the best solution. Furthermore, this Class was to include all sensible features planned for the Class 211 – and IKL was commissioned to start work in 1987. At the same time, the Ministry of Defence decided to speed up work on the new class, and on all components and systems with good reason. The Federal Navy needed new, modern submarines. It was contractually obliged to incorporate the Norwegian command and weapons control system made by Kongsberg Defence & Aerospace AS, determined for installation in the ill fated Class 210 project. And the German submarine shipyards (HDW and TNSW) were suffering from a lack of orders – their Swedish competition (Kockums) had managed to snatch a lucrative contract from under their noses. Kockums had managed to sell the Australian Navy six large Collins Class submarines. But from the outset, the boats, an enlarged version of the Swedish „Västergötland" class, sailed under an unlucky star - which gave the German shipyards a sense of „Schadenfreude". Technical problems arose at an early stage, already in the construction phase, and they dragged on to the delivery of the boats. Even in 2011, THE AUSTRALIAN wrote: „Not a single submarine seaworthy"[2]. The problems were accompanied by allegations of foul play and a biased Australian selection committee – especially as HDW/IKL's offer was initially considered to be the best of seven shipyards. In an irony of fate, in 1999, soon after HDW took over Kockums, the shipyard had to sort welding shortcomings in sections provided by Kockums to Australia.

In 1987, now that the chance of a new order had passed, design work focused in on new submarines for the German Navy. The size of the boat, which was to operate in the Baltic Sea, played an important role. Fitted with an external air independent propulsion plant, it was to take over the tasks of the Class 206s, and that meant deployment in the shallow waters of the western Baltic Sea together with its approaches, and in the deep waters of the eastern Baltic. In the German Navy's opinion, it should not exceed the outer dimensions of its predecessor.

Faced with this prerequisite, the designers, as a logical consequence, initially opted for a wider boat. The new Russian THYPOON Class submarines had made their first appearance. The world's largest submarine giants comprised two large pressure hulls next to each other and IKL quickly recognized that this type of boat could be built, but had many disadvantages. Such a design would be too complicated and too expensive. And it was the latter which the Navy did not want to hear.

So they stuck to a single pressure hull solution, fabricated of an austenitic steel alloy that is characterised by its high strength and elasticity. This alloy is not only advantageous for diving in different depths and pressures, but also in the case of groundings or collisions. It is non-magnetic, and together with non-magnetic equipment installed inside a

*Collins submarines off the coast of Western Australia – not seaworthy?* (Royal Australian Navy/CPOIS David Connolly)

boat, delivers a low magnetic signature which, in its turn, provides an effective shield against magnetic mines. This austenitic steel alloy had been specially developed by the German industry for submarines. The pressure body's survivability has been calculated with a safety factor margin of twice the approved maximum diving depth and the destruction depth. In addition, the pressure hull and the boat's equipment are largely shock resistant.

The pressure hull has cylindrical cross-section which conically tapers aft. The larger cylindrical part has a lower and upper deck. The floor of the latter is elastically suspended in the boat as a structural measure against noise and shock. It's here, midships where the command and control centre, navigation, weapons and ship control systems are stationed. Electronic equipment is slung beneath the floor. Accommodation for the crew and spare torpedoes are further forward, and the six torpedo tubes are built into the forward bulkhead.

Behind the conning tower, the after-body which has an increasingly smaller diameter, mostly contains the unmanned propulsion systems. It is surrounded by a free-flooding outer shell that houses the two oxygen tanks and the hydride cylinders.

The conning tower posed a special challenge, as it's required for operations above the surface, and when dived, for snorkelling and periscoping. It houses the bridge for surface sailing, and hoisting masts fur sub-sea operations. The size and height of a sail naturally influences a boat's

*The conical aftbody and X-rudder of a HDW Class 212A submarine.* (YPS Peter Neumann)

dived resistance. It has considerable influence on speed, trim, and fuel consumption, thus in consequence, the size of fuel and oxygen tanks, the number of hydride storage cylinders for hydrogen, and battery capacities required for defined mission purposes. Doing away with the sail is not an option, and ideas and designs to discard it have had short half-lives. Thus the Class 212 engineers sought for alternative solutions to reduce the tower's height, and came up with ideas such as hinged hoisting masts and an elevating bridge. At the end of the day, they managed to shorten the sail's hight to the satisfaction of the German Navy.

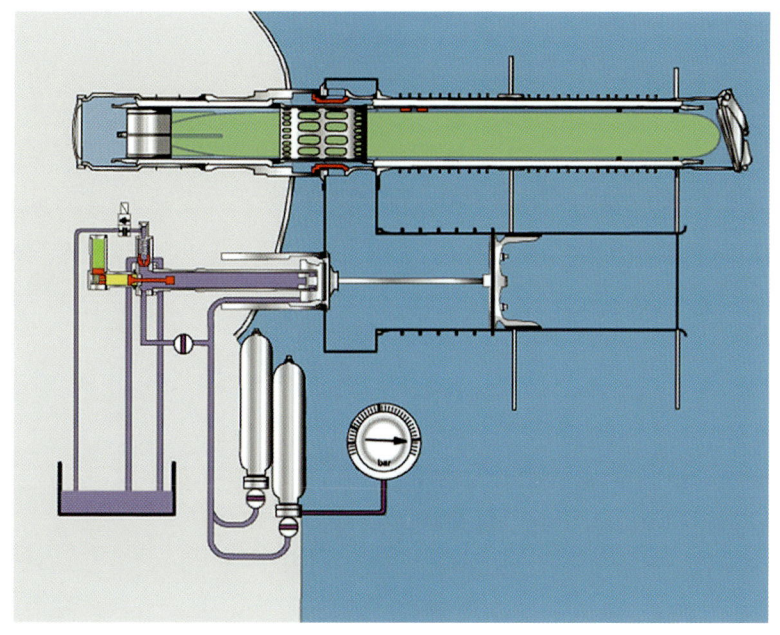

*The pressurized water torpedo launching system of a Class 212A submarine. (Graphic HDW)*

An X-rudder is fitted almost at the stern and provides excellent manoeuvrability. In comparison to a more conventional cross-rudder, the X-rudder's four rudder blade surfaces are larger and generate more leverage and grip which permit sharp changes of course. The rudder has been positioned ahead of the propeller to ensure it an (almost) swirl-free water inflow. And being forward of the prop, it does not emit rudder-noise associated with propeller slipstream.

The pressurized water torpedo launching system is yet another noteworthy innovation. Once developed by MaK, this technology had been further developed by HDW after acquiring the former's torpedo tube assembly division. Here the torpedo is ejected from the tube at high speed with high pressured water, and only starts its drive when it has put enough distance behind itself and the boat. In all other known launching technologies, the torpedo exits the tube under own power, and owing to loud propeller noise, enables detection of the submarine. What is more, the HDW ejection system has significant advantages when launching torpedoes in shallow water.

## NOISE REDUCTION

The engineers did everything possible to reduce noise emissions, and in the process reduced other emissions such as magnetism, radar, infra-red (heat dissipation) to the lowest possible levels. Today, these submarines, as previously said, emit less energy than a single LED bulb! Engineers have placed special emphasis on making the boats extremely quiet. Thus, they have gone to great lengths to eliminate any noise made by the boat moving through the water, or from its machinery. It's all about silencing drives and systems. Every piece of machinery, every device, module, pipe and cable is elastically mounted. Hatches are flush, and the hull smoothed to avoid acoustic seepage. All these measures have reduced the noise signature to a minimum, which can hardly be detected. They enlarge the reach of the submarine's own sonar and at the same time reduce the risk of discovery.

A critical issue for a submarine's detection by an opponent's sonar, is the signal that an (own) submarine bounces back, which makes it vital to reduce (own) signals as far as possible, and place great emphasis on a noise-optimized hull shape. Reducing „reflection effects" as well as the application of special sonar-absorbing materials on the submarine's exterior surfaces is an important task. In the case of the HDW Class

212 boats, hydrodynamics and signature strengths defined the shape of the hull.[3]

A further measure to reduce self-made noise is the new boat's outer cladding, or skin that envelopes the pressure hull. Made of FRP, this novelty has smooth, clean surfaces which lower water resistance and are harder to detect with sonar. The outer cladding covers the oxygen tanks, connectors, winches, spills, mooring cleats, decoys etc. Doors and items protruding from the pressure hull are hidden behind flush closing hatches and flaps. In order to produce the individual components, HDW set up its own state-of-the-art FRP workshops, and manufactures moulded cladding components with surfaces that are smoother than of steel – unless it is burnished at extremely high costs. As sea water flows around both sides of cladding, there is no risk of crushing at great water depths.

However, the new boat grew in size. IKL presumed the air-independent propulsion would need more weight and volume. The electronics for the new weapons and guidance technology, the automation and the additional installations for power and cooling would require more space, and finally the crew were to provided more comfortable accommodations. Hot bunking where two crew share a bed was to become a thing of the past. Not only was there enough space for each of the 28 crew to have his/her own bunk, but there was also space enough for the crew to eat in two mess-rooms. Speaking of food, the cook was to have an ultra-modern galley that would turn a housewife green with envy. Living conditions were to improve further with a shower on board, the first since the days of the Imperial Navy.

*Flaps on the smooth FRP external hull cladding of a HDW Class 212A submarine conceal the anchoring gear, mooring bollards, removable stanchions etc. (YPS Peter Neumann)*

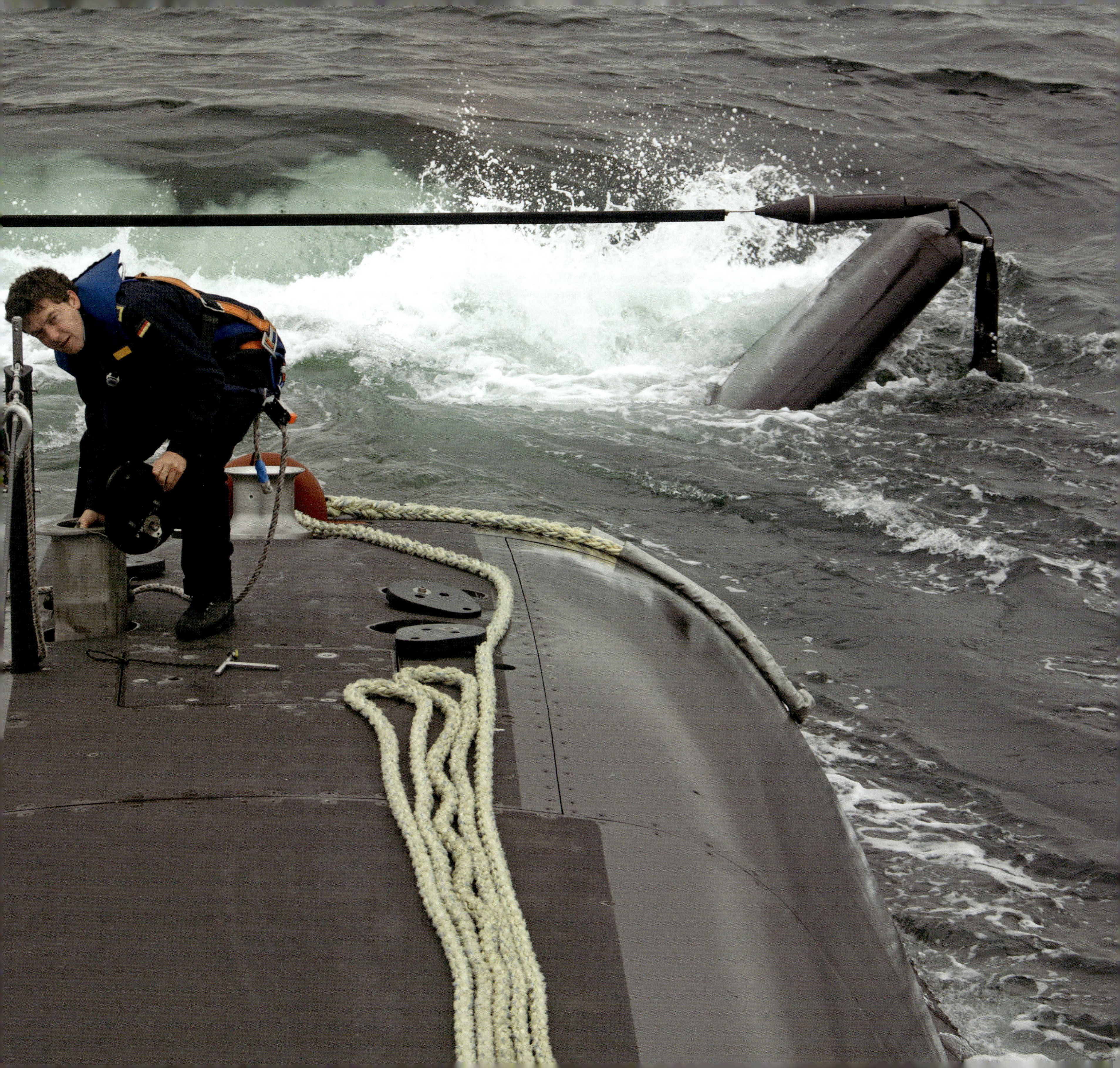

# The Class 212A Becomes Reality

The new submarine was finally on the long road to being built. It had indeed taken a long time to get the planning right, sort out problems and find the straight path leading to the new boats. And now, the road had become the destination, albeit which was still far away. In 1987 IKL was commissioned to develop the Class 212, of which six boats were to be built.

At the same time, on request of the Ministry of Defence, the two submarine shipyards (HDW and TNSW) formed a consortial working group, the "ARGE 212", led by the former. It had the given the job to approve the concept and define the work on behalf of the BWB, and subcontract it out to other partners within the industry. IKL was assigned with the definition and construction, the lion's share. Further assignments were given to major players such as Siemens, MTU, Kongsberg Defence & Aerospace AS, Gabler Maschinenbau, STN Atlas Elektronik and Zeiss Optronic. The consortium had the duty of fixing prices, coordinate deadlines/agendas, look after logistics, documentation and construction plans.

This was followed by several design loops, and a model of the CIC was built and found to be good. After completion of the definition phase and the transfer of the definition documents, building contracts with HDW and Thyssen Nordseewerke (TNSW) were signed in spring 1991. The first boat was to be delivered in 1995. Meanwhile the number of new submarines had been raised. A second batch of six boats was to follow the first batch of six, according to the planning in 1990. But things worked out differently. As the USSR folded in 1991, the world's political stage changed and an age of détente seemingly started. This was not missed in Kiel. ANNA KARENINA was a Russian ferry that moored opposite to the yard, and traded between Kiel and Leningrad. One day her able crew replaced the vessel's home-port "Leningrad" with "St. Petersburg", much to the delight of Kiel's submarine citizens.

The resulting consequences for the submarine shipyards were, however, painful. The eagerly awaited orders were repeatedly delayed, the boats had lost their urgency to politicians. In the face of the humongous costs for the German unification, the sizable costs for new submarines faded in importance. And this gave the executive decks of the two shipyards little joy, even though they were awarded with a presumed lost contract to build three DOLPHIN Class submarines for Israel. But it also had an up-side that components intended for the Class 212 boats could be tested up front on the Israeli boats.

Meanwhile, busy hustle and bustle began behind the scenes, with the ambition to realize the German Na-

*Hull optimisation: Class 212 tank test model in the HSVA.* (YPS Peter Neumann)

vy's order, which was finally announced on 6 July 1994 with a volume of 2.6 billion DM for a first batch of four Class 212 submarines. Two were to be built at HDW, and two at TNSW. The announcement also included building a second batch, somewhere in the far future.

IKL now entered troubling times, it had no business. But in 1993 it relocated from Lübeck to the safe haven of HDW, and in 1994, the shipyard had acquired all shares of the renowned engineering company. In 1997 IKL was deleted from the commercial register. In Kiel, IKL's able employees were welcome, their invaluable expertise strengthened HDW's capabilities – and nobody in Kiel had the intent of losing them – to the French competition?

On 1 July 1998, the actual building of the first section for the first boat kicked off as Defence Minister Volker Rühe pushed the frame welding robot's starting button. In the meantime, the German Class 212 codification became "HDW Class 212A", as the Italian Navy had signed up in the construction programme. The design was revised to suit their purposes for a boat that could go even deeper, and the German Navy followed suit. Thus a Class 212 boat was never built. Fincantieri, a shipyard in La Spezia, built the two ordered Italian boats, and two more are currently in the books. HDW supplies both the Fuel Cell system and the bow section with torpedo tubes.

On 20 March 2002, Bärbel Kaempf, wife of the Head of the BMVg's Armament Department, Ministerial Director Dr. Jörg Kämpf, christened the first Class 212A boat "U 31", in a names giving ceremony at HDW. In his speech, Hannfried Haun, Deputy CEO of HDW, stressed how the cornerstone for long-term employment had been laid with the decision to deploy the Fuel Cell. And he also emphasized how many sub-suppliers throughout Germany benefited from building submarines.

U 31's christening was a milestone on its way to commissioning in October 2005, and after the ceremony, the boat was subjected to extensive harbour and sea trials. But in truth, testing had begun long ago, in January 2002. The German Navy's requirements placed on external air independence, extremely low signatures and advanced weapon and sensor systems had resulted in a high degree of integration. The classic separation between "platform" and "payload" was no longer applicable – rather, the system had to be considered as a whole. And it had been a challenge to the shipyards and their suppliers.

Extra diligence was lavished on newly developed components. Countless questions had to be given satisfactory answers, which were not only theoretical. Thus, two fully-integrated shore-based test systems – the Fuel Cell test block and a Command and Weapon Control System (CWCS) – were built to respond to practical details long before the boat was launched. This saved time and money.

The young submarine's real life began on 20 April 2002 as the boat was "splashed" and practical testing seamlessly continued, as the integration and starting-up procedures had already started in January when the boat was still in the building shed. The in-water functionality tests moored alongside the fitting out quay were to prove that all systems worked not only on their own, but interact-

*Christening U 31 on 20 March 2002. (YPS Peter Neumann)*

*Testing U 31: Hoisting manoeuvre in the Eckernförder Bay. (YPS Peter Neumann)*

ed without any problems. And of course they also had to fulfil strict test specifications. This was completed in early 2003. The first German Navy crew had spent four weeks in HDW's "naval training centre" and had become acquainted with the boat and its systems. They were to operate the submarine during the forthcoming sea trials, which started with shallow diving in the western Baltic. The entire ship's technology and operations were up on the bench. The boat was a tight squeeze as, in addition to the crew, shipyard employees, sub-suppliers and, last but not in any way least, BWB approval staff had been shipped aboard.

End of July 2003, U 31 left home waters for the first time, bound for Norway – and for its second trials series, namely deep water testing where it was provisionally based in Kristiansand, Stavanger and Bergen. Here, the Norwegian Navy helped its German colleagues and enabled them to use its facilities. Acoustics, sonar and weapon control systems were in for deep water testing, preferably in the Skagerrak. And U 31 launched its first practice torpedoes. But not everything went according to plan. The boat was supposed to be delivered in the following March, but actually entered service together with U 32 on 19 October 2005. Nobody was surprised as the novel boat was in every way a revolutionary step in submarine construction. The problems which dogged it during trials had been unpredictable, but were solved, much to the benefit of succeeding boats.

Especially those problems that were not of a technical nature belonged to the category of unpredictable problems. For example, as U 31 was moored in a guarded area rented by HDW at Kristiansand, the Norwegian press published rumours that the boat was actually powered by a nuclear reactor, causing public opinion to become uncomfortable. A specially scheduled press conference turned the tide as Norwegian journalists convinced themselves that, owing to its Fuel Cell technology, U 31 was actually extremely friendly to the environment.

## THE NEW SUBMARINE GENERATION: HDW CLASS 212A

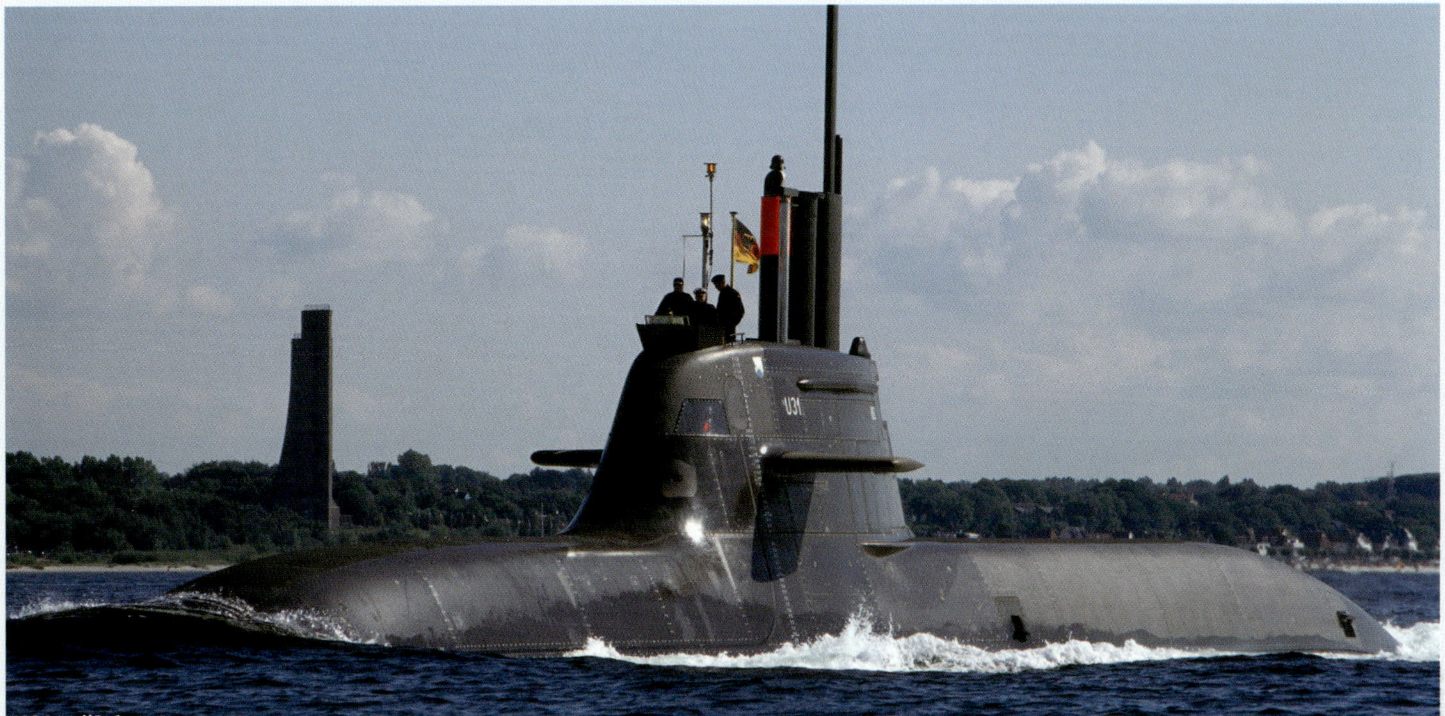
U31

U 31 off Laboe. (YPS Peter Neumann)



The Naval Forces magazine celebrated the new submarine class, at that time still Class 212, in 1995 as the "ultimate underwater weapon system":

> *"This submarine can detect and identify ships from a hidden position and launch torpedoes long before the opponent has recognised what's actually going on. On the basis of a broad deployment profile and with regard to possible future threats, the design focuses on three main characteristics: overall low signatures, prolonged underwater endurance with AIP, effective sensors and the weapon system."* [1]

This new revolutionary submarine class marked the beginning of a generation of submarines which bridge the gap between a conventional diesel-electric and nuclear powered boat with a design that differs from all predecessors.

### HDW CLASS 212A (1. BATCH) MAIN DATA

**MAIN TASKS**

- Independent, largely undetectable, long-lasting loitering in operational areas without regional limitation.
- Undetectable reconnaissance and monitoring of sea areas where other naval forces cannot or should not be used.
- Tie down enemy naval forces.
- Backing up sea areas and key positions against attack from enemy surface and submarine vessels, as well as preventing unfettered enemy use of sea areas and sea lanes.

**KEY TECHNOLOGIES ON THE HDW CLASS 212A SUBMARINES**

| | |
|---|---|
| Fuel Cell plant | Siemens, HDW |
| PERMASYN® motor | Siemens |
| Sonar systems | ATLAS ELEKTRONIK |
| Optical systems | Carl Zeiss Optronics |
| Torpedo weapon systems | ATLAS ELEKTRONIK, HDW |
| Torpedo defence systems | Whitehead Alenia Sistemi Subacquei |
| Helicopter defence (IDAS) | Diehl BGT Defence |

**MAIN SPECIFICATIONS**

| | |
|---|---|
| Length over all | approx. 65 m |
| Height including sail | approx. 11.5 m |
| Hull diameter | max 7 m |
| Displacement, surfaced | approx. 1,450 t |
| Displacement, submerged | approx. 1,830 tonnes |
| Diving depth | about 400 m |
| Crew | 28 persons |
| Pressure hull | nonmagnetic steel |
| Command and weapons control system | Kongsberg |

**PROPULSION SYSTEM[3]**

| | |
|---|---|
| PERMASYN® drive motor | 1,700 kW |
| Fuel Cell system | 9 modules each of 34 kW |
| Diesel generator | MTU 16V365 Piller Generator 1,050 kW |
| Drive batteries | Hawker/VARTA |
| Low-noise 7 blade skew-back propeller | |
| Max surfaced speed | 12 knots |
| Max dived speed | 20 knots |

*U 31 pushing at speed.* (YPS Peter Neumann)

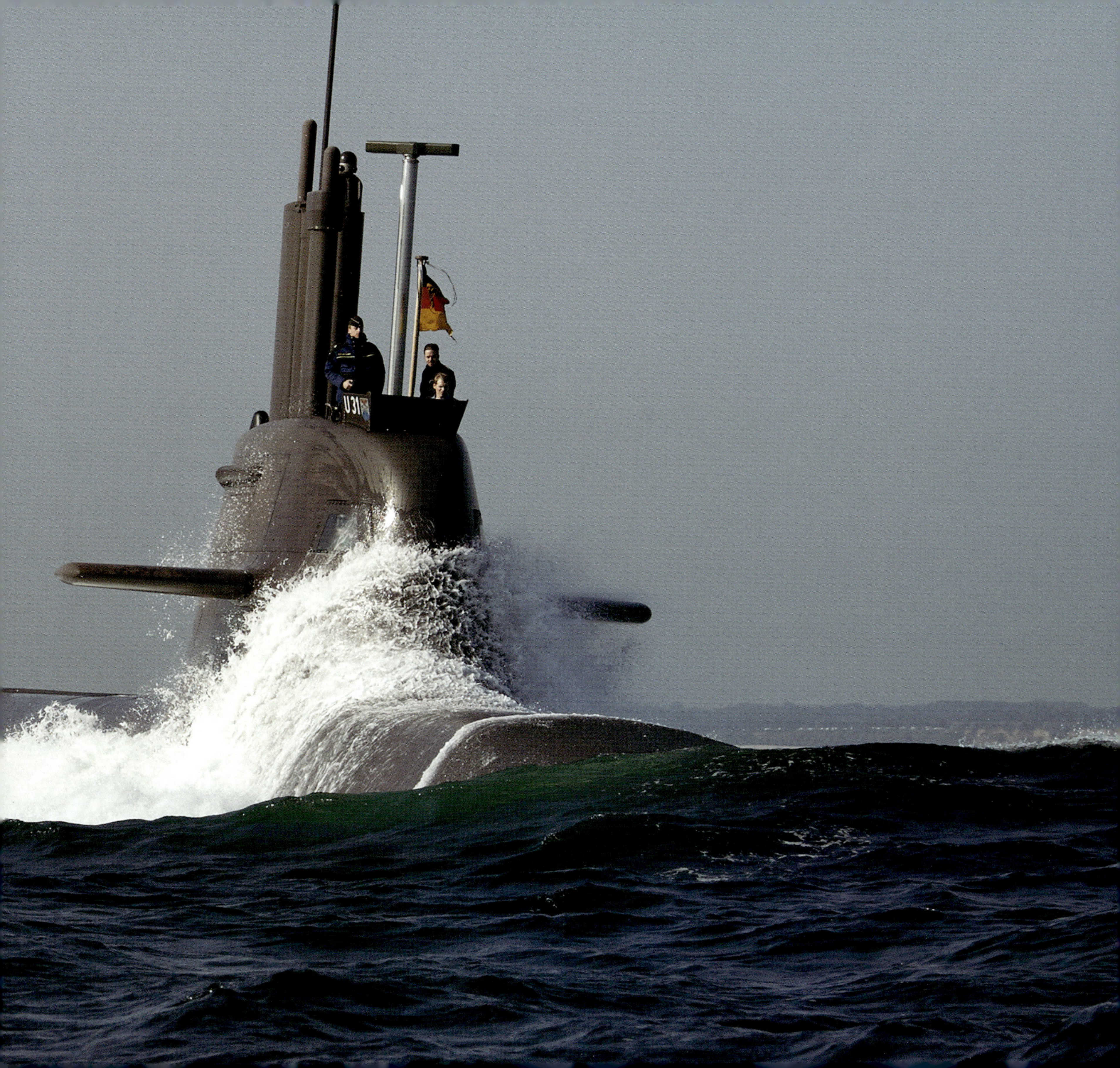
U31

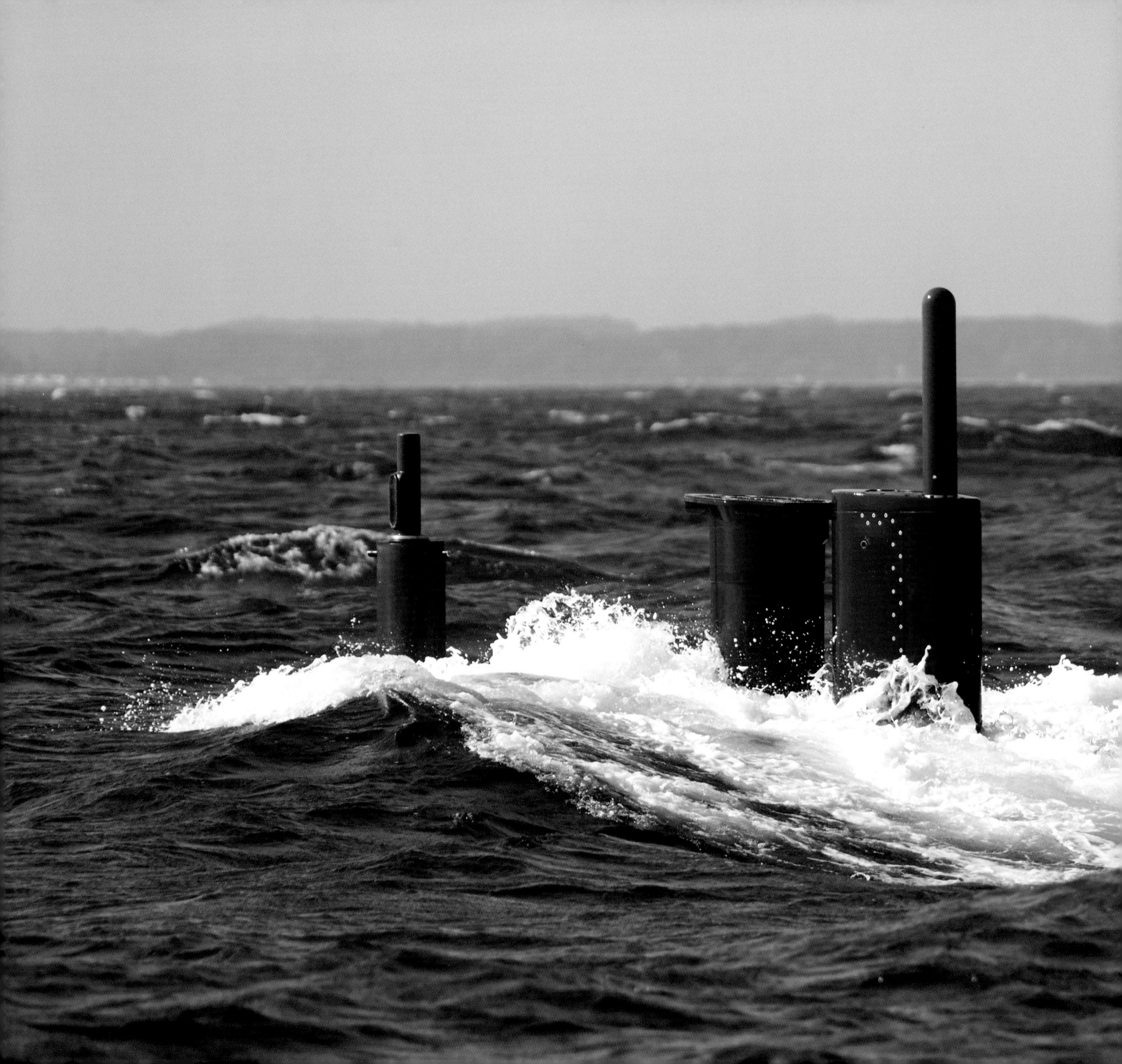

### ARMAMENT
6 x 533 mm torpedo tubes, pressurized water launching system,

### INTEGRATED SONAR SYSTEM
DBQS 90 FTC (ATLAS ELEKTRONIK) passive ranging sonar PRS, distance measurement system, intercept (CIA), sonar flank array sonar (FAS), towed array sonar (TAS), mine avoidance system MAS, own noise monitoring system ONA

### PERISCOPE SYSTEMS
SERO 14 observation Periscope with thermal image detection, SERO 15 attack periscope with laser rangefinder (both Carl Zeiss Optronics)

### INTEGRATED RADIO MESSAGING SYSTEM
HF, VHF, UHF, VLF, INMARSAT-C, UHF-SATCOM, GMDSS (global maritime distress and safety system)

### NAVIGATION SYSTEM
Inertial navigation platform (LITEF), course and location reference system
Electromagnetic log, navigation radar (Kelvin Hughes ELNA), depth sounder, GPS, AIS

### HOISTING MASTS
Snorkelling and radar mast (Riva Calzoni)
FM masts (Gabler Maschinenbau)

*HDW Class 212A periscope, snorkel and UHF/VHF masts (from left to right).*
(YPS Peter Neumann)

## THE COMMAND AND WEAPONS CONTROL SYSTEM (CWCS)[4]

The command and weapon control system on the first batch of HDW Class 212A boats comprises a standard CWCS the integrated sonar system, and the periscopes. The standard CWCS was developed by Kongsberg, a Norwegian technology corporation, on the basis of a 1983 agreement, and it connects the sensors (sonar, navigation, electronic support measures and periscope systems) via a data bus to effectors (torpedo system) and the submarine's bridge systems.

## THE BUILT-IN SONAR SYSTEM DBQS 40

This system enables detection in the medium and low frequency range, and and comprises the towed array sonar, flank array sonar, passive sonar, the distance measurement system, the intercept sonar, the mine detection sonar and the own noise monitoring system. Detection results, target parameters and systems status are graphically displayed on three consoles with high resolution colour raster displays. Furthermore, operaters have an accoustic tracking system running on an electronic ring memeory for audio analaysis, conditions the sound distribution of the sound can be determined and displayed. Hydrophones on the outside of the pressure hull and interior sound sensors monitor the submarine's own noise.

## PERISCOPES

The periscope system comprises a SERO 15 attack periscope fitted with optical and laser rangefinders. The observation periscope has a SERO 14 optical rangefinder, thermal imaging (IR) and combined EloUm electronic support measures, and GPS antenna.

*Periscope watch in the CIC.* (YPS Peter Neumann)

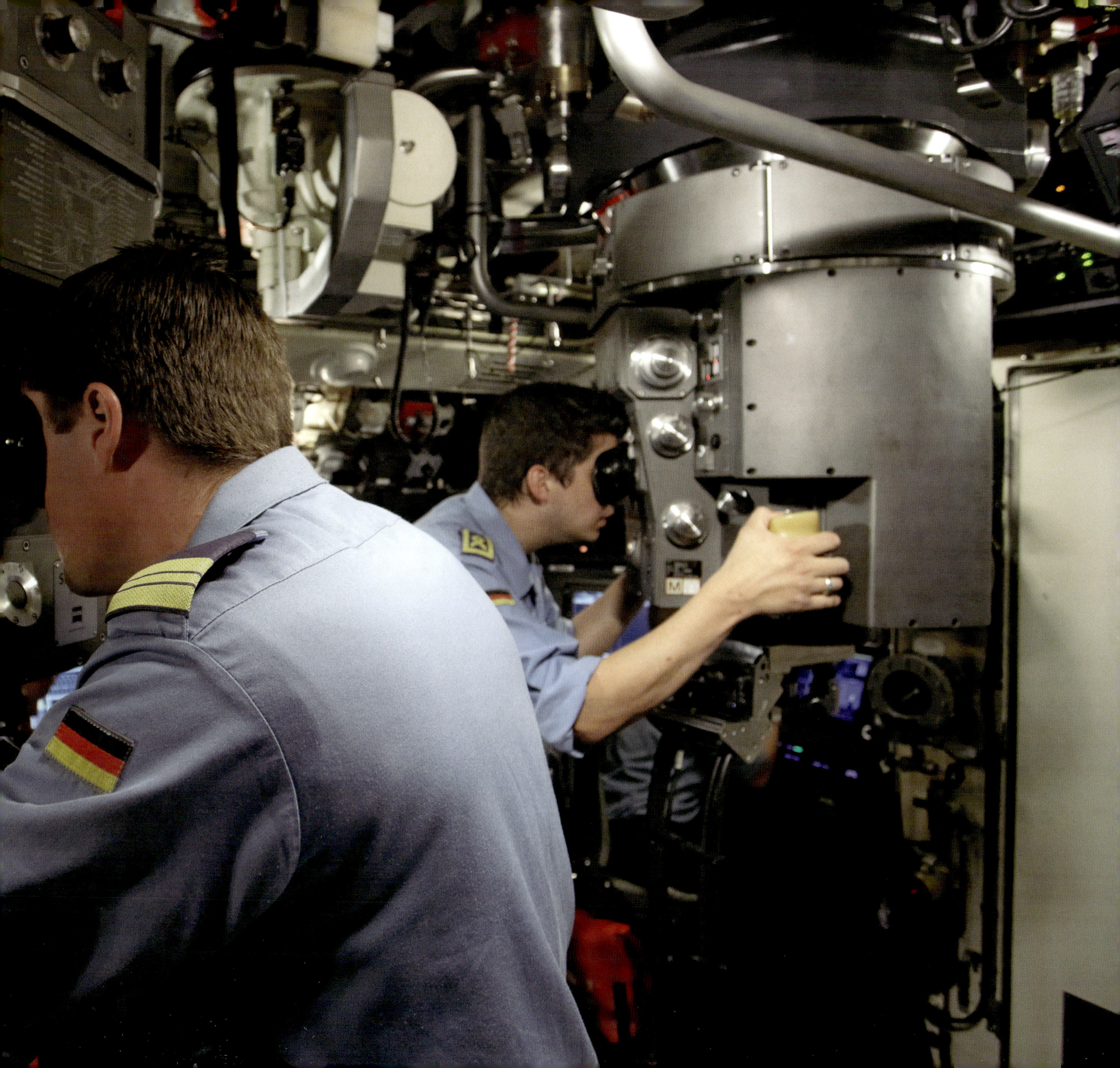

## ILLU – "INTEGRIERTER LENK- UND LEITSTAND U-BOOT" OR THE INTEGRATED STEERING AND CONTROL SYSTEM OF A SUBMARINE

Thanks to the high levels of automation provided by the ILLU automation system, relatively few personnel are required to operate the many and complex drive chain, electric, other equipment and systems required to operate the boat. In order to keep the boat under control in any situation, ILLU monitors, controls and commands about 50 units of ship-technical hardware.

The ILLU automation system is centralized into two consoles, namely one for driving/steering the boat, and the second manages ship technical issues. Both are located in the CIC, and each is operated by a single person.

The individual automation sub-systems of each unit is decentralized and located at, or close to the equipment it is designed to steer. A redundant data bus allows data traffic between the sub-systems and the ILLU.

ILLU automated operations take a big burden of submariners, and makes lives a lot easier, as regularly confirmed in service reports and duty reviews. And it reduces crew sizes.

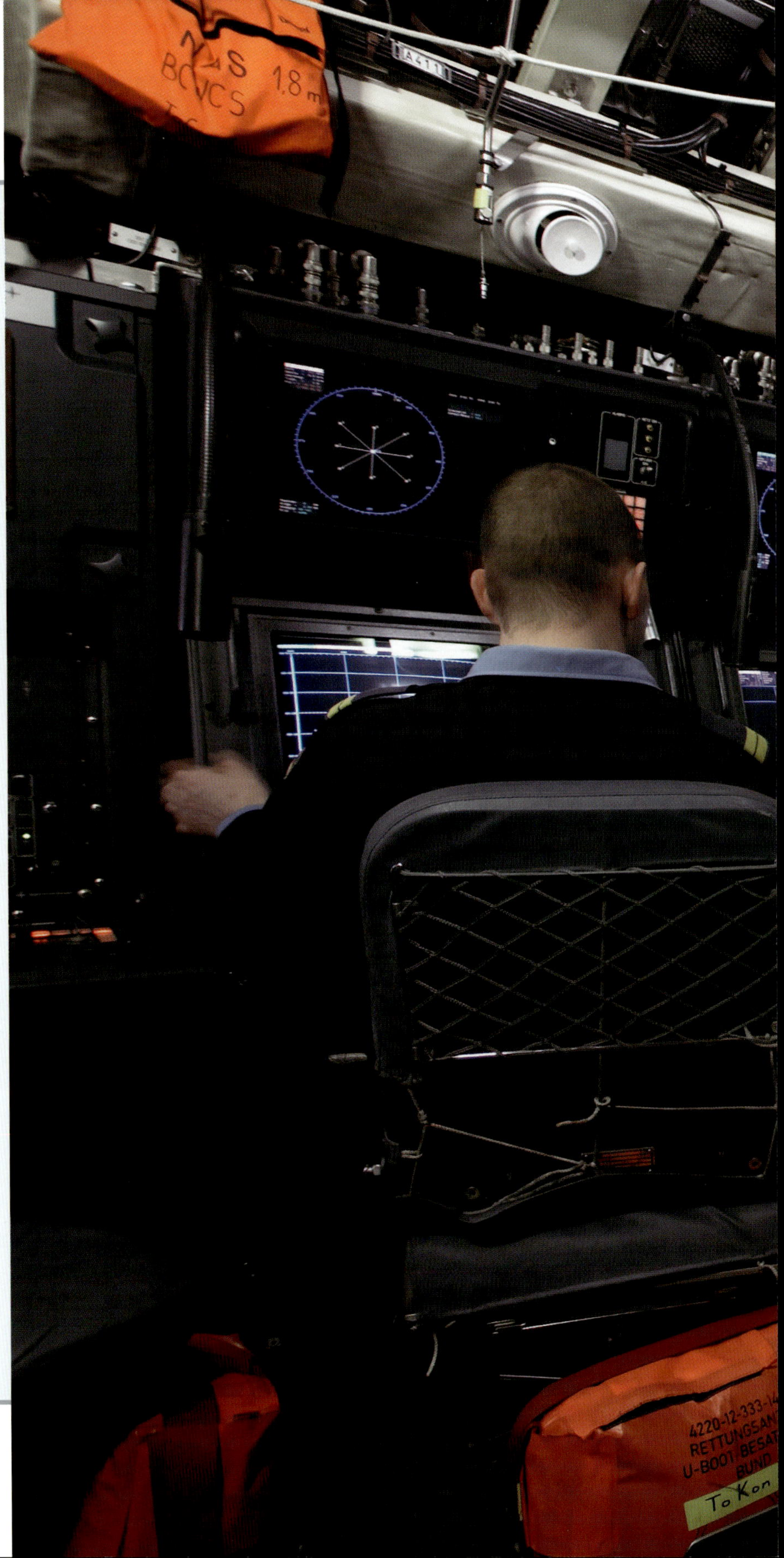
1.8 m
To Kon

*Consoles in a HDW Class 212A CIC.* (YPS Peter Neumann)

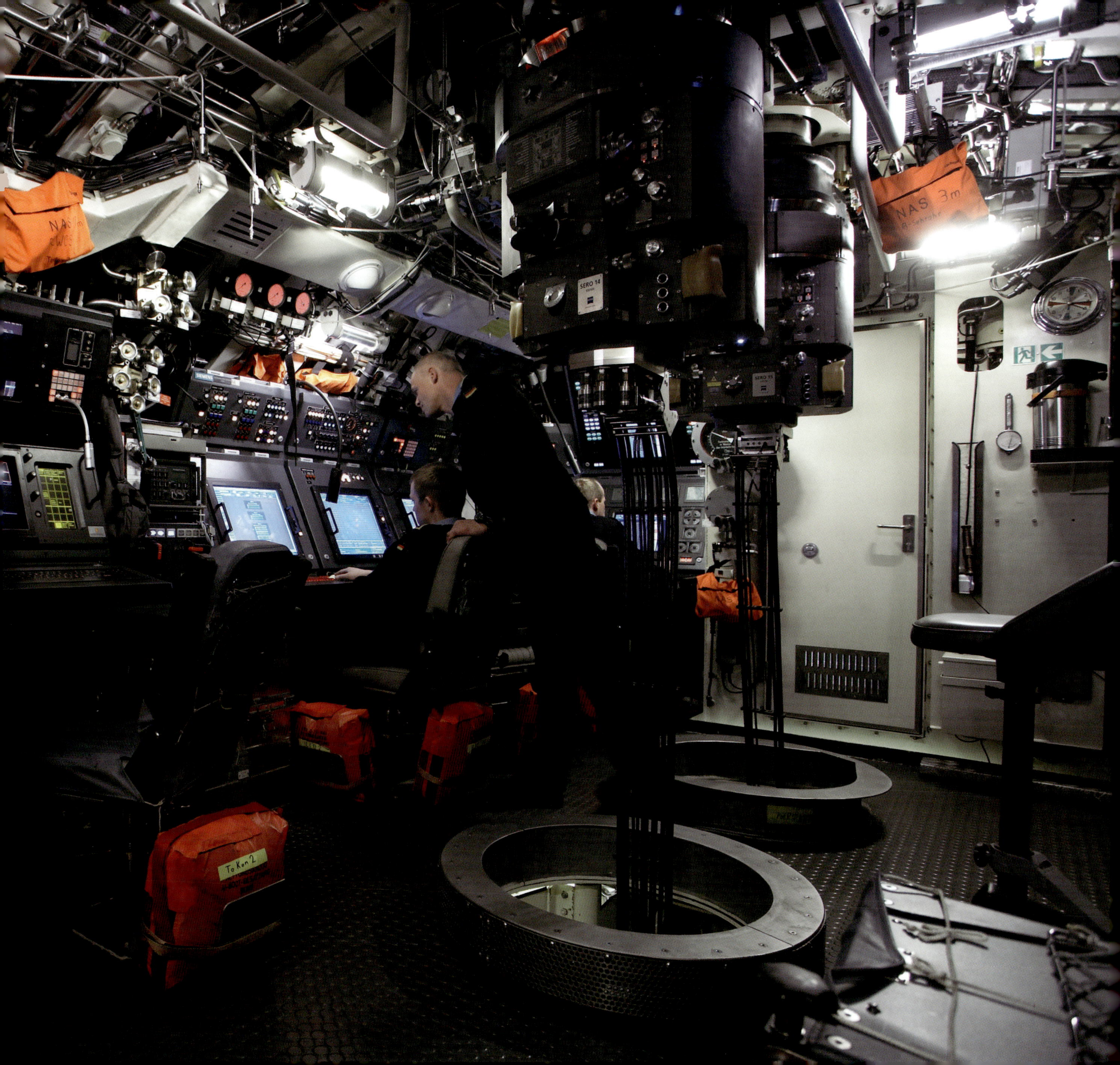
SERO 14
SERO 15
NAS 3m
To Ken 2

## HDW CLASS 212A SUBMARINES. THE SECOND BATCH.

Initially, the German Defence budget plans for the second batch of Class 212A submarines consisting of four boats, did not work out. In fact, in order to fulfil commitments and replace older units, the German Navy required 12 boats in all, which also have not become reality. The current new defence concept was passed in 2011 in the course of a hasty re-orientation of German military services as six boats were believed to sufficient, and the two boats of the second batch ordered in 2006 are not that much consolation. (The Italian Navy also ordered two further unchanged Class 212A boats.)

The new German boats feature a number significant changes. Their basic physical structure, apart from a two meter lengthening, has remained the same, as the Fuel Cell systems too. However, technological progress surged ahead during the building of the first batch of boats, and deployment scenarios changed. Thus the new boats have been adapted to become even more effective with the capability to be an integral part of network centric operations. Changes include: [5]

- the installation of a communication system for network centric operations
- the installation of an integrated sensor management and weapon command and control system made in Germany
- the replacement of the flank array with a spatial side antenna
- an optronics mast has replaced the periscope

*U 35, the first of the second batch boats, is shadowed by a navy support vessel as she leaves Kiel for sea trials.* (YPS Peter Neumann)

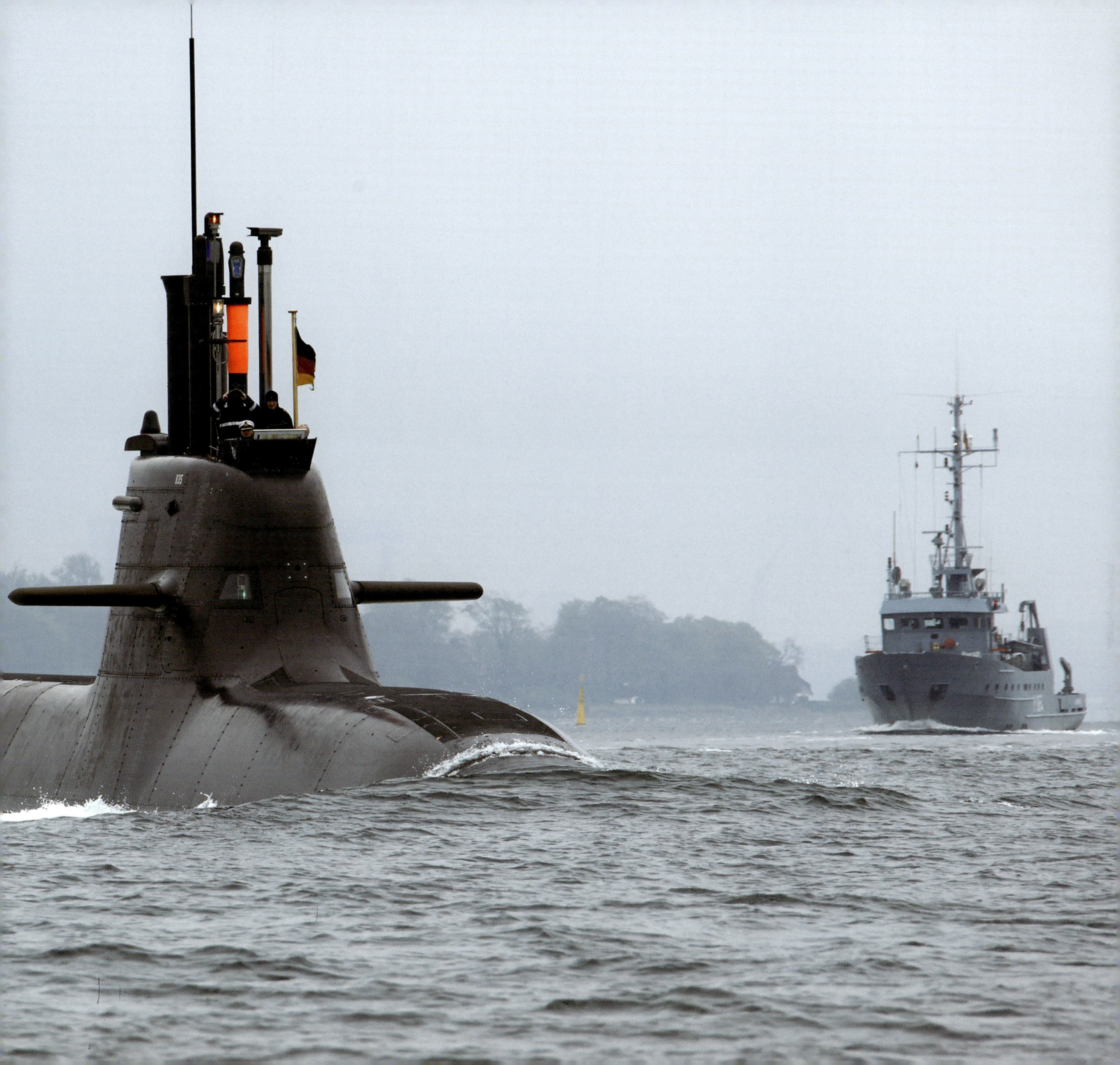

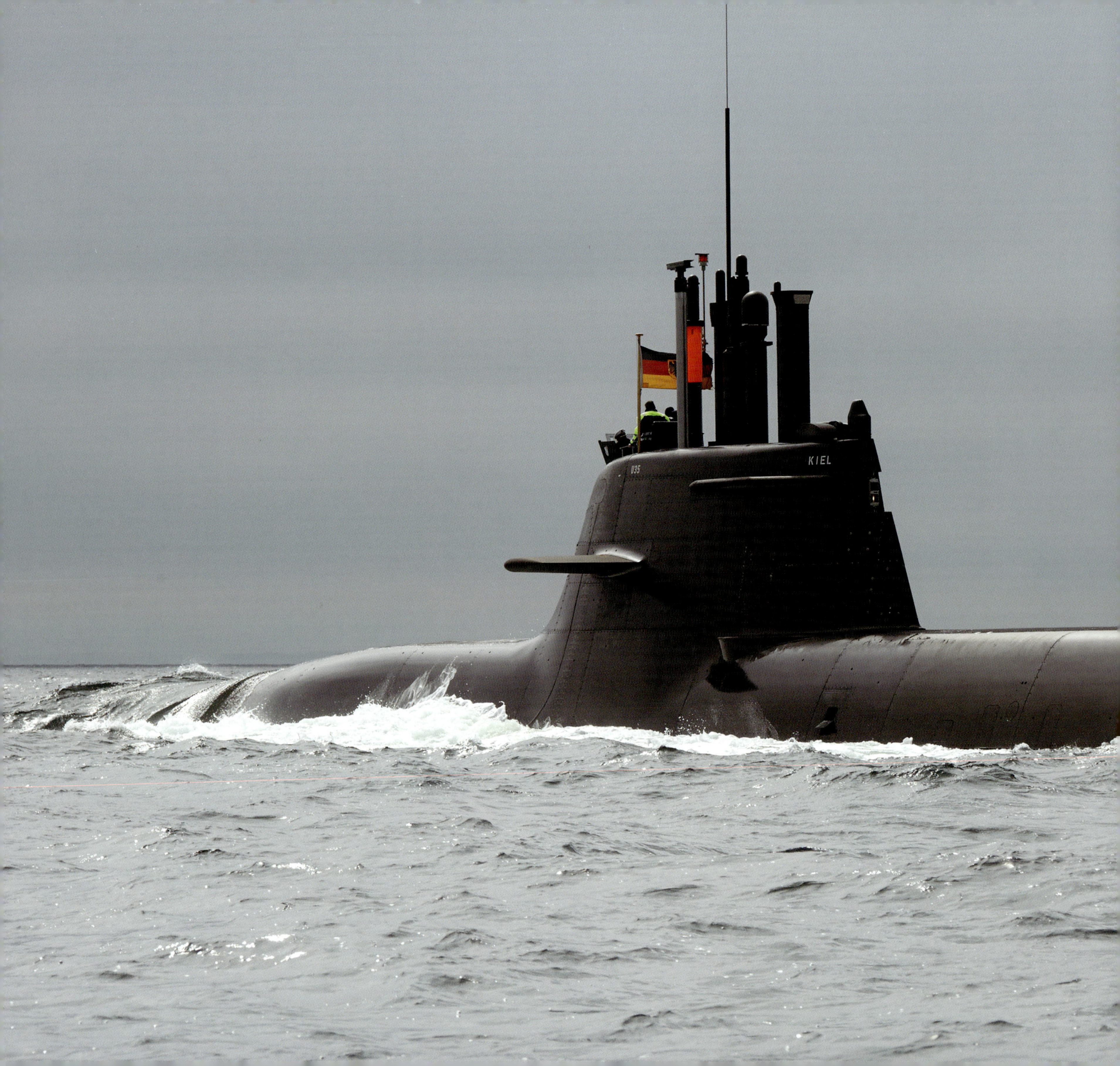
U35
KIEL

- the installation of a telecommunications mast rigged with a towable buoy for communications from the deep named CALLISTO, which is planned and in development.
- the integration of a lock for special navy forces
- tropicalisation.

Thus the new boats are better adapted for deployment across the world than those of the first batch. Enhanced communication systems include the NATO tactical data link "Link 11/16" as well a IFF (Identification, Friend or Foe) equipment. Moreover, in current development and in the test phase is a telecommunications mast that will release and tow a buoy which rises to the surface from the deep. Fitted with a SHF SATCOM antenna, it will link the boat to other participants for network-centric operations. Named CALLISTO the new system, owing to its complexity, still has a few problems that are being solved.

The ISUS 90 weapon command and control system made ATLAS ELEKTRONIK has replaced the Norwegian build system installed in the first batch. It integrates acoustic, optical and electronic signals and runs on eight consoles. ISUS 90 controls ship and navigation systems, as well as the wide-ranging wire-guided torpedoes and missiles. A spatial side antenna has been fitted for the first time, instead of a flank array. Its performance is superior to current standard systems, and it can serve as an Advanced Ranging Sonar, (ARS).

*U 35 on trials off the coast of Schleswig-Holstein.* (YPS Peter Neumann)

The latest Carl Zeiss Optronics periscope SERO 400 and optronics mast OMS 100 deliver eagle-eyed results. According to one of U 31's past commanders, already the previous periscope generation SERO 14 and SERO 15 made his US Navy comrades turn green with envy – they would very much liked to have had them too. Carl Zeiss of Oberkochen, with the new hull-penetrating SERO 400 periscope and the non-hull-penetrating OMS 100 optronics mast, has introduced a number of decisive improvements to its predecessors. For example, the SERO 400's battery-buffered emergency function, as its optical and control components remain functional, allows uninterrupted observation in the case of a main power breakdown. In addition, a fibre optic gyroscope has replaced the previous mechanical gyro, which without being picked by up sonar, soundlessly stabilises the periscope and optronics mast systems. In addition, their non-magnetic construction minimises radar detection.[6] Furthermore, automatic functions ensure fast surveillance and observation. The period of mast exposure above the surface is extremely short.

The inclusion of a lock in the sail for submerged disembarkation/retrieval of special embarked forces gave reason for the boat's lengthening of three frames. This entrance can accommodate four persons; furthermore the boats are equipped with pressure-resistant containers for their mission equipment.

The second batch boats have been tropicalised for deployment in warm seas. Better insulation materials/technologies to the pressure hull, as well as improved climate control and air cooling systems ensure tolerable working conditions aboard.

Additionally, the boats have larger bunker capacities for enlarged operation ranges around the world.

In a nut shell, the new boats are contemporary, if not ahead of their times. They are well prepared for the future as they have been designed and built to accommodate upgrades and retrofit programmes for equipment such as towed array sonars or submarine defence gear, one of which is the IDAS missile. It enables a submarine to retaliate against threats from air and sea born submarine hunters, and, with limitation, attack land targets.

*A hatch in the stern of the second batch boats enables fast stretcher transports in a special rescue basket.*

*(YPS Peter Neumann)*

*Right: Flow-optimised outer cladding of GRP enveloping the pressure hull and sail structure reduces noise to a minimum.*

*(YPS Peter Neumann)*

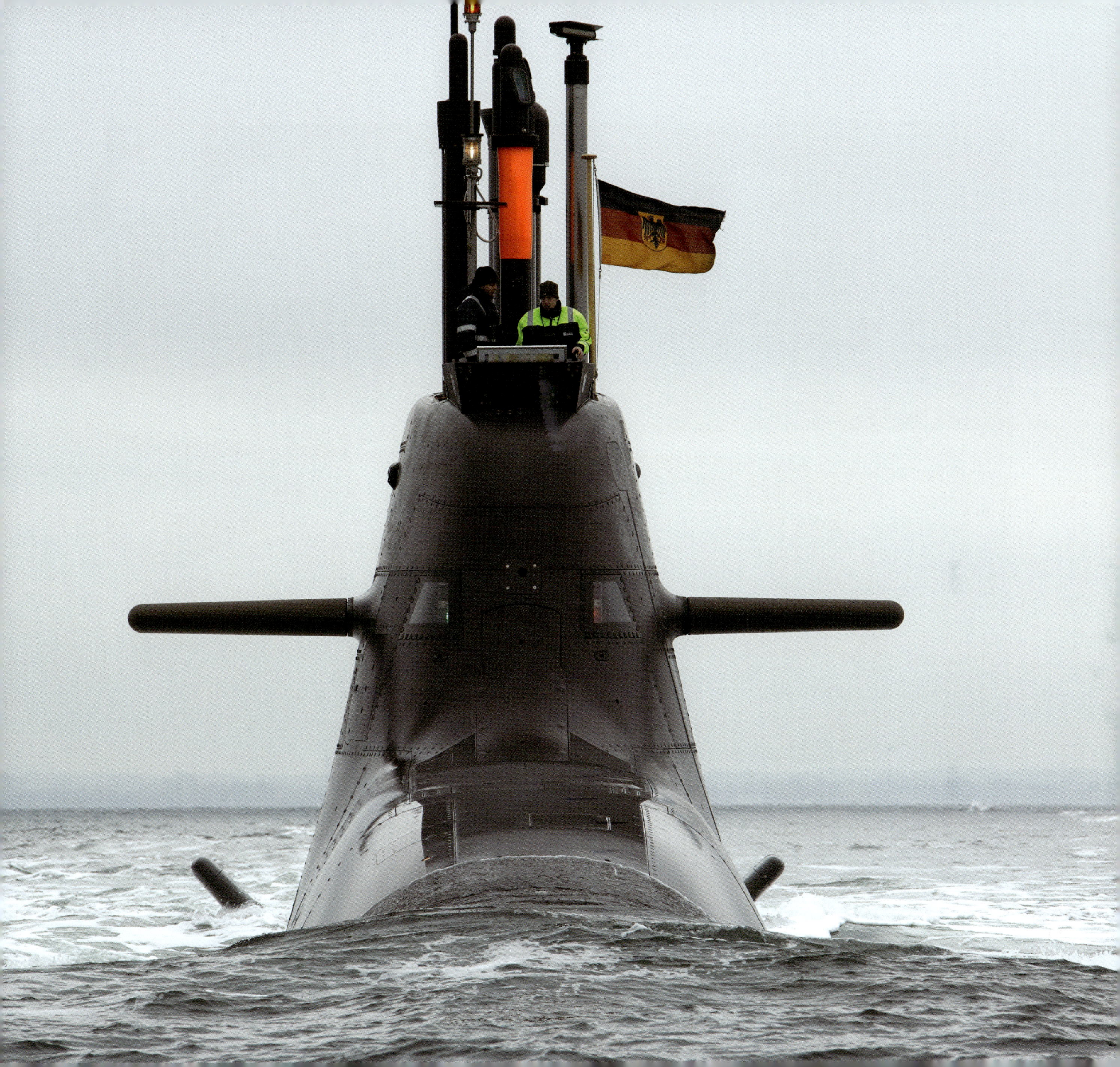

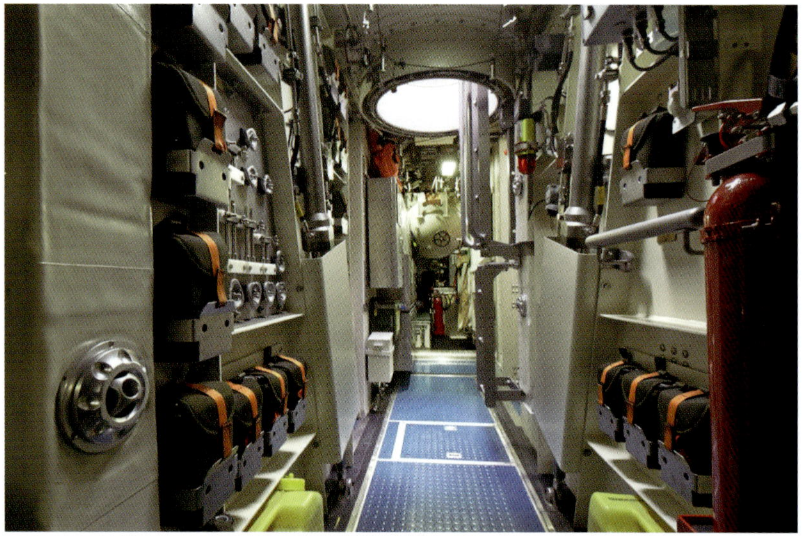

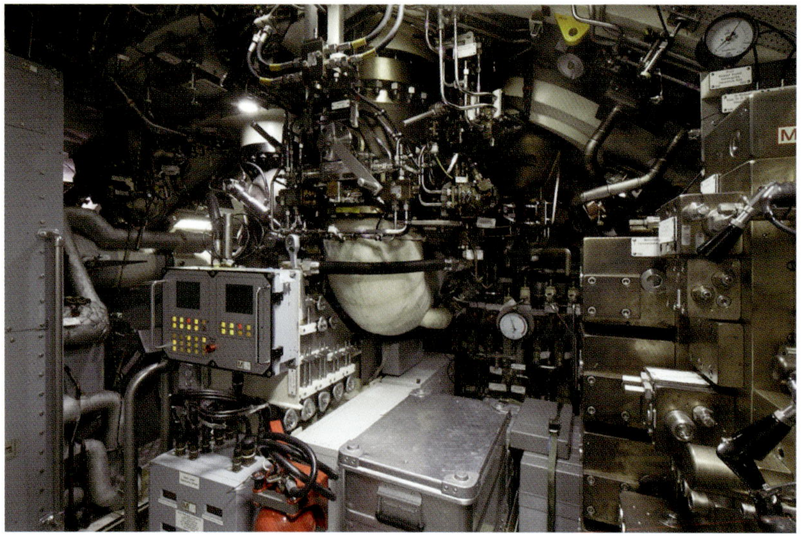

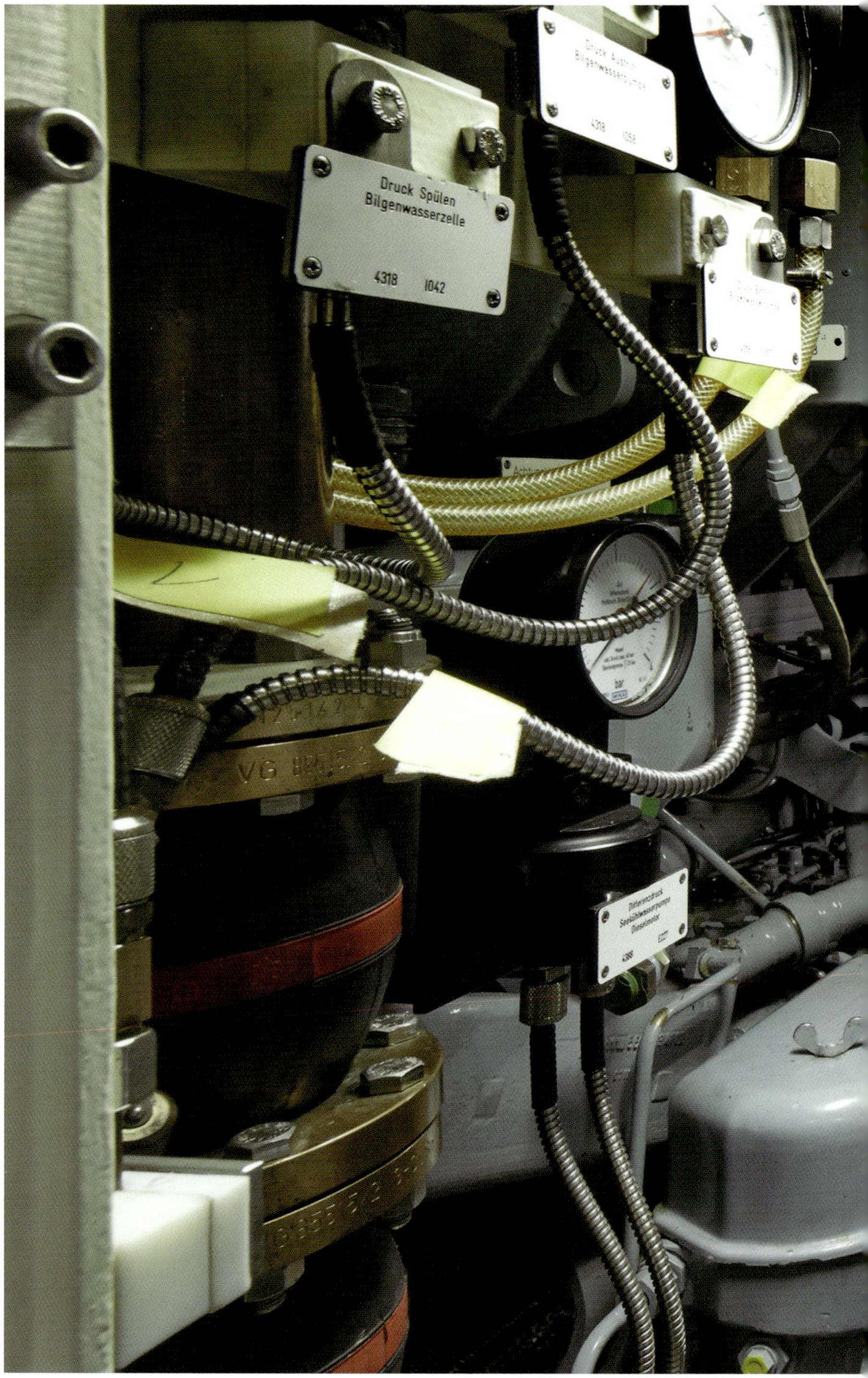
Druck Spülen
Bilgenwasserzelle
4318 1042

*Tour around a second batch HDW Class 212A submarine (U 35).*

*Top: view down the upper deck's main corridor, looking forward, where daylight floods in through the entry hatch. Below: The snorkel intake and exhaust outlet systems. The submarine's MTU diesel engine is depicted on the right.* (YPS Peter Neumann)

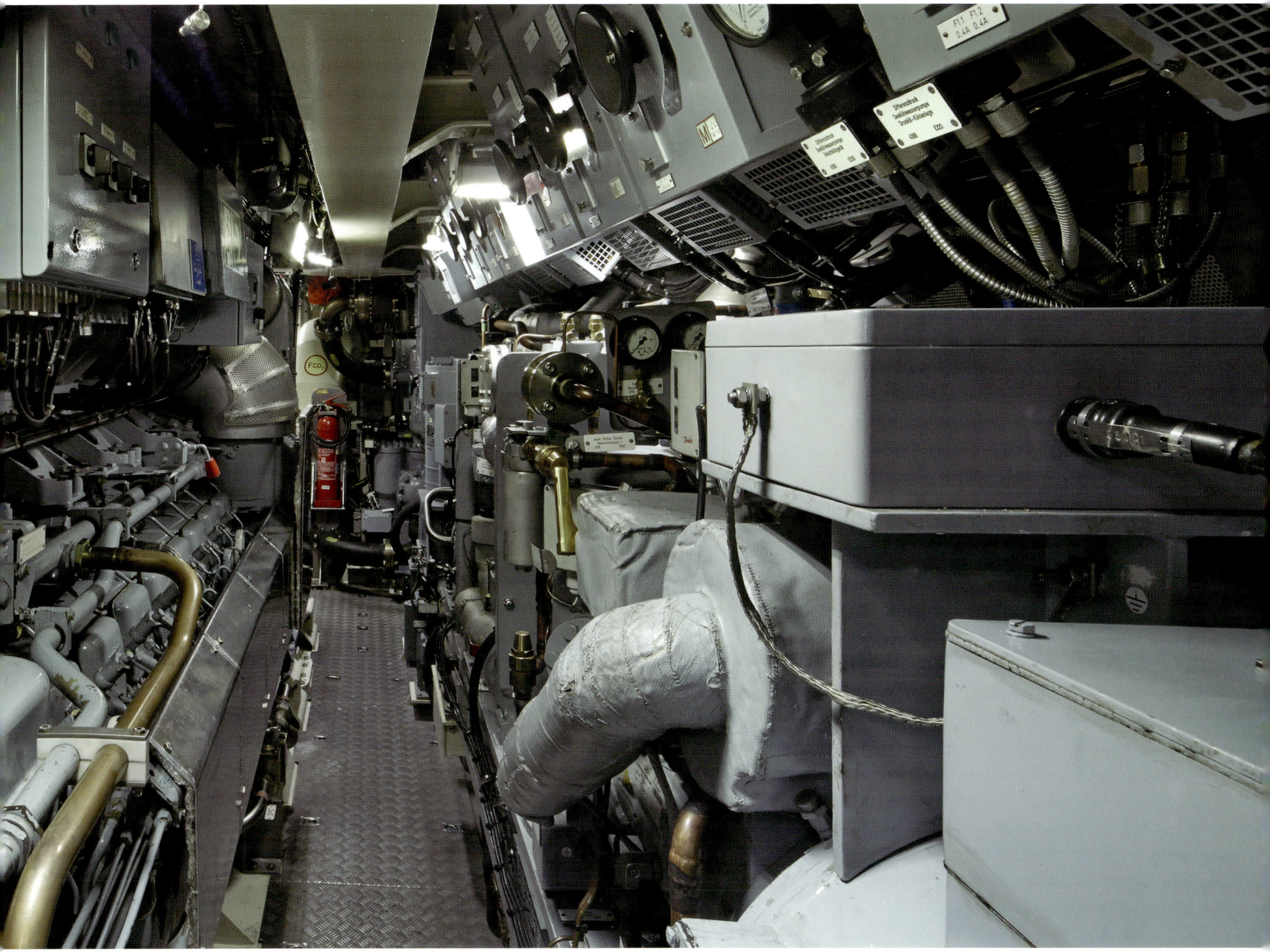
F1.1 F1.2
0.4A 0.4A

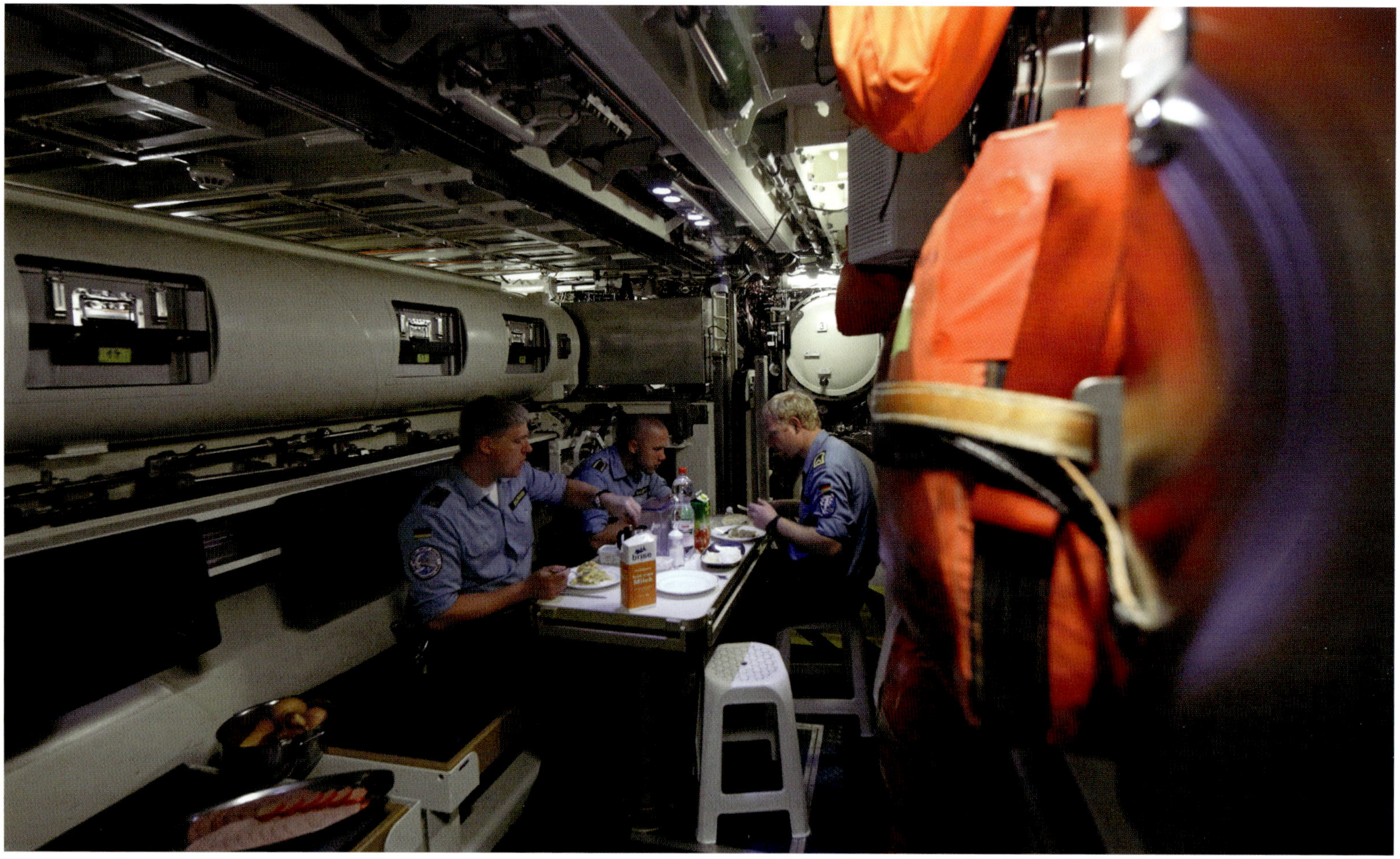

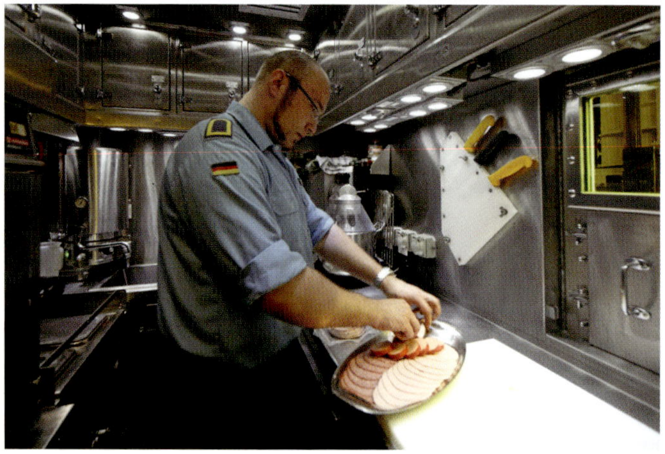

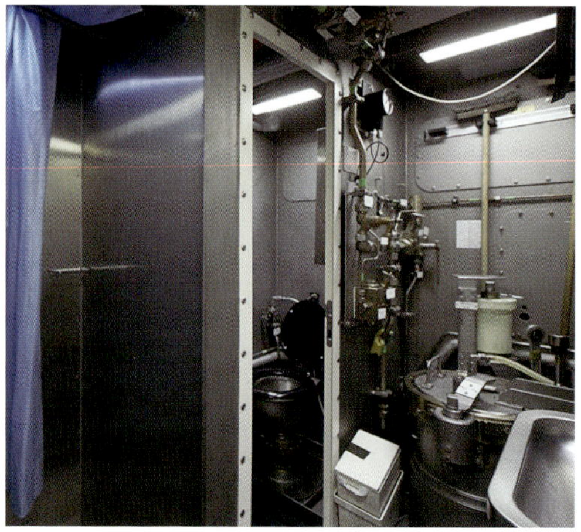

*The new HDW Class 212A boats offer more comfort than former classes. Top: The crew mess. Below left: The galley. Below right: shower and WC. Opposite: Officer's cabin, double bunks and a desk.*

*(YPS Peter Neumann)*

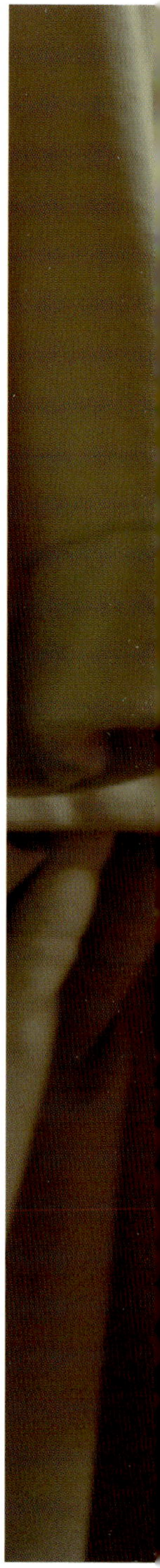

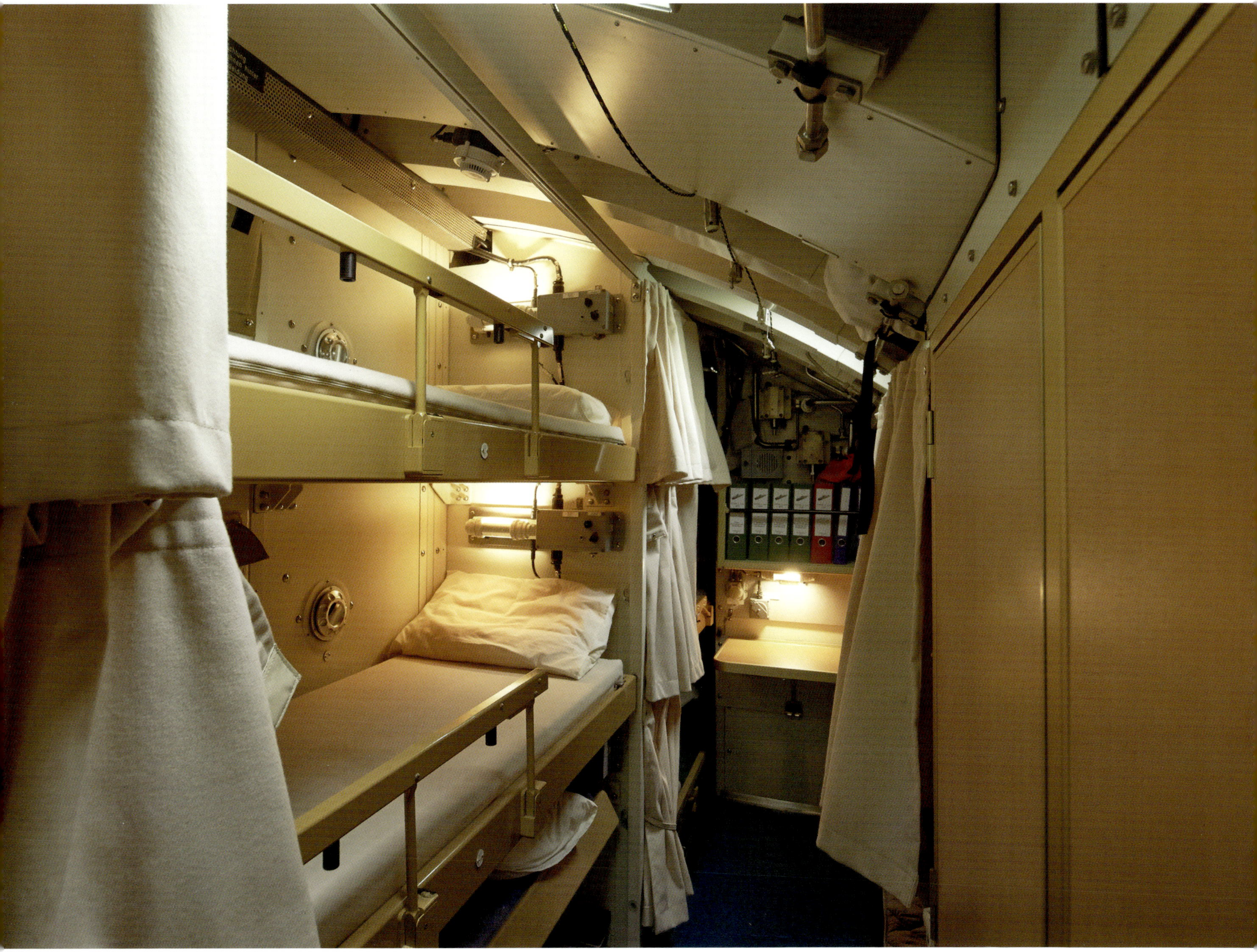

# HDW's Class 214 Submarines – Fuel Cell Technology for the World

The German Navy's new Fuel Cell technology was an international sensation. But that was not everything. It became evident during the SubCon 95 and SubCon 99 (a regular international conference for submariners), that foreign navies were not only interested in new boats fitted with the technology, but actually wanted to acquire them. HDW was the only shipyard in the world that was capable to offer production-ready Fuel Cell technology, and accordingly it was logical to address the demand – with the new HDW Class 214 submarine "designed for the world".

Including the 21st century, over 60 Class 209 submarines have proved their merits on four continents, making them, together new Class 212 boats, cornerstones for a new design, which HDW merged into a simple formula: Class 209 + Class 212 = Class 214. The result is an air-independent, non-nuclear blue water submarine with exceptional anti-submarine-defence capabilities, with a comparably low displacement, extremely good stealth properties and an excellent payload for weapon systems and sensors. It is a new and modern approach to maritime warfare, and is capable of responding to current global threats in coastal waters, ranging from terrorism, asymmetric warfare, national conflicts and organised crime to piracy scenarios.

In truth however, the HDW Class 214 is far more than the sum of Class 209 plus Class 212A. Both classes greatly exceed their abilities and potentialities. Endurances under water are significantly larger, acoustic, thermal and magnetic signatures are *petite*, the boats can dive deeper – and have greater fighting prowess. Thus, this new design has in turn opened a new chapter in German submarine construction that has become yet another success story – with a somewhat dogged start.

The Greek Navy was first client and placed 15 February 2000 the order for three boats, for HDW a major breakthrough. The first boat was to be built in Kiel, and numbers two and three at the Hellenic Shipyard in

*The Greek adventure: HDW built cutting-edge submarine production facilities for the Hellenic Shipyards in Skaramagkas.* (YPS Peter Neumann)

Skaramangkas, a port town in the west of Athens. As part of the deal, HDW was obliged to convert the Greek shipyard into a modern submarine yard, which sounded good. In 2002 HDW took over Hellenic Shipyards, the Greek Navy ordered yet another boat, and at considerable expense, HDW turned the dilapidated shipyard into a gem. This did not particularly impress the yard's workforce, who, together with the state owned ETBA Bank, had been the previous owners within a joint workers' cooperative. After the sale had been consummated, the shipyard workforce continued to believe it was still landlord, a situation which led to ugly confrontations that ranged from strikes, blockades of the administration building to violent attacks on directors of the new board. Nobody can claim the intervening police excelled, and not even mediation efforts of the European metalworker's trade union impressed the Greek employees. The then General Secretary gave up in despair, it was simply not possible to converse with his Greek colleagues.

But this was not all. Financial irregularities forced the HDW group to open legal proceedings against the ETBA Bank. Even the first submarine PAPANIKOLIS made headlines as the Greek Navy refused to accept it long after completion, and were not inclined to settle accounts, supposedly owing to shortcomings. But as the specialist press pointed out, low tide in the Greek Treasury's coffers was probably more likely to have caused the bickering. Five years had to pass after delivery before the boat was paid for and sailed to Greece. But by then, the Class 214 had long established an excellent reputation, as for example with the Korean Navy.

As the PAPANIKOLIS was under construction the Korean, Turkish and Portuguese Navy ordered boats. In December 2013 the Singapore Navy also signed the contract for two, but not all boats carry the designation "214". Special customer requirements lead to modifications often requiring other names, so for example, the Singapore boats will be classified as "HDW Class 218SG".

In conclusion, despite a rather unfortunate start, the Class 214 boats have become a notable success with four boats for Greece, nine for Turkey, two boats Portugal, two for Singapore.

*Long unpaid for: the Hellenic Navy's PAPANIKOLIS – the first Class 214 boat on sea trials in Norway.* (YPS Peter Neumann)

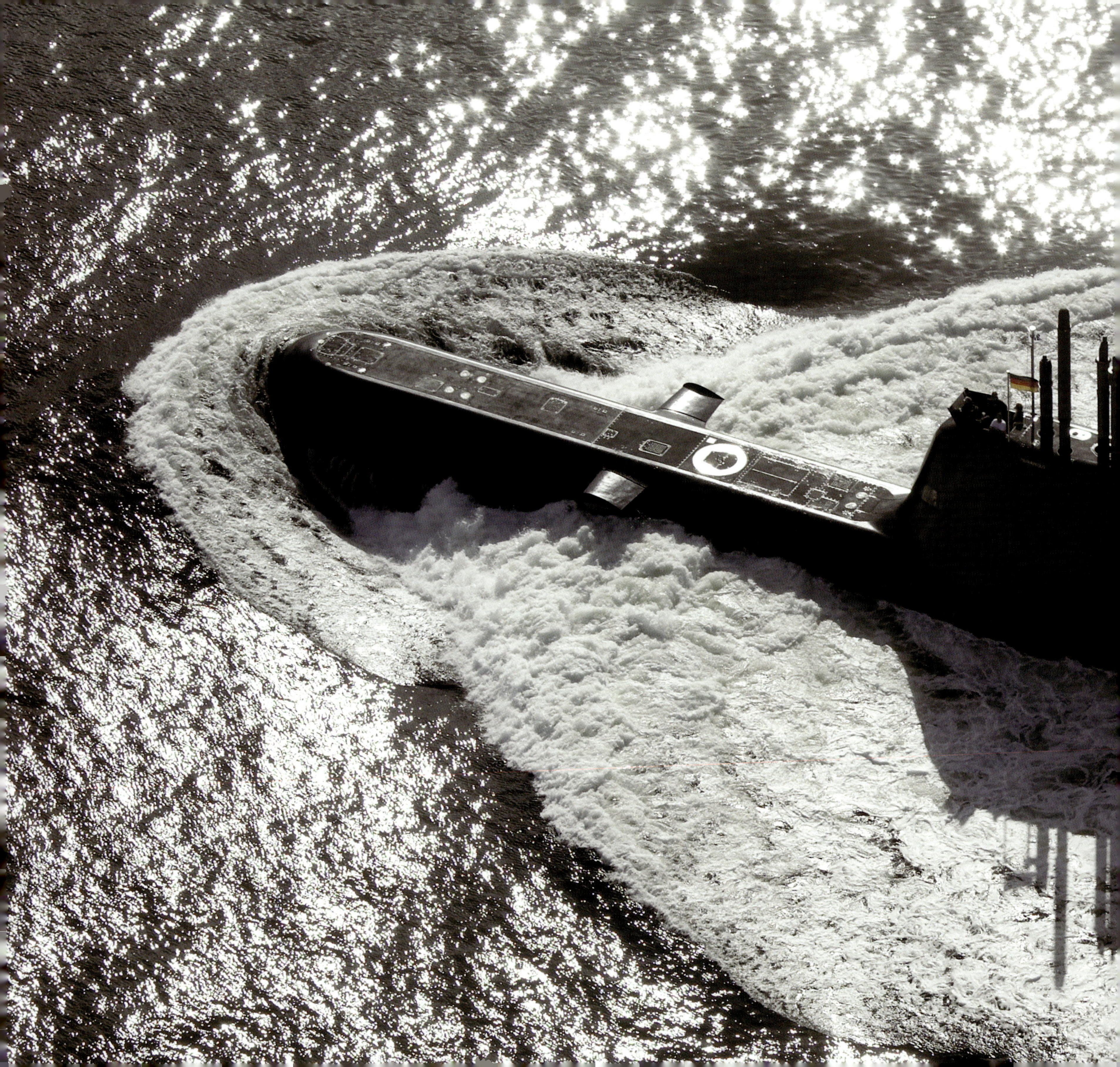

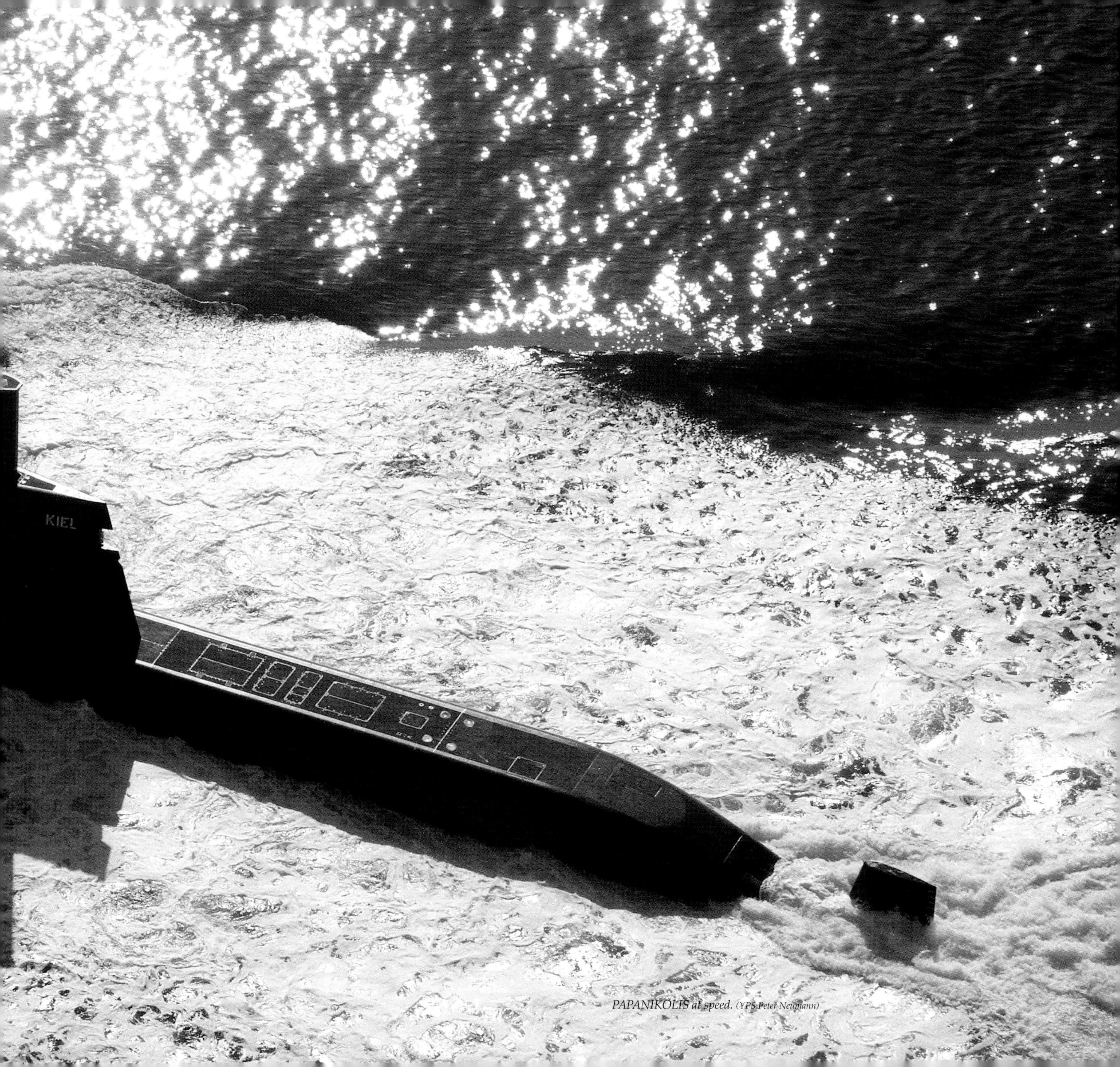
KIEL

*PAPANIKOLIS at speed.* (YPS Peter Neumann)

## THE CHALLENGE:
## SYSTEM INTEGRATION AND MODULARISATION

From the outset, HDW engineers backed two horses, namely modular design and systems integration, two disciplines which at first glance are not easily yoked together, as the greater the modularity is, the more difficult it becomes to integrate single modules within the system. [1] Every naval client has different necessities, different budgets and demands individual solutions, which the engineering teams solved with expertise and experience.

Optional outfitting with, for example CIRCE, an anti-torpedo self-defence system, a diver lock, or an emergency main ballast tank blow system with high pressure inert gas requires plenty of flexibility. Its about creating a design that permits the installation of additional systems and equipment after delivery, and that as easily as possible. And so the Class 214 has been designed and engineered to accommodate weapons, sensors, electronics and ship systems of the future, at a later stage. Such measures guarantee long life times.

The boats' unique charachteristics are a result of close co-operations between the shipyard, suppliers and authorities. The boats can dive deeper, as the steels used in the pressure hull, HY 80 and HY 100, which permit diving depths of over 400 metres, have been optimised in collaboration with the Government and industry. The air independent power plant's performance has been increased, and its price reduced, with a Fuel Cell developed by Siemens. It delivers 120 kW per module. Extensive model testing at the Hamburg Ship Model Basin (HSVA) and the Hydronautics Research Inc. (Maryland, USA) has optimized the hull lines's hydrodynamic qualities, and thus increased acoustic stealth properties. Propeller cavitation noise has also been reduced in comparison to the already quiet performances of previous boat classes. And finally, the Class 214 submarine was the first to be fitted with an anti-torpedo self-defence system and ATLAS ELEKTRONIK's latest command and control system, ISUS 90.

All this has led to a boat that can remain longer at sea, with a sea endurance of 50 days, and a crew of 30 plus five additional persons. Dived, it can sprint at 16 to 20 knots over hours, and that repeatedly. The boat can run at two to six knots dived, with the Fuel Cell, during patrol and interception missions. According to official statements, depending on the amount of hydrogen and oxygen shipped aboard, Class 214 boats can master three week deployments dived, without having to use the snorkel, but there are hints that it could be a lot longer. Thus a Class 214 boat can fully exploit its advantages in the third dimension – unseen, unheard, and hidden in unknown depths. Should it be necessary, it can vacate deployment areas, with full batteries, at high speeds over several hours. And finally, full diesel tanks permit 12,000 mile ranges at six knots.

Long submarine operations strain crews, and accordingly, living and working conditions, as on the Class 212A boats, have been made subject to improval. The CIC's layout accommodates the full watch, working at ergonomically designed consoles. Equipment such as the Optronic mast, a non-pressure-hull penetrating device combining every feature of a conventional periscope, but with additional functions that include, for example, rolling video recording, is not only state-of-the-art, but a saver of space to the benefit of the crew. All ship, radio, sailing and navigational operations are monitored and conducted from the CIC midships, thus reducing the required watch time spent aft in the engine room. This arrangement has another benefit: Living quarters have been allocated forward, far from noise sources. It's a comfortable place to watch TV or listen to the radio. Obviously every crew member has his/her own bunk. And three showers, three toilet/wash-rooms, a well equipped galley with several cold rooms and washing machine with tumble-dryer ensure that long missions are reasonably comfortable affairs.

# HDW CLASS 214 SUBMARINE [2]

## MAIN TASKS

- ▶ The modular weapon and sensor mix has been designed to fulfil every conceivable mission which includes operations against surface ships and submarines, secret service assignments, reconnaissance and monitoring of sea areas etc.
- ▶ In addition, a Class 214 submarine is built to participate in training and combat missions within larger groups, as well as conduct covert mine laying operations.

## MAIN ACHIEVEMENTS

- ▶ Significantly increased underwater endurance and low probabilities of detection, not least thanks to the Fuel Cell plant.
- ▶ Increased diving depths and overall efficiency compared to HDW Class 209 boats.
- ▶ Minimal thermal, acoustic and magnetic signatures.

## MAIN SPECIFICATIONS

| | |
|---|---|
| Length over all: | approx. 65 m |
| Height including sail: | approx. 13 m |
| Hull diameter: | approx. 6.3 m |
| Displ. surfaced: | approx. 1,850 t |

*PAPANIKOLIS, HDW Class 214 #1.*
(YPS Peter Neumann)

| | |
|---|---|
| Displ. dived: | approx. 1,930 t |
| Diving depth: | over 400 m |
| Crew: | 27 (+ 10) persons |
| Pressure hull: | ferromagnetic steel |

## WEAPON COMMAND AND CONTROL SYSTEM

ISUS 90 (Integrated sensor, command and control and weapon engagement system)

## PROPULSION SYSTEMS

| | |
|---|---|
| Drive-motor (PERMASYN®) | 3,900 kW |
| Fuel Cell plant | 2 Modules, each 125 kW |
| Diesel generator | 2 x MTU 16V396 |
| Drive batteries | 450 - 900 V |

Low-noise 7 blade skew-back propeller

| | |
|---|---|
| Max surfaced speed | 12 knots |
| Max dived speed | 20 knots |

## ARMAMENT

8 x 533 mm torpedo tubes, pressurized water launching system for all torpedo types.

8 storage racks for reserve torpedoes, of which four are for fast reloads.

## UPGRADES AND OPTIONS (EXAMPLES)

Radio buoy, towed array sonar (TAS), mine avoidance sonar, degaussing system, lithium-ion batteries, torpedo defence system, special forces equipment, pressure launching system for weapons and missiles, mine laying systems, second communications mast (SATCOM and HF).

*In contrast to the Class 212A specifications, only general data is listed here as every nation's Class 214 boat has its own needs and requirements. Accordingly, the boats have different configurations, and data is not available to the public.*

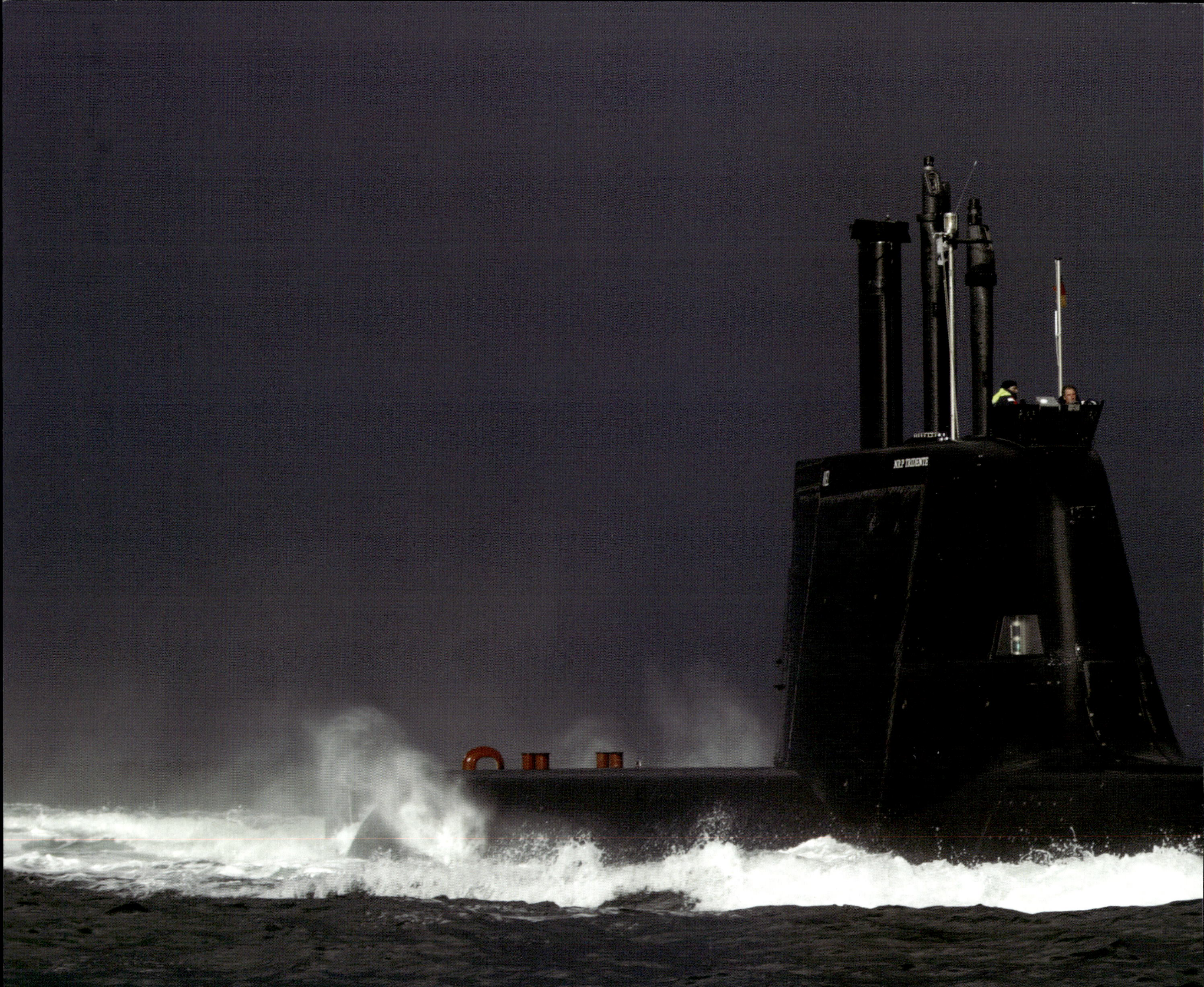
NRP TRIDENTE

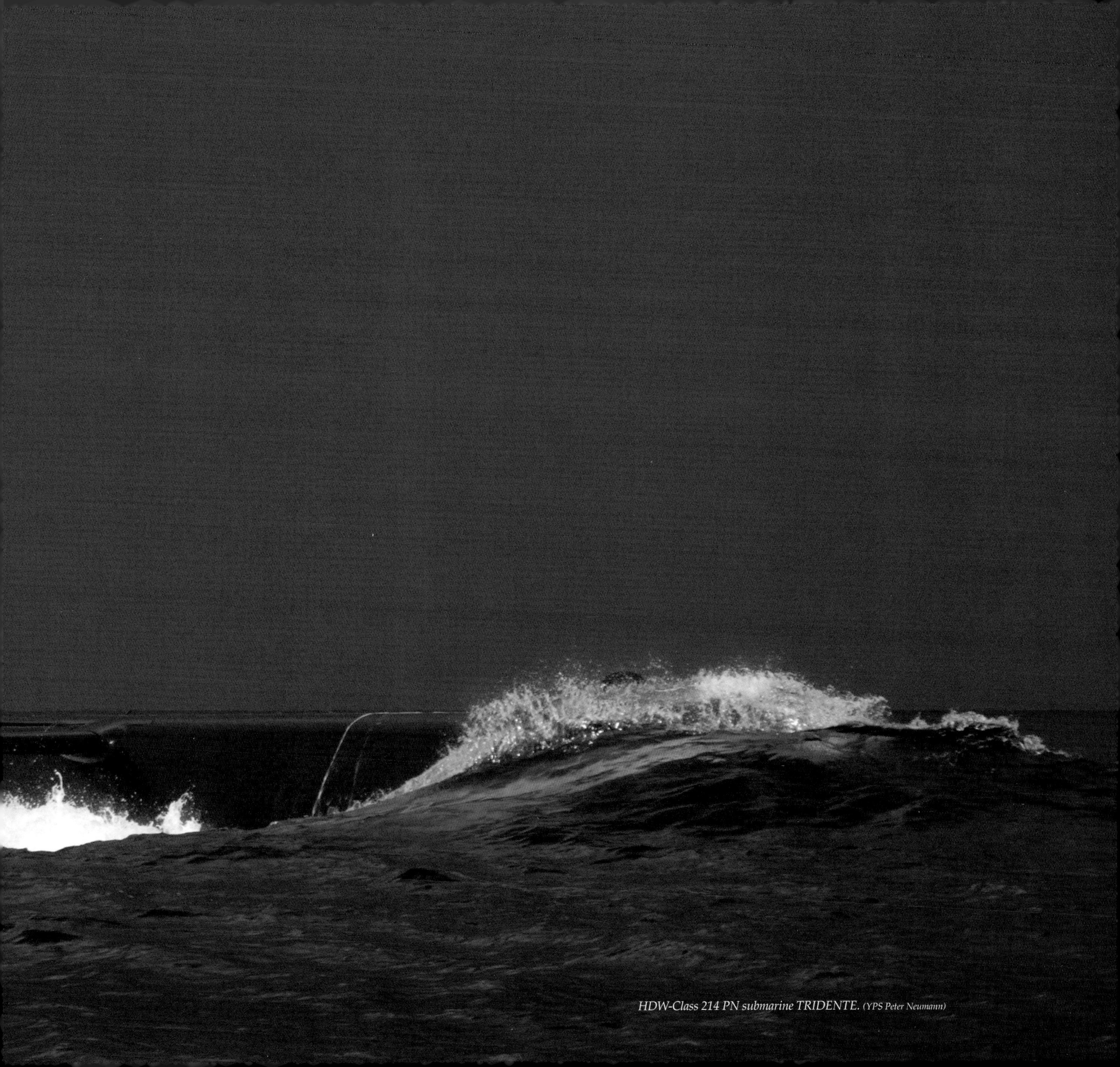

*HDW-Class 214 PN submarine TRIDENTE.* (YPS Peter Neumann)

# Still on Paper: HDW Class 210mod and Class 216 Submarines

The sustained demand for submarines, especially in the Pacific region, is leading to new submarine types and designs, as the navies of different countries confront different threat scenarios and conduct different missions in different waters. Moreover, different governments have differently sized defence budgets. Thus, for example, Australia plans to replace its COLLINS class submarines with much larger boats that will be suitable for long operations in the deep Pacific Ocean. Other nations are looking at small, compact submarines better suited for littoral waters, and that fit better to smaller budgets. In response to the latter, the German submarine industry is now talking about two further submarine types, the HDW Class 216 and HDW class 210mod.

## HDW CLASS 210MOD – A COMPACT, POWERFUL AND INEXPENSIVE PERFORMER

This new submarine class is optimal for operations in coastal water and peripheral seas, but can equally well be deployed in warm tropical waters or the deep sea. These boats can either be built in Kiel, or locally assembled from material packages. This compact boat's performance exceeds those of the Class 209, which, with more than 60 units, despite modernisations, are starting to show their age. This new class, according to Thyssen Marine Systems, is the perfect answer for navies intending to set up a submarine force, or complement a AIP submarine fleet with conventional diesel-electric boats. This class also offers an interesting alternative to a "mid-life conversion", the upgrading of an older boat after long service, if future costs of the old boat are taken into account.[1]

The Class 210mod's design has its roots in the proven Norwegian Ula Class boats. However, the new design has been supplemented with features and components found on

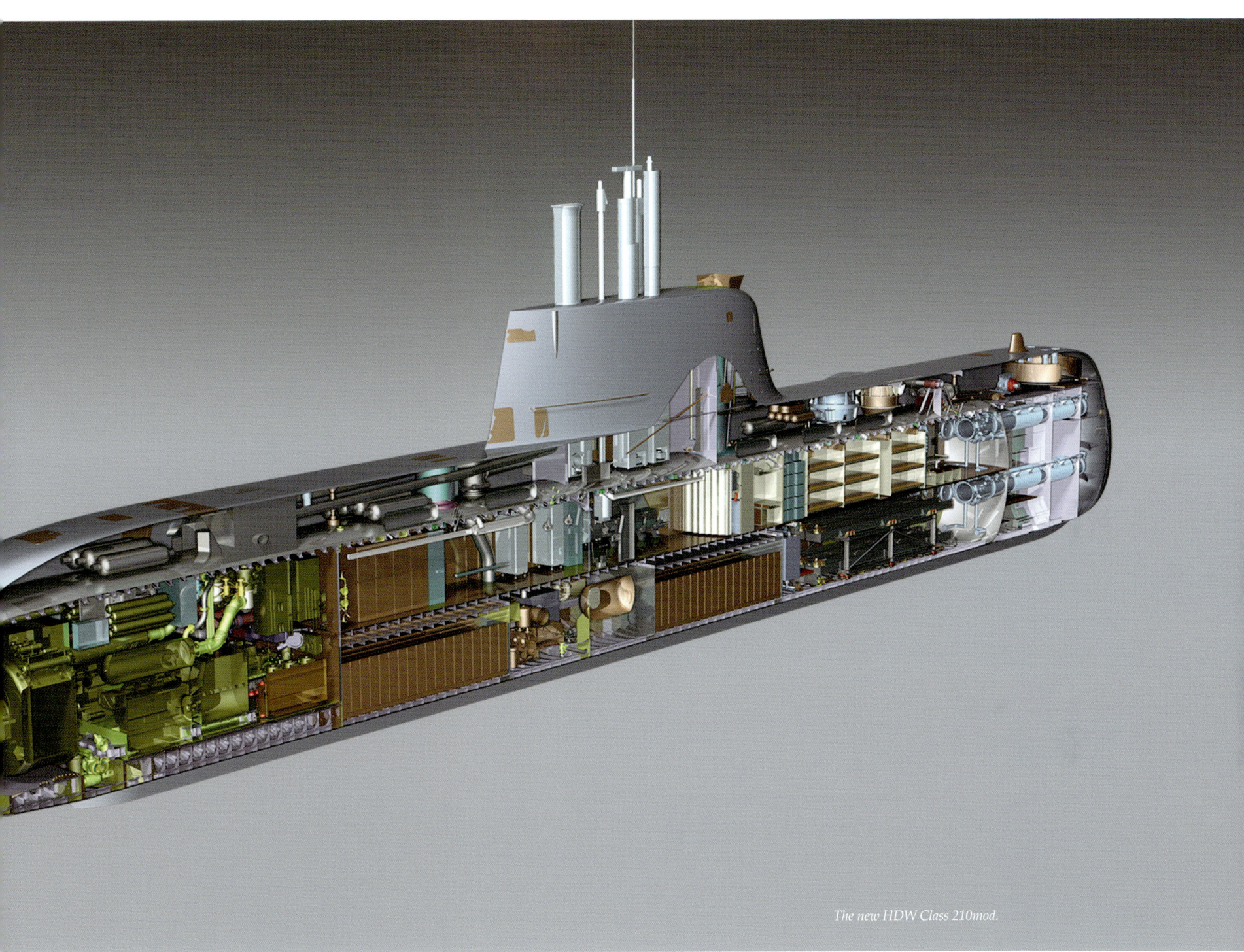
*The new HDW Class 210mod.*

Class 212A and Class 214 boats, such as the Permasyn® motor, modern management and sensor systems, hoisting masts, with which exception of the periscope, do not penetrate the pressure hull. The design has a slender hull shape, which together with a composite propeller, emits low signatures. As on a Class 212A and 214 boat, the degree of automation is high. The boat will be fitted with a HABETaS® emergency escape system, as well a diver's lock. But what the boat does forego, is an AIP system, for cost reasons.

The X-rudder, which has proved to be extraordinarily successful on the Class 212A boats, and delivered them enormous manoeuvrability abilities, is also on the Class 210mod's special features list. The boat's compact design, an approximate displacement of 1,150 tonnes, a powerful motor and small draft makes it predestined for shallow water missions. However, as the proven HY80 steel alloy will be used, the boat will be able endure depths of up to 250 metres.

New lithium-ion batteries have come aboard for underwater operations. They are significantly smaller than the lead-acid batteries previously in use. They can store three times as much energy as the former. This equates into less and shorter snorkelling periods and longer dives, especially at speed. Furthermore, lithium-ion batteries do not gas and are maintenance free when in operation; an automatic battery management system constantly monitors the cells to ensure safety.

The Combat Information Centre (CIC) can be called the brain centre of any submarine. This is where the commander and his officers of the watch monitor the information needed to operate the boat and its weapons, and which is gleaned from the sonar system, above water sensors, steering and communication systems, and those for the weapons. The CIC is clearly structured to keep track of data and information inflow. The main system is the command and weapons deployment system.

Its sonar and weapons management information can be distributed to two consoles each, or alternatively run on three or four multi-function consoles. Two consoles on the stb side of the boat are reserved for navigation. Electronic charts and AIS are standard. As in the Class 214, the 216's CIC has a one-man helming station.

The Class 210mod has a separate engine control station forward of the engine room. It features two systems management consoles, of which one is sufficient for normal operations. The second provides redundancy and can be used for on-board training. The ship systems are largely automated, and control the diesel generator, battery cooling system and exhaust system as well as monitoring the bilge.

The Class 210mod's sail is of GRP, and its air-draft is as low as those on a Class 214 boat, which is robust, light, easy to maintain – and has poor acoustic reflection properties. It houses the hoisting gear (snorkel, periscopes and radar and communication masts), and has enough surplus space to accommodate up to three masts in future upgrades. The conning-tower is also fitted with the HABETaS® emergency escape system, with which the crew can exit the boat at 300 metres.

Four bow torpedo tubes for standard heavyweight torpedoes are located in two levels forward of the crew quarters, and can release a variety of self-launching torpedoes. Furthermore, the boat has the space to store six further weapons, two of which are in quick loading stations. And the design will be able to fire missiles such as the IDAS.

Living and working conditions have paid a role in the design of this boat which has sufficient bunks for each crew member on a two watch system (21 persons), or on a three watch (15 persons) system. Thus the Class 210mod boats have mission endurances of about 30 days.

THE HDW CLASS 210MOD SUBMARINE

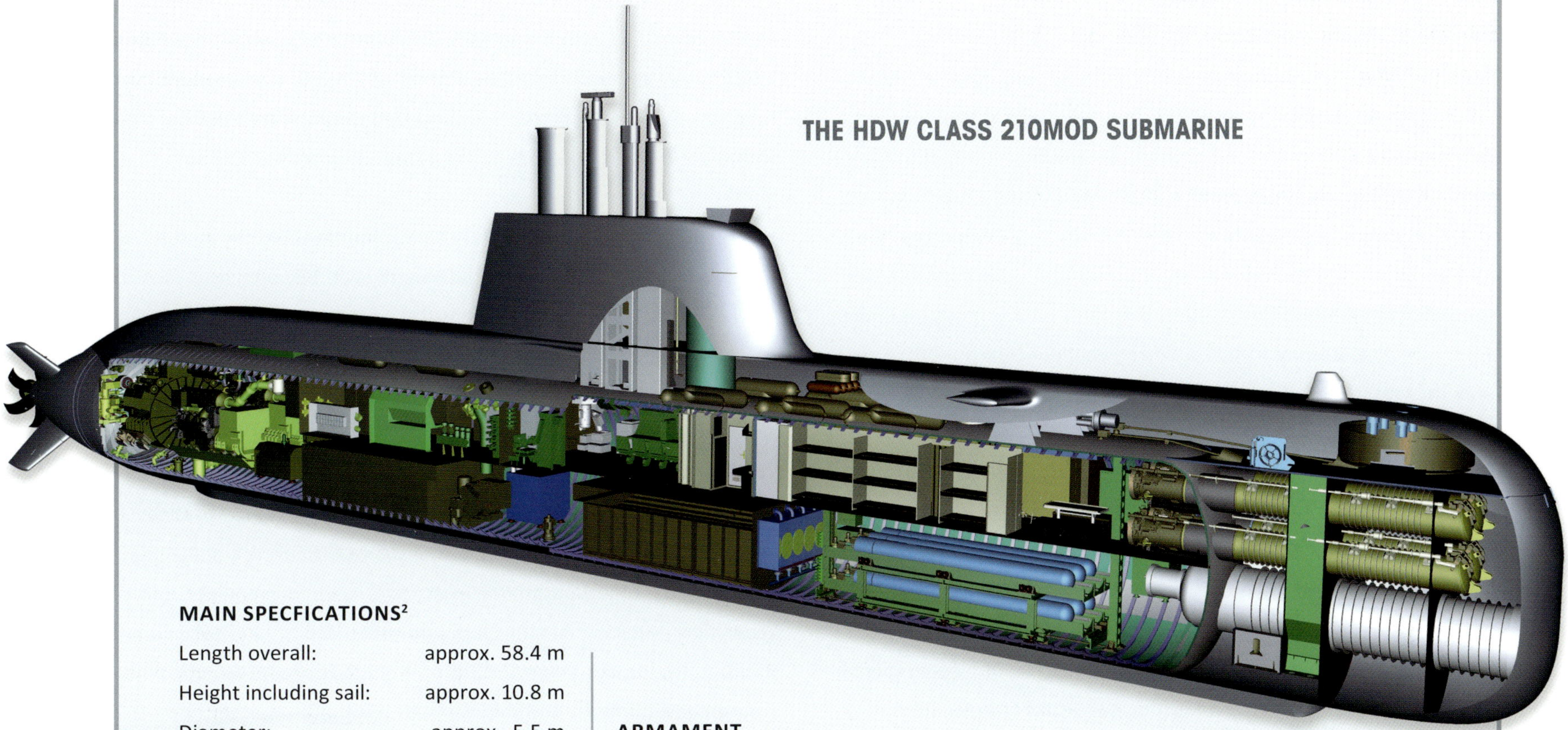

**MAIN SPECFICATIONS**[2]

| | |
|---|---|
| Length overall: | approx. 58.4 m |
| Height including sail: | approx. 10.8 m |
| Diameter: | approx. 5.5 m |
| Displacement, surfaced: | ca. 1,150 t |
| Diving depth: | ca. 250 m |
| Crew: | 27 (+ 10) persons |
| Pressure hull: | ferromagnetic Stahl |

**PROPULSION SYSTEM**

PERMASYN® drive motor

Diesel generators: 2 x MTU 16V396

Batteries: Litium-Ion

Low noise 7 blade skew-back propeller

Speed: undisclosed

**ARMAMENT**

4 standard torpedo tubes for self-launching torpedoes

Space for six reserve weapons, with two at quick loading stations

**AUTOMATION SYSTEMS**

Central command, ship and weapon control system

**INTEGRATED SONAR-SYSTEM**

Cylindrical hydrophone, interception sonar

**INTEGRATED RADIO COMMUNICATION SYSTEMS**

VLF, HF, VHF, UHF, INMARSAT-C[3], GMDSS[4], AIS

**NAVIGATION SYSTEM**

Inertial navigation system, EM-Log, navigation radar, echo-sounder, GPS, ECDIS5

## HDW CLASS 216 SUBMARINE – 20,000 LEAGUES UNDER THE SEA

Since the 1950s, Jules Verne's vision in the above novel has been met by nuclear submarines that can operate submerged as long as they want, on a global scale, until the rations are depleted. Meanwhile, now that the cold war has been ended, it has become increasingly evident that nukes are not all that suitable for every scenario, owing to high signatures. They are also extremely expensive, and ultimately, after service life, the safe disposal of the reactors is in the best case, difficult and costly, or in the worst case dangerous as in Russia, where, abandoned in out of the way bays, they rot to pieces.

Smaller diesel-electric or AIP-driven boats (such the HDW Classes 209, DOLPHIN, 212A or 214, and in the near future, the 210mod), dominate shallow coastal seas, where nuclear-powered submarines cannot operate. New requirements are emerging in the Pacific region as leading industrial nations define the need for units that are able to conduct long-term covert reconnaissance operations far from home, transport and support special forces, or launch a surprise attack with missiles.[6] Such mission definitions exceed the possibilities and capabilities of today's compact Class 212A or 214 submarines, which were they to fulfil the profile, would need even larger ranges and endurances, be able to sustain high transit speeds over long periods, have larger reconnaissance and weapon capacities, be fitted with sea and land missiles – and offer a larger crew comfortable amenities.

HDW's Class 216 fits the mission. This design profits from the accrued experience gathered from the large number of boats operated by numerous navies, the lessons learnt during construction, and from the unbroken line of development by IKL and HDW. Research, sometimes over decades, at HDW and its industrial partners, pays off too. This new design combines the proven with recent and future innovations.

With a displacement of approximately 4,000 tonnes and a length of about 90 metres, it is twice the size of any previous submarine built in Kiel. But size is not everything and results from the necessary space for propulsion, power generation, storage systems for electric power and fuel, a variety of different payloads, the weapon command and control systems – and well appointed crew accommodations. The boat has two full heigh decks for the ship and weapon

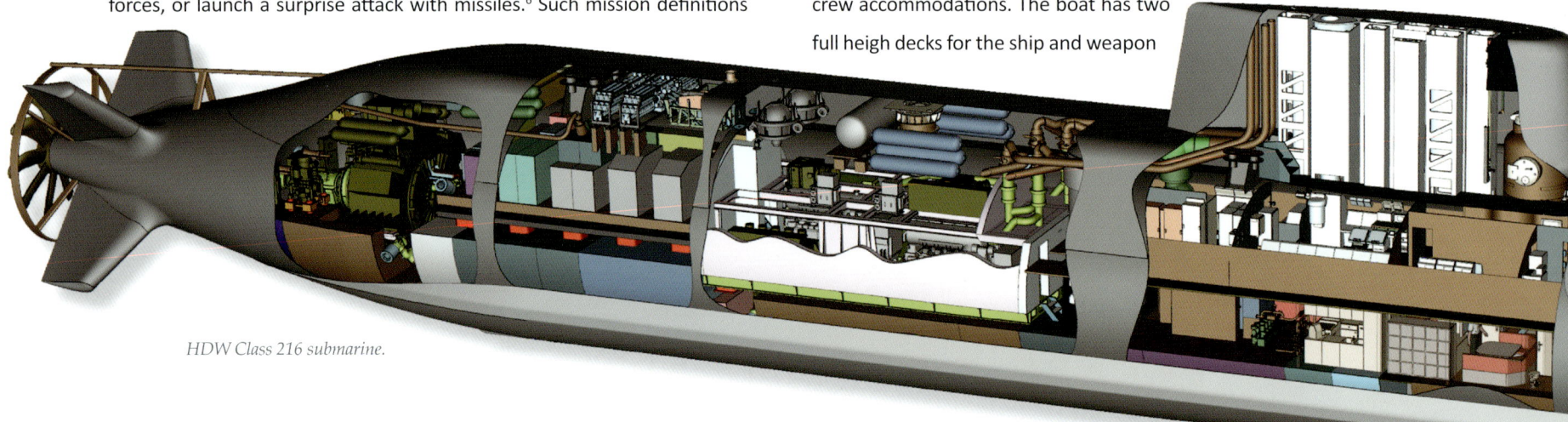

*HDW Class 216 submarine.*

systems, and its accommodation and recreational areas are separate. Ditto the CIC, which is no longer part of the transit passageway between for and aft.

Crew accommodations have enormous influence on crew moral, and are thus an extremely important issue on a boat designed for missions that can last up to 80 days – time enough the circle the globe. As it is becoming increasingly difficult for navies to recruit sufficient proficient personnel, the boat can be manned with 33 persons running a three-watch system. They have ten bedrooms with up to six bunks. Five additional full-size bunks and 16 provisional cots will be provided for "passengers" such as special forces, divers, trainees etc. Good food and little exercise build flab, which can be worked off in the fo'c'sle, in a gym. Two generous messes serve as common and dining rooms. But the messes can be also used for briefings, or as cinemas. Adjacent is the well equipped galley with large storage rooms. A further "general purpose" room next to the CIC provides space for either more accommodations, a meeting room, further radio and reconnaissance paraphernalia, or it can be used as a sick bay/hospital.

The pressure hull is made of the proven high-strength HY80 steel, and owing to tightly spaced stiffener rings and hull skin dimensions, forgoes deep frames, which thus results in less restrictions to the interior design. The hull is dived by a pressure proof bulkhead separating the living from the operation areas. In the event of uncontrollable water ingress, the boat has two pressure resistant departments that withstand the outside pressure until the destruction depth is reached; both departments are equipped with emergency escape systems docking facilities for deep-sea rescue vehicles.

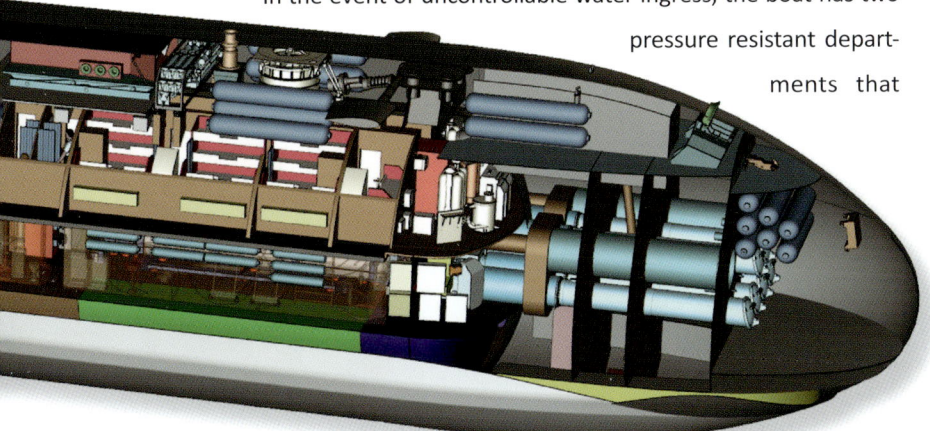

The boat is highly manoeuvrable, in both deep and shallow water, owing to the X-rudder configuration, which enables small turning radiuses and rapid depth changes. The proven Permasyn® motor enables dived speeds of over 20 knots under water; modern lithium-ion batteries store the electric power for propulsion and other consumers. Four powerful diesel generators charge the batteries, and energy-efficient consumers ensure low levels of snorkelling. The lithium-ion battery technology in conjunction with the Fuel Cell system is a perfect symbiosis and enables the boat to keep its cover over four weeks without having to snorkel. Oxygen is stored aboard in its liquid state, where as the hydrogen is no longer kept in hydride cylinders, but made from methanol in an on-board methanol reformer, the residual $CO_2$ exhaust dissolves into the sea without trace. HDW has invested time and research into this technology, and has build a functional test rig, which is now paying off.

## HIGH-TECH IN THE CIC

Seven multifunctional consoles serve as a "Human Machine Interface (HMI)" within the integrated sonar and weapons management system, and open structures simplify the integration of all information systems. The data obtained from the acoustic sensors, the navigation management system and the weapons management system are automatically monitored for plausibility, analysed, classified and placed at the operator's disposal. Advanced ATLAS ELEKTRONIK sensors, such as the Enhanced Flank Array Sonar (EFAS), a conformal array sonar in the bow (replacing the circular base sonar), and an aft directed sonar panel co-operate and create a highly sensitive acoustic sensor network. Last but not least, high-frequency seabed navigation sonar and forward-facing "close proximity" sensors are used for navigation. Thus, the boat can circumvent mines and assist in diver operations or the deployment of unmanned vehicles.

For visual operations the boat is equipped with two optronics masts made by Carl Zeiss, which are equipped with ESM (electronic support measures) sensors, including an early warning system monitoring the entire surroundings and air space, HDTV channel, infrared camera and laser range finders. The radio room provides analogue, digital, and IP-based communication (Internet) converge. Three telecommunications masts cover all frequency ranges.

The CIC is separated from the ship systems control centre by a transparent sliding wall that separates tactical operations from ship systems operations, for undisturbed communications within the respective teams. But if required, both can be easily linked. The helmsman has his working station in the ship systems control centre, and owing to high levels of automation, only two are required to monitor and control the boat's ship systems. The engine room remains largely unmanned, apart from inspections.

A modern submarine must be flexible and easily prepared for a large variety of deployments. Accordingly, navies are now focusing on "flexible payloads"—the possibility of bringing a wide assortment of equipment on board. In response, the Class 216 boat has a large, vertically arranged pressure lock (Vertical Multi-Purpose Lock – VMPL) aft of the CIC, with which the boat can be adapted to varying mission requirements with payload modules, such as for example, mine laying equipment, docking stations for unmanned underwater vehicles (UUV), a diver lock for 20 men, cruise missiles launchers, or additional fuel tanks. Two modular platforms on the upper decks are at disposal for anti-torpedo modules, for a UUV garage, for pressure resistant containers of special forces, etc.

The torpedo storage compartment and torpedo transport skids have been designed for maximum flexibility – the latter can be converted during a mission to accommodate lightweight torpedo modules. And thus not only

*The first methanol reformer test plant at HDW was a bulky piece of equipment, yet to big for an on-board installation.* (YPS Peter Neumann)

are torpedoes stored here, but mines, missiles and other equipment too. Furthermore, the compartment can be fitted with additional bunks – or even used for garbage storage.

Gabler Maschinenbau will supply a novel multi-purpose hoisting container-mast that is deployed at periscope depth, and depending on the mission, it will be able to accommodate a weapon station, three air-borne drones, a laser communication terminal or additional electronics.

One of a submarine's greatest assets is noiseless stealth. But signature reduction measures are more difficult to implement on larger boats than on smaller units, as they naturally have a larger signature potentials. And so HDW has used every possibility to lower the signatures of their new Class 216 submarine. Measures start with angled surfaces. GRP and anti-sonar coatings provide protection to the sail and deck, and the hoisting masts are cladded with radar absorption material. Every item that can emit noise is sound proofed and decoupled from the hull with anti-noise mountings. Sensors monitor own air and structure borne noise, and their effects on underwater sensors are registered and compensated by the sonar system.

The pressure hull is made of ferric steel, its magnetic field is reduced to a minimum with a degaussing system. The sail and hoisting masts have hydrodynamically optimised profiles – and last but not least, the diesel exhaust is cooled to lower the infra-red signature.

## HDW CLASS 216 SUBMARINE

**MAIN TASKS**

The modular weapon and sensor mix and the AIP plant make the HDW Class 216 predestined for anti-surface ship warfare and submarine defence, reconnaissance, surveillance and target acquisition, land target attacks, support of special forces operations, the deployment of unmanned vehicles, mine laying and detection.

**KEY TECHNOLOGIES**

PERMASYN® drive technology, lithium-ion batteries, composite propeller, integrated weapon control system, HABETaS® emergency escape system, methanol reformer, large number of extra bunks.

**MAIN SPECIFICATIONS**

(as far as known)

| | |
|---|---|
| Length over all: | approx. 89 m |
| Diameter: | approx. 8 m |
| Height including sail: | ca. 15 m |
| Displacement: | approx. 4,000 t |
| Crew: | 33 persons (+21) |
| Pressure hull: | ferromagnetic steel |

**PROPULSION SYSTEM**

PERMASYN® drive motor
Fuel Cell plant
Diesel-generator
Lithium-Ion batteries
Noiseless composite propeller
Speed, dived: over 20 knots

**INTEGRATED RADIO MESSAGING SYSTEM**

VLF, HF, VHF, UHF, INMARSAT-C, GMDSS, AIS

**ARMAMENT**

6 weapon tubes with launching systems for torpedoes, mines and missiles.

High weapon payload and corresponding storage capacities.

Flexible storage space for 18 reserve weapons.

Additional weapon modules for the Vertical Multi-Purpose Lock (VMPL)

# Tomorrow's Submarine Technology Today

The myths surrounding the "Grey Wolves" of the Second World War in omnipresent newspaper articles, and blogs and U-tube clips abundant in the internet, have little to do with the success and excellent reputations of German submarine designers, builders and their modern submarines. Rather more, this success and excellence is founded on intensive research and development, technological brilliance, highly professional, modern building facilities, on over the accrued expertise from more than century of submarine engineering and operations. It is based on co-operations with a parent navy, namely the German Navy as well as with customer navies, on thinking ahead into future scenarios, on technical developments which have constantly led to revolutionary boats – and above all, hard work.

Intensive research and development is key to the solution of future demands placed on modern submarines, and so developers are working on projects not only to the benefit of present and future boats and navies, but also upgrade existing boats. HDW's book "Silent Fleet"[1], now in its sixth edition, provides a constantly updated overview of new technologies – providing they are not protected by military secrecy. But even so, the published facts are exciting enough.

## STEALTH

Stealthy secrecy is a submarine's core capacity; the modern submarine's special values are that it is quieter than the surrounding sea, it is undetectable to infra-red sensors measuring thermal radiation, it is perfectly shaped to avoid sonar detection, and its noiselessness.

Development never stops. For certain, navies operating German submarines

*State-of-the-art building facilities at ThyssenKrupp Marine Systems in Kiel.* (YPS Peter Neumann)

– and not just them – acknowledge the German submarine's stealth. On the other hand, attack submarine developers are not asleep either, and improving stealth characteristics is accordingly the highest priority in German research and development. It is not about just dampening existing signatures, but about finding new ways to eliminate them.

The underlying principle of a HDW design is to keep the boat as small as possible – that is an effective method to reduce hull signal strengths. Another approach is the development of coating materials which absorb sonar and radar beams. And HDW builds completely non-magnetic boats – e.g. the HDW Class 212A submarines for the German Navy, which have been further refined and perfected.

Signature reduction not only effects the boat as a whole, but each individual system, every component and device built into the boat. And these include propellers, cable trays and the development of ultra low noise machinery such as pumps, sea-cocks, shut-off valves, flaps, drives, compressors etc. Bear in mind, modern batteries and air-independent power plants have done their bit to increase the stealth features, others should not lag.

## THE COMPOSITE PROPELLER

The recently developed composite propeller is a significant noise reducer. Great effort went into tackling the homogenization and pre-swirl of propeller inflow to minimise stress variations on each blade as it revolves, and thus optimize propeller efficiency.

Copper/aluminium/manganese alloys of conventional propellers have been replaced with modern flexing composite materials which lend propeller blades properties that move the loud cavitation point up into higher speeds



## ACOUSTIC COATINGS

Today, a modern conventional submarine is practically impossible to detect with passive sensor. However, despite the risk of giving its position away first, active sonar detection has become increasingly ubiquitous, and as hunting for submarines with it is practically unavoidable, active sonar detection has become a submarine's main threat. In addition to playing down silhouettes, acoustic coating materials that absorb sonar and radar beams are effective countermeasures which HDW has been developing since 2007.

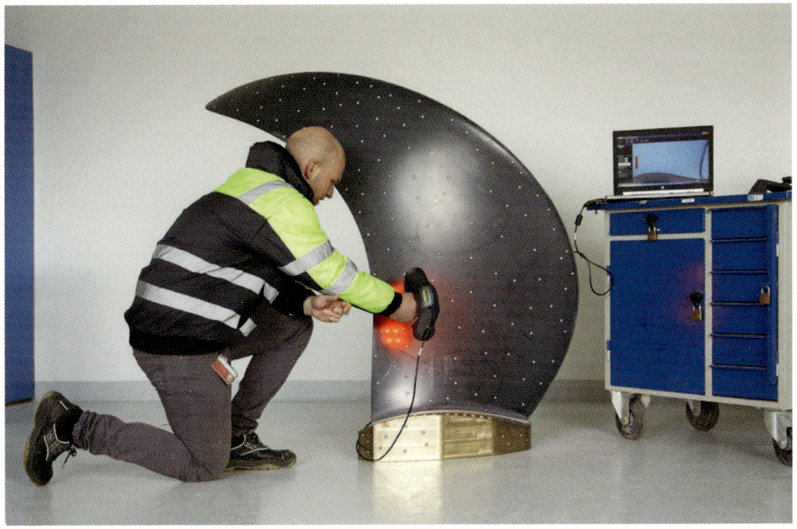

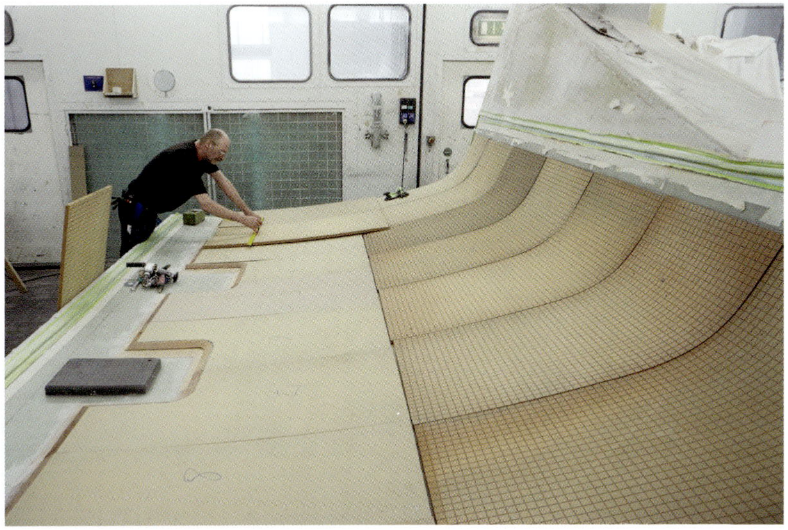

*Measuring the manufacturing accuracy on a composite propeller blade, GRP submarine cladding.* (YPS Peter Neumann)

*Pre-Swirl ruders on U 35. (YPS Peter Neumann)*

## THE PRE-SWIRL RUDDER

A rotating submarine propeller leaves a swirl in its wake which sequesters off some of the propeller's propulsion energy. In order to counteract the effect, much of this energy can be recovered with pre-swirl rudders – fins – that smoothen the water flow and thus deliver a performance increase of up to 10%. The second batch Class 212A boats were the first to benefit from this technology.

## LITHIUM-ION BATTERIES

We have got used to the rechargeable Lithium-Ion batteries that provide the power for every day electronic devices. Now we especially appreciate the fact that the annoying memory-effect of past rechargeable batteries is a thing of the past. But submarines had to wait for this energy storage technology. There is more to it than just scaling up a small home computer battery. And so HDW entered a cooperation with the German battery manufacturer GAIA in 2005 to develop a Lithium-Polymer battery solution for submarines

In comparison to a conventional lead-acid battery, the Lithium-Ion battery has a higher volumetric energy density, better voltage stability, needs less auxiliary systems (which are also simpler), needs no maintenance, has a longer life – and is beneficial to a submarine's overall stealth characteristics. The new standard submarine cell is cylindrically shaped and has a capacity of 2,000 watt hours. Depending on the size of the submarine, several thousand cells can be accommodated into modules, each of 20 cells on board.

The cells have demonstrated striking performances and proven their reliability. Equipped with solar cells and Lithium-Ion batteries,

TÛRANOR PLANETSOLAR, an experimental catamaran, circumnavigated the globe to demonstrate the feasibility of an emission-free world. Its battery engineering had been developed by HDW and installed according to their submarine safety standards and integration procedures. The successful world tour proved that the batteries and HDW's integration concept are highly functional – it remains to be noted that the catamaran also survived the Horn of Africa's pirate-infested waters.

## HYDROGEN MADE IN A METHANOL REFORMER

The best, safest and easiest solution to store hydrogen for AIP is metal hydride cylinders. On the other hand, for those navies preferring larger submarines with extended endurances and higher AIP speeds, the on-board production of hydrogen from hydro-carbonates with a reformer is an alternative that can have advantages over cylinder-stored hydrogen.

ThyssenKrupp Marine Systems has developed and tested a shore-based methanol reformer that produces high quality hydrogen on demand for the Siemens Fuel Cell. An installation-capable prototype with all its necessary auxiliary systems, such as a CO2 dissolution unit as well as the methanol and oxygen supply systems, is now in the final test phase. Installed on board, the reformer will be encapsulated, and provided with all safety systems.

## ARMAMENT: DEVELOPING WEAPON TUBES

HDW upholds its own tradition with the in-house development and production of torpedo and weapon tubes. Amongst its own customized testing facilities is a system installed in a former dry dock to analyse ejection parameters and trajectory characteristics on up to full scale model torpedoes.

The shipyard's state-of-the-art building facilities have delivered submarines with up to ten launching tubes, which can be fitted with a variety of launchers such as an ejection system in which pressurized air interact with a missile, a hydro-mechanical system in which hydraulic cylinders launch missiles and mines via a wire, or a system in which weapon launching is achieved with by a piston with a lever reaching through a slot into a hydraulic cylinder. The Class 212A boats are fitted with a water discharge system in which pressurized water acts directly on the weapon, and only after it has put enough room between itself

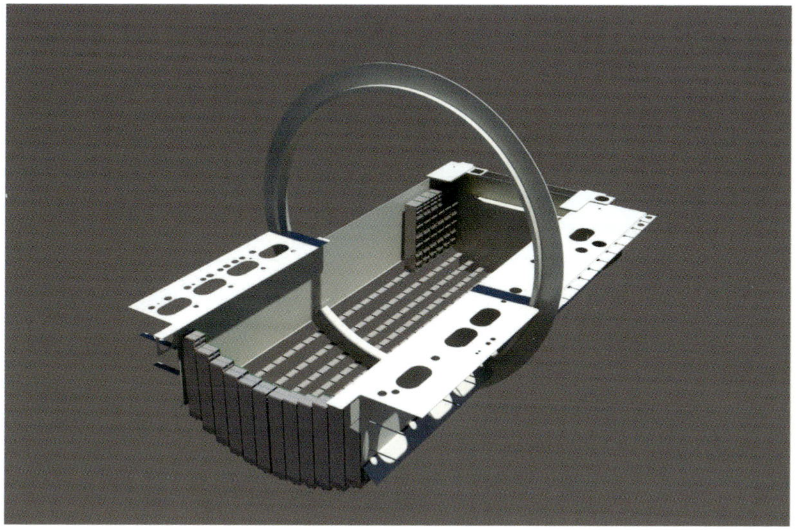

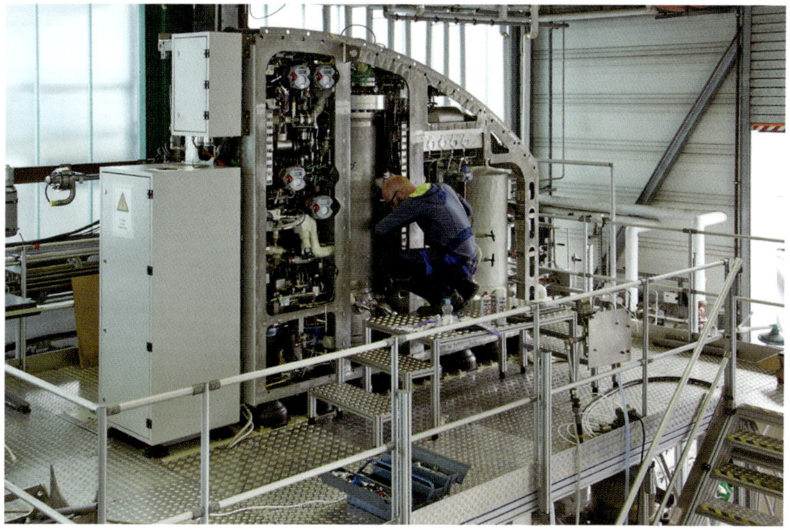

*Left: Lithium-Ion battery arrangement.* (ThyssenKrupp Marine Systems). *Right: Installation ready methanol-reformer test rig.* (YPS Peter Neumann)

*Torpedo tube assembly in Kiel.* (YPS Peter Neumann)

and the submarine, does the engine fire up – and so does not unmask the submarine's launching position.

Current weapon tube research and development concentrates on hunter-helicopter, surface warship and coastal targeting missiles – such as the Interactive Defence and Attack System (IDAS) for submarines with launchers for four autonomous missiles installed in a weapon tube. ThyssenKrupp Marine Systems is also working on start and retrieval equipment for unmanned underwater vehicles that can fit into a weapon tube too. And finally, development is leading to larger diametered weapon tubes, which, as locks, will be suitable for divers, underwater vehicles etc.

## IDAS – THE INTERACTIVE DEFENCE AND ATTACK SYSTEM FOR SUBMARINES

A submarine's most dangerous foe is the ASW-helicopter, against which they have been pretty much defenceless. Now ThyssenKrupp Marine Systems/HDW, Diehl BDT Defence and Kongsberg have developed a unique countermeasure – IDAS. Tested on a Class 212A boat, it passed tests and is now being prepared for serial production. IDAS offers submariners an array of completely new weapon deployment options. The missile, which so far has no competitors, combats threats from the air, fights ships and hits coastal targets with high accuracy.

The submarine does not have to surface to deploy the multi-purpose missiles, but can launch them from a standard torpedo tube, from safe depths.

The IDAS missile has an autopilot and infrared imaging for autonomous control and navigation, but thanks to an innovative fibre-optic link, can be monitored throughout the whole of its flight from within the submarine. The operator can select or change the target, correct the point of impact, or abort the mission. The target approach control, the search head's precision and a small warhead result in high weapon-effectivity paired with limited collateral damage.

IDAS DIEHL
GUIDED TEST MISSILE

*The IDAS guided missile.* (Archive ThyssenKrupp Marine Systems)

The system comprises three components: the launch container, the missiles and a management system. After ejection (from a torpedo tube), the IDAS missile unfolds wings and rudders, ignites a rocket motor, climbs to the surface, and after becoming airborne, sets course for the target.

Furthermore, IDAS is the first guided missile able to "fly" through water without requiring any additional shielding which saves costs and storage space requirements – and it increases a submarine's tactical flexibility.[2]

IDAS is far more than a pure self defence system for submarines. It is an absolute novelty. Emerging scenarios reveal how escalation-capable weapons that enlarge a submarine's weaponry are urgently needed. Intelligent, highly accurate guided missiles with small warheads will play important roles in the future.

Detection
Ejection
Surface
Target recognition
Destruction

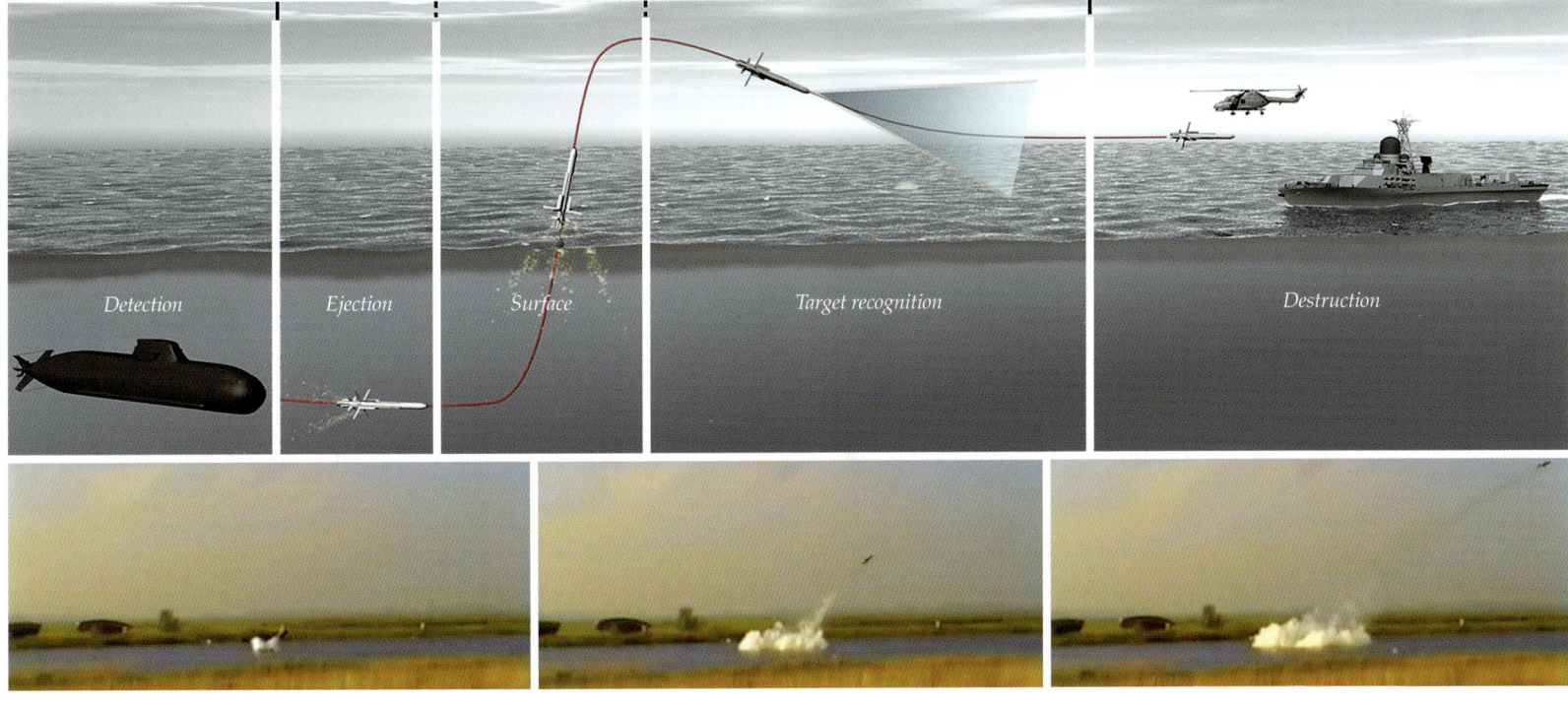

*Test launching an IDAS missile.* (Archive ThyssenKrupp Marine Systems)

*HABETaS®* *(Archive ThyssenKrupp Marine Systems)*

## HABETaS® RESCUE SYSTEM

The German Navy's credo for submarine operations is "safety before rescue". Thus boats built in Germany are inherently safe. Yet there are navies which would like to see additional security – and a rescue system such as HABETaS® does ease crew minds. It exceeds possible escape depths of any other current system. In the unlikely case that a HDW submarine has to be evacuated, crews have excellent survival chances, HABETaS® enables escape from 300 meters depths, in free ascent.

In simulations, escape depths of 550 metres have been achieved, far beyond the attested maximum of 180 meters, and thus a new standard for submarine rescue has been set. HABETaS® can be installed on any new submarines, and retrofitted to older boats. It is a joint development between HDW, AMITS, a British company, and the Ballonfabrik Augsburg (BfA). In 2009 the Dutch Navy ordered 8 units, and the rescue system's effectiveness has been since confirmed in a joint exercise between the Royal Netherlands Navy and the Royal Norwegian Navy in 2012.

## HOISTING MASTS

HDW has maintained a long partnership with Gabler Maschinenbau, manufacturers of submarine hoisting masts required for snorkelling, radar, telecommunication antennas, etc.

Demands for more flexibility, more reliability, more sensors and lower costs have led to new masts designs, characterized by the guide trunks's rectangular design. In most cases, all components such as cable guides can be installed inside the guide trunk, which results in a very compact layout. This raises the packing density inside a sail, and depending on the type of boat, permits the installation of one or two more masts. A further advantage is the short replacement time required for each unit, which translates into mission driven configurations and minimized time in dock.

## AUV LAUNCH AND RECOVERY SYSTEMS[3]

In armed forces, unmanned, autonomous systems are becoming ever more omnipresent for air, land and sea operations, and in a far-sighted move in 1997, HDW started its development for the integration of unmanned underwater vehicles (UUV)[4]. They can extend the roles of covertly operating submarines as they can deliver sensors close to shore, inside harbours, fjords and river estuaries without exposing the submarine. And they can prepare and assist amphibious and Special Forces operations.

In 2008 HDW initiated a further program for the development of launch and recovery systems for boats deploying, for example, Diehl BTG Defence's unmanned Autonomous Undersea Vehicle (AUV) DAVID, which has the dimensions of a small torpedo, or a larger, externally mounted ATLAS ELEKTRONIK SeeOtter MK II. These systems are suitable for installation in new submarines, as well as for retrofitting to older boats.

*Latest generation hoisting masts on U35 (YPS Peter Neumann)*

# A Future within Competitive Markets

Progress is both incessant and perpetual. Experts estimate ThyssenKrupp Marine System's technological lead on submarines to be approximately one decade. But that is no reason to sit back and watch competitors. The technical advantage alone is not the main reason why clients acquire new German submarines.

They all acknowledge German submarine technology, and place orders in Germany owing its good submarine building reputation paired with the German submarine flotillas' experience. But they are not always willing or able to pay German prices due to tight defence budgets or empty public purses.

The market for submarines is growing, and it is highly competitive. But in the meantime, newcomers have also established themselves in addition to the traditional providers, and this does not make life any easier for the world's market leader for non-nuclear powered submarines in Kiel. Russia has been elbowing itself into the international market. Korea offers a licensed Class 209 copy. Japan is trying hard too, and the People's Republic of China is a force to be reckoned with. Furthermore, in summer 2014, Saab took over ThyssenKrupp Marine System's subsidiary Kockums in a brutal manner, and so Sweden falls into the ranks of competitors too.

This makes it all the more important to promote research and development, and to continue to offer new products. UUVs, unmanned underwater vehicles, for example, will play a far greater role in the future than today. However the future will not only consist of military vessels. The civil sector also holds great opportunities. Because in the 21st century, the interest in exploration and extraction of resources in oceans is becoming greater than ever. Sea mining today is not only hotly debated, but is vigorously pursued by industrialised nations, and Germany is one of them that is increasing its participation. This will lift the demand for vehicles and machinery that can operate under water, a field in which ThyssenKrupp Marine Systems is already actively involved.

Finally, the cost pressure on shipyards remain unbroken. Here the key factors are the optimisation of production processes, reduction of costs and above all, to maintain strict adherence to scheduling. After all, no customer is willing to wait unduly for his submarine – be it the best German technology or not.

This has been understood by the Kiel shipyard, and it's doing its homework. In over 175 years of history, it has shown itself to be surprisingly versatile, and that it was always willing and able to break new ground. Its true tradition is constant change. For the future, one can hope that German politics will continue to support the issues involved, respect them and not give away or surrender unique key technologies invented by Germany's industrial community.

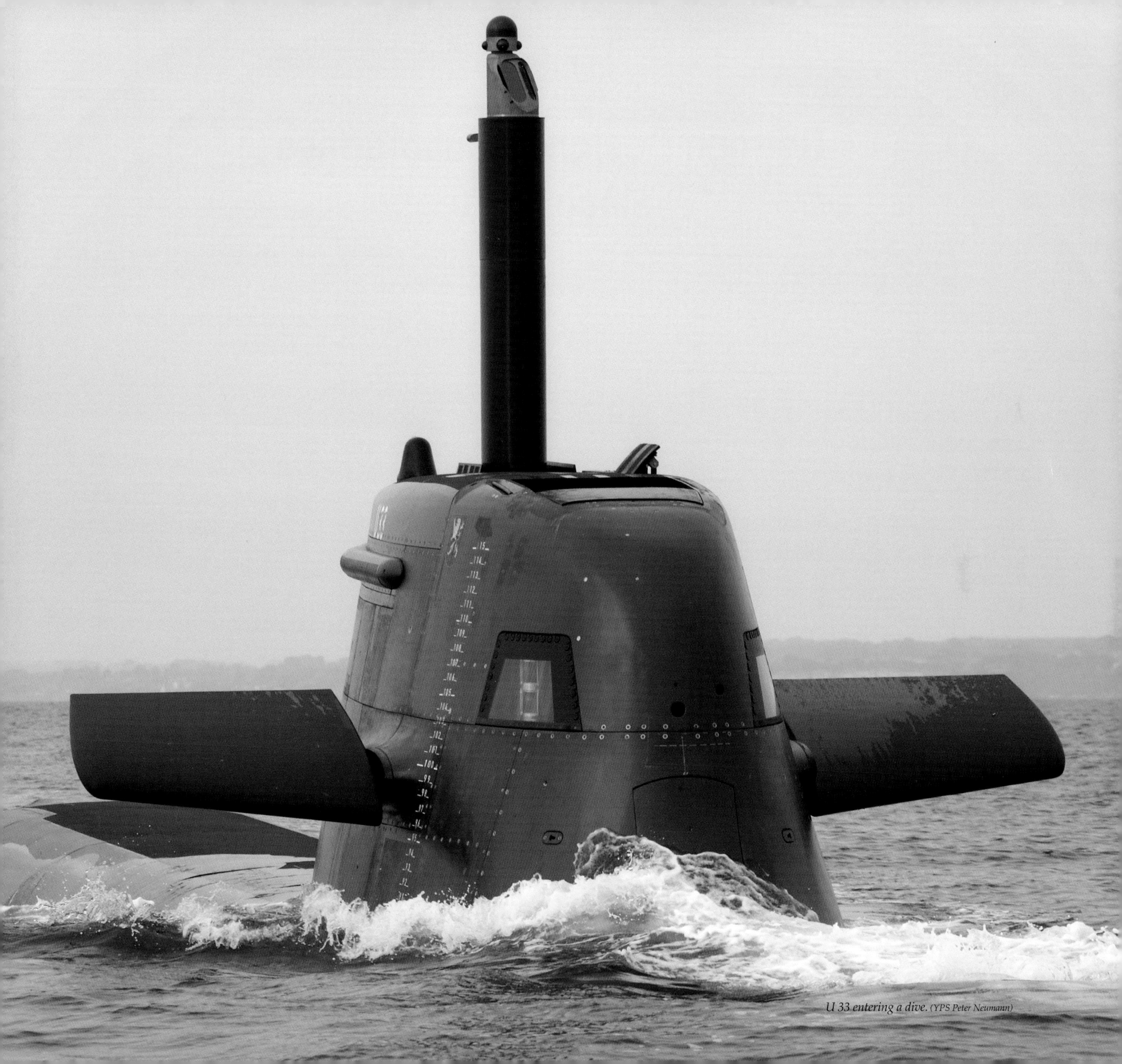

*U 33 entering a dive.* (YPS Peter Neumann)

# German Designed Submarines Since 1960

| Yard Nr. | Name | Hull Nr. | Nation | HDW Class | Built by | Com-missioning | Decom-missioning | Remarks |
|---|---|---|---|---|---|---|---|---|
| HDW 1150 | U1 | S180 |  | 201 | HDW | 21.03.1962 | 22.07.1963 | |
| | U1 | S180 |  | 201 | HDW | 03.04.1965 | 15.03.1966 | |
| | U1 | S180 |  | 205 | HDW | 06.06.1967 | 29.11.1991 | |
| HDW 1151 | U2 | S181 |  | 201 | HDW | 13.05.1962 | 15.08.1963 | |
| | U2 | S181 |  | 205 | HDW | 11.10.1966 | 19.03.1992 | |
| HDW 1152 | U3 | S182 |  | 201 | HDW | 10.07.1962 | 15.09.1964 | |
| HDW 1153 | U4 | S183 |  | 205 | HDW | 19.11.1962 | 01.08.1974 | |
| HDW 1154 | U5 | S184 |  | 205 | HDW | 04.07.1963 | 17.05.1974 | |
| HDW 1155 | U6 | S185 |  | 205 | HDW | 04.07.1963 | 23.08.1974 | |
| HDW 1156 | U7 | S186 |  | 205 | HDW | 16.03.1964 | 30.09.1965 | |
| | | | | | | 22.05.1968 | 12.07.1974 | |
| HDW 1157 | U8 | S187 |  | 205 | HDW | 22.07.1964 | 09.10.1974 | |
| | Techel | S172 |  | 202 | Atlas | 14.10.1965 | 15.12.1966 | |
| | Schürer | S173 |  | 202 | Atlas | 06.04.1966 | 15.12.1966 | |
| HDW 1158 | U9 | S188 |  | 205 | HDW | 11.04.1967 | 03.06.1993 | |
| HDW 1159 | U10 | S189 |  | 205 | HDW | 28.11.1967 | 04.03.1993 | |
| HDW 1160 | U11 | S190 |  | 205 | HDW | 21.06.1968 | 30.10.2003 | |
| HDW 1161 | U12 | S191 | 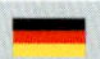 | 205 | HDW | 14.01.1969 | 30.04.1971 | |
| | | | | | | 08.01.1974 | 14.07.2005 | |
| RNSW 351 | KNM Kinn | S 316 |  | 207 | RNSW | 08.04.1964 | 20.02.1980 | |
| RNSW 352 | KNM Kya | S 317 | 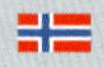 | 207 | RNSW | 15.06.1964 | 07.09.1989 | Transferred to Denmark |
| | KDM Spingeren | S-324 |  | | | 17.10.1991 | 25.11.2004 | |
| RNSW 353 | KNM Kobben | S 318 |  | 207 | RNSW | 17.08.1964 | 2000 | Transferred to Poland |
| RNSW 354 | KNM Kunna | S 319 |  | 207 | RNSW | 29.10.1964 | 2001 | Transferred to Poland |
| | ORP Kondor | 297 |  | | | | 20.10.2003 | |

| Yard Nr. | Name | Hull Nr. | Nation | HDW Class | Built by | Commissioning | Decommissioning | Remarks |
|---|---|---|---|---|---|---|---|---|
| RNSW 355 | KNM Kaura | S 315 | 🇳🇴 | 207 | RNSW | 05.02.1965 | 31.05.1990 | Transferred to Denmark |
| RNSW 365 | KNM Ula | S 300 | 🇳🇴 | 207 | RNSW | 07.05.1965 | 26.10.1990 | |
| | KNM Kinn | S-316 | 🇳🇴 | | | | | Renamed KMN Kinn in 1987 |
| RNSW 357 | KNM Utsira | S 301 | 🇳🇴 | 207 | RNSW | 08.07.1965 | 12.12.1991 | |
| RNSW 358 | KNM Utstein | S 302 | 🇳🇴 | 207 | RNSW | 15.09.1965 | 23.11.1990 | |
| RNSW 359 | KNM Utvaer | S 303 | 🇳🇴 | 207 | RNSW | 01.12.1965 | 30.10.1987 | Transferred to Denmark |
| | KDM Tumleren | S-322 | 🇩🇰 | | | 20.10.1989 | 17.08.2004 | |
| RNSW 360 | KNM Uthaug | S 304 | 🇳🇴 | 207 | RNSW | 16.02.1966 | 16.12.1987 | Transferred to Denmark |
| | KDM Saelen | S-323 | 🇩🇰 | | | 10.10.1990 | 21.12.2004 | |
| RNSW 361 | KNM Sklinna | S 305 | 🇳🇴 | 207 | RNSW | 27.05.1966 | 09.01.1989 | |
| RNSW 362 | KNM Skolpen | S 306 | 🇳🇴 | 207 | RNSW | 17.08.1966 | 08.11.1989 | Transferred to Poland |
| | ORP Sep | 295 | 🇵🇱 | | | 16.08.2002 | | |
| RNSW 363 | KNM Stadt | S 307 | 🇳🇴 | 207 | RNSW | 15.11.1966 | 12.05.1987 | |
| RNSW 364 | KNM Stord | S 308 | 🇳🇴 | 207 | RNSW | 14.02.1967 | 12.05.1987 | Transferred to Poland |
| | ORP Sokól | 294 | 🇵🇱 | | | 04.06.2002 | | |
| RNSW 365 | KNM Svenner | S 309 | 🇳🇴 | 207 | RNSW | 12.06.1967 | | Transferred to Poland |
| | ORP Bielik | 296 | 🇵🇱 | | | 08.09.2003 | | |
| | Narvhalen | S320 | 🇩🇰 | 205i | Orlogsv. | 27.02.1970 | 2003 | |
| | Nordkaperen | S321 | 🇩🇰 | 205i | Orlogsv. | 14.02.1967 | 2003 | |
| HDW 1221 | Glafkos | S-110 | 🇬🇷 | 209/1100 | HDW | 05.11.1971 | | |
| HDW 1222 | Nirefs | S-111 | 🇬🇷 | 209/1100 | HDW | 10.02.1972 | | |
| HDW 1223 | Triton | S-112 | 🇬🇷 | 209/1100 | HDW | 08.08.1972 | | |
| HDW 1224 | Proteus | S-113 | 🇬🇷 | 209/1100 | HDW | 23.11.1972 | | |
| HDW 29 | A.R.A. Salta | S-31 | 🇦🇷 | 209/1200 | HDW/Tanador | 23.08.1974 | | |
| HDW 30 | A.R.A. San Luis | S-32 | 🇦🇷 | 209/1200 | HDW/Tanador | 23.08.1974 | | |
| HDW 31 | U13 | S192 | 🇩🇪 | 206 | HDW | 19.04.1973 | 23.09.1997 | |
| HDW 32/RNSW 441 | U14 | S193 | 🇩🇪 | 206 | RNSW | 19.04.1973 | 26.03.1997 | |
| HDW 33 | U15 | S194 | 🇩🇪 | 206A | HDW | 17.07.1974 | 14.12.2010 | |
| HDW 34/RNSW 442 | U16 | S195 | 🇩🇪 | 206A | RNSW | 09.11.1973 | 31.03.2011 | |
| 35 | U17 | S196 | 🇩🇪 | 206A | HDW | 28.11.1973 | 14.12.2010 | |
| HDW 36/RNSW 443 | U18 | S197 | 🇩🇪 | 206A | RNSW | 19.12.1973 | 31.03.2011 | |

| Yard Nr. | Name | Hull Nr. | Nation | HDW Class | Built by | Com- missioning | Decom- missioning | Remarks |
|---|---|---|---|---|---|---|---|---|
| 37 | U19 | S198 | 🇩🇪 | 206 | HDW | 09.11.1973 | 03.06.1998 | |
| HDW 38/RNSW 444 | U20 | S199 | 🇩🇪 | 206 | RNSW | 24.05.1974 | 26.09.1996 | |
| 39 | U21 | S170 | 🇩🇪 | 206 | HDW | 16.08.1974 | 03.06.1998 | |
| HDW 40/RNSW 445 | U22 | S171 | 🇩🇪 | 206A | RNSW | 26.07.1974 | 31.12.2008 | |
| 41 | U25 | S174 | 🇩🇪 | 206A | HDW | 14.06.1974 | 31.12.2008 | |
| HDW 42/RNSW 446 | U24 | S173 | 🇩🇪 | 206A | RNSW | 16.10.1974 | 31.03.2011 | |
| 47 | U27 | S176 | 🇩🇪 | 206 | HDW | 16.10.1974 | 13.06.1998 | |
| HDW 48/RNSW 447 | U26 | S175 | 🇩🇪 | 206A | RNSW | 13.03.1975 | 09.11.2005 | |
| 49 | U29 | S178 | 🇩🇪 | 206A | HDW | 27.11.1974 | 31.12.2006 | |
| HDW 50/RNSW 448 | U28 | S177 | 🇩🇪 | 206A | RNSW | 18.12.1974 | 30.06.2004 | |
| HDW 51/RNSW 450 | U23 | S172 | 🇩🇪 | 206A | RNSW | 02.05.1975 | 31.03.2011 | |
| HDW 52/RNSW 449 | U30 | S179 | 🇩🇪 | 206A | RNSW | 13.03.1975 | 28.02.2007 | |
| | Gal | | 🇮🇱 | 540 | Vickers | 01.01.1977 | 1999/2000 | |
| | Tanin | | 🇮🇱 | 540 | Vickers | 1977 | 1999/2000 | |
| | Rahav | | 🇮🇱 | 540 | Vickers | 12.1977 | 1999/2000 | |
| HDW 53 | BAP Islay | SS-35 | 🇵🇪 | 209/1200 | HDW | 22.08.1974 | | |
| HDW 54 | BAP Arica | SS-36 | 🇵🇪 | 209/1200 | HDW | 24.01.1975 | | |
| HDW 61 | A.R.C. Pijao | S-28 | 🇨🇴 | 209/1200 | HDW | 14.05.1975 | | |
| HDW 62 | A.R.C. Tayrona | S-29 | 🇨🇴 | 209/1200 | HDW | 18.07.1975 | | |
| HDW 65 | TCG Atilay | S-347 | 🇹🇷 | 209/1200 | HDW | 12.03.1976 | | |
| HDW 66 | TCG Saldiray | S-348 | 🇹🇷 | 209/1200 | HDW | 15.01.1977 | | |
| HDW 67 | Sábalo | S-31 | 🇻🇪 | 209/1300 | HDW | 06.08.1976 | | |
| HDW 68 | Caribe | S-32 | 🇻🇪 | 209/1300 | HDW | 11.03.1977 | | |
| HDW 91 | Shyri | S-101 | 🇪🇨 | 209/1300 | HDW | 05.11.1977 | | |
| HDW 92 | Huancavilca | S-102 | 🇪🇨 | 209/1300 | HDW | 16.03.1978 | | |
| HDW 95 | TCG Batiray | S-349 | 🇹🇷 | 209/1200 | HDW | 07.11.1978 | | |
| HDW 96 | TCG Yildiray | S-350 | 🇹🇷 | 209/1200 | Gölcük | 01.01.1982 | | Material Package |
| HDW 106 | Poseidon | S-116 | 🇬🇷 | 209/1100 | HDW | 22.03.1979 | | |
| HDW 107 | Amfitriti | S-117 | 🇬🇷 | 209/1100 | HDW | 14.09.1979 | | |
| HDW 108 | Okeanos | S-118 | 🇬🇷 | 209/1100 | HDW | 15.11.1979 | | |
| HDW 118 | Pontos | S-119 | 🇬🇷 | 209/1100 | HDW | 29.04.1980 | | |

| Yard Nr. | Name | Hull Nr. | Nation | HDW Class | Built by | Com- missioning | Remarks |
|---|---|---|---|---|---|---|---|
| HDW 131 | BAP Casma/Angamos | SS-31 | Peru | 209/1200 | HDW | 19.12.1980 | |
| HDW 132 | BAP Antofagasta | SS-32 | Peru | 209/1200 | HDW | 19.12.1980 | |
| HDW 133 | BAP Chipana | SS-34 | Peru | 209/1200 | HDW | 28.10.1982 | |
| HDW 134 | BAP Pisagua | SS-33 | Peru | 209/1200 | HDW | 12.07.1983 | |
| HDW 135 | Cakra | S 401 | Indonesia | 209/1300 | HDW | 08.07.1980 | |
| HDW 136 | Nanggala | S 402 | Indonesia | 209/1300 | HDW | 21.10.1980 | |
| HDW 171 | TCG Dagonay | S-351 | Turkey | 209/1200 | Gölcük | 01.11.1985 | Material Package |
| HDW 181 | Thomson | S-20 | Chile | 209/1400 | HDW | 07.05.1984 | |
| HDW 182 | Simpson | S-21 | Chile | 209/1400 | HDW | 18.07.1985 | |
| TNSW 463 | A.R.A. Santa Cruz | S-41 | Argentina | TR 1700 | TNSW | 15.10.1984 | |
| TNSW 465 | A.R.A. San Juan | S-42 | Argentina | TR 1700 | TNSW | 18.11.1985 | |
| | | | Argentina | TR 1700 | | | |
| | | | Argentina | TR 1700 | | | |
| | | | Argentina | TR 1700 | | | |
| | | | Argentina | TR 1700 | | | |
| HDW 186 | Shishumar | S-44 | India | Type 1500 | HDW | 22.09.1986 | |
| HDW 187 | Shankush | S-45 | India | Type 1500 | HDW | 20.11.1986 | |
| HDW 188 | Shankul | S-47 | India | Type 1500 | Mazagon | 28.05.1994 | Material Package |
| HDW 189 | Shalki | S-46 | India | Type 1500 | Mazagon | 07.02.1992 | Material Package |
| TNSW 480 | KNM Ula | S-300 | Norway | Ula Class | TNSW | 27.04.1989 | |
| TNSW 481 | KNM Uredd | S-305 | Norway | Ula Class | TNSW | 03.05.1990 | |
| TNSW 482 | KNM Utvaer | S-303 | Norway | Ula Class | TNSW | 08.11.1990 | |
| TNSW 483 | KNM Uthaug | S-304 | Norway | Ula Class | TNSW | 07.05.1991 | |
| TNSW 484 | KNM Utstein | S-302 | Norway | Ula Class | TNSW | 14.11.1991 | |
| TNSW 485 | KNM Utsira | S-301 | Norway | Ula Class | TNSW | 30.04.1992 | |
| HDW 197 | Tupi | S 30 | Brazil | 209/1400 | HDW | 06.05.1989 | |
| HDW 198 | Tamoio | S 31 | Brazil | 209/1400 | Arsenal de Marinha | 12.12.1994 | Material Package |
| HDW 215 | TCG Dolunay | S-352 | Turkey | 209/1200 | Gölcük | 01.06.1991 | Material Package |
| HDW 219 | Timbira | S 32 | Brazil | 209/1400 | Arsenal de Marinha | 22.10.1997 | Material Package |
| HDW 220 | Tapajó | S 33 | Brazil | 209/1400 | Arsenal de Marinha | 21.12.1999 | Material Package |

| Yard Nr. | Name | Hull Nr. | Nation | HDW Class | Built by | Com-missioning | Remarks |
|---|---|---|---|---|---|---|---|
| HDW 242 | Chang Bogo | | 🇰🇷 | 209/1200 | HDW | 02.06.1993 | |
| HDW 243 | Lee Chun | | 🇰🇷 | 209/1200 | Daewoo | 30.04.1994 | Material Package |
| HDW 244 | Choi Museon | | 🇰🇷 | 209/1200 | Daewoo | 27.02.1995 | Material Package |
| HDW 245 | TCG Preveze | S-353 | 🇹🇷 | 209/1400mod | Gölcük | 23.09.1994 | Material Package |
| HDW 246 | TCG Sakarya | S-354 | 🇹🇷 | 209/1400mod | Gölcük | July 1995 | Material Package |
| HDW 249 | Park Wi | | 🇰🇷 | 209/1200 | Daewoo | 03.02.1996 | Material Package |
| HDW 250 | Lee Jongmu | | 🇰🇷 | 209/1200 | Daewoo | 01.09.1996 | Material Package |
| HDW 251 | Jeong Un | | 🇰🇷 | 209/1200 | Daewoo | 29.08.1997 | Material Package |
| HDW 265 | Dolphin | | 🇮🇱 | Dolphin | Dolphin Consortium | 27.07.1999 | |
| HDW 266 | Leviathan | | 🇮🇱 | Dolphin | Dolphin Consortium | 15.11.1999 | |
| HDW 290 | Tikuna | S 34 | 🇧🇷 | 209/1400mod | Arsenal de Marinha | 16.12.2005 | Material Package |
| HDW 291 | Lee Sunsin | | 🇰🇷 | 209/1200 | Daewoo | 15.06.1999 | Material Package |
| HDW 292 | Na Deayong | | 🇰🇷 | 209/1200 | Daewoo | 01.05.2000 | Material Package |
| HDW 293 | Lee Eokgi | | 🇰🇷 | 209/1200 | Daewoo | 01.11.2001 | Material Package |
| HDW 294 | TCG 18 Mart | S-355 | 🇹🇷 | 209/1400mod | Gölcük | 28.07.1998 | Material Package |
| HDW 295 | TCG Anafartalar | S-356 | 🇹🇷 | 209/1400mod | Gölcük | 22.07.1999 | Material Package |
| HDW 317 | Tekumah | | 🇮🇱 | Dolphin | Dolphin Consortium | 25.07.2000 | |
| HDW 318 | U 31 | S181 | 🇩🇪 | 212A | ARGE 212A | 19.10.2005 | |
| HDW 319 | U 32 | S182 | 🇩🇪 | 212A | ARGE 212A | 19.10.2005 | |
| HDW 320 | U 33 | S183 | 🇩🇪 | 212A | ARGE 212A | 13.06.2006 | |
| HDW 321 | U 34 | S184 | 🇩🇪 | 212A | ARGE 212A | 03.05.2007 | |
| HDW 344 | Salvatore Todaro | S526 | 🇮🇹 | 212A | Fincantieri | 28.03.2006 | |
| HDW 345 | Scirè | S527 | 🇮🇹 | 212A | Fincantieri | 19.02.2007 | |
| HDW 350 | TCG Gür | S-357 | 🇹🇷 | 209/1400mod | Gölcük | 21.04.2006 | Material Package |
| HDW 351 | TCG Çanakkale | S-358 | 🇹🇷 | 209/1400mod | Gölcük | 22.06.2006 | Material Package |
| HDW 352 | TCG Burakreis | S-359 | 🇹🇷 | 209/1400mod | Gölcük | 01.11.2006 | Material Package |
| HDW 353 | TCG I.Inönü | S-360 | 🇹🇷 | 209/1400mod | Gölcük | 27.06.2007 | Material Package |
| HDW 361 | Papanikolis | S120 | 🇬🇷 | 214 | HDW | 27.10.2010 | |
| HDW 362 | Pipinos | S121 | 🇬🇷 | 214 | HSY | 06.10.2014 | Material Package |
| HDW 363 | Matrozos | S122 | 🇬🇷 | 214 | HSY | | Material Package |
| HDW 365 | SAS Manthatisi | S 101 | 🇿🇦 | 209/1400mod | GSC | 03.11.2005 | |

| Yard Nr. | Name | Hull Nr. | Nation | HDW Class | Built by | Com- missioning | Remarks |
|---|---|---|---|---|---|---|---|
| HDW 366 | SAS Charlotte Maxeke | S 102 | South Africa | 209/1400mod | GSC | 14.03.2007 | |
| HDW 367 | SAS Queen Modjadji | S 103 | South Africa | 209/1400mod | GSC | 22.05.2008 | |
| HDW 371 | Sohn Wonil | | South Korea | 214 | Hyundai | 26.12.2007 | |
| HDW 372 | Jeong Ji | | South Korea | 214 | Hyundai | 02.12.2008 | |
| HDW 373 | An Junggeun | | South Korea | 214 | Hyundai | 30.11.2009 | |
| HDW 383 | N.R.P. Tridente | | Portugal | 209PN | GSC | 17.06.2010 | |
| HDW 384 | N.R.P. Arpão | | Portugal | 209PN | GSC | 22.12.2010 | |
| HDW 398 | U35 | | Germany | 212A | ARGE 212A | 23.03.2015 | |
| HDW 399 | U36 | | Germany | 212A | ARGE 212A | | |
| HDW 400 | INS Tanin | | Israel | Dolphin AIP | ThyssenKrupp Marine Systems | 30.06.2014 | |
| HDW 401 | INS Rahav | | Israel | Dolphin AIP | ThyssenKrupp Marine Systems | | |
| HDW 402 | | | Israel | Dolphin AIP | ThyssenKrupp Marine Systems | | |
| HDW 410 | | | Turkey | NTSP | Gölcük | | |
| HDW 411 | | | Turkey | NTSP | Gölcük | | |
| HDW 412 | | | Turkey | NTSP | Gölcük | | |
| HDW 413 | | | Turkey | NTSP | Gölcük | | |
| HDW 414 | | | Turkey | NTSP | Gölcük | | |
| HDW 415 | | | Turkey | NTSP | Gölcük | | |
| HDW 416 | Pietro Venuti | S528 | Italy | 212A | Fincantieri | | |
| HDW 417 | Romeo Romei | S529 | Italy | 212A | Fincantieri | | |
| HDW 426 | Kim Jwajin | SS076 | South Korea | 214 | DSME | 31.12.2014 | |
| HDW 427 | Yun Bonggil | | South Korea | 214 | Hyundai | | |
| HDW 428 | Ryu Gwansun | | South Korea | 214 | DSME | | |
| HDW 429 | | | South Korea | 214 | | | |
| HDW 430 | | | South Korea | 214 | | | |
| HDW 431 | | | South Korea | 214 | | | |
| HDW 447 | Confidential | | | 209/1400mod | ThyssenKrupp Marine Systems | | |
| HDW 448 | Confidential | | | 209/1400mod | ThyssenKrupp Marine Systems | | |
| HDW 449 | Confidential | | | 209/1400mod | ThyssenKrupp Marine Systems | | |
| HDW 450 | Confidential | | | 209/1400mod | ThyssenKrupp Marine Systems | | |
| HDW 453 | Confidential | | | 218 | ThyssenKrupp Marine Systems | | |
| HDW 454 | Confidential | | | 218 | ThyssenKrupp Marine Systems | | |

# List of Footnotes

### CHAPTER 1
### LEVIATHAN ERWACHT

1. Padfield, War beneath the Sea, p. 479
2. Harris, The Navy Times Book of Submarines, p.38
3. Herold, Der Kieler Brandtaucher, p.99
4. Herold, Der Kieler Brandtaucher, p. 95
5. Herold, Der Kieler Brandtaucher, p. 98
6. Fulton, Torpedo war and submarine explosions, p. 177 ff.
7. Harris, The Navy Times Book of Submarines, p.132 ff
8. Harris, The Navy Times Book of Submarines, p.132 ff

### CHAPTER 2
### THE ROLE OF THE SUBMARINE IN MODERN SCENARIOS

1. The Global Submarine Market
2. Nechaj, radio Stimme Rußlands, 1.8.2012
3. Wolf, Washington Post 1.8.2012
4. Thiede, Zükünftige maritime Operationen, p.8
5. Thiede, Zükünftige maritime Operationen, p.8/9
6. Worcester, The Role of the Submarine
7. Koldau, Mythos U-Boot, p. 55
8. Worcester, The Role of the Submarine
9. Stuve, The increasing importance of conventional submarines, p. 21
10. Stuve, The increasing importance of conventional submarines, p. 17
11. The role of submarines in warfare
12. The role of submarines in warfare
13. The role of submarines in warfare
14. Stuve, The increasing importance of conventional submarines, p. 19
15. Sun Tzu, Die Kunst des Krieges
16. Not just a powerful weapon
17. Submarines make sense

### CHAPTER 3
### GERMANY BUILDS SUBMARINES

1. Mallman Showell, The submarine century, p. 21
2. Busley, Moderne Unterseeboote, p. 124
3. Rössler, U-Bootbau, Bd. 1, p. 24
4. Rössler, U-Bootbau Bd. 1, p.27/Ostersehlte, Von Howaldt zu HDW, p.168
5. Rössler, U-Bootbau, p. 24
6. Rössler, U-Bootbau, Bd. 1, p. 27/28
7. Rössler, U-Bootbau, Bd. 1, p.30
8. Rössler, U-Bootbau, Bd. 1, p.28/Ostersehlte, Von Howaldt zu HDW, p. 167
9. Rössler, U-Bootbau, Bd. 1, p.130 / Van der Vat, Stealth, p. 137
10. Van der Vat, Stealth, p. 37
11. Rössler, U-Bootbau, Bd. 1, p.134 / Van der Vat, Stealth, p. 138
12. Nohse, Rössler, Konstruktionen für die Welt, p. 12
13. Rössler, U-Bootbau, Bd. 1, p.134.
14. Nohse, Rössler, Konstruktionen für die Welt, p. 14
15. Nohse, Rössler, Konstruktionen für die Welt, p 17
16. zit. nach: Nohse, Rössler, Konstruktionen für die Welt, p 18

### CHAPTER 4
### THE TYPE XXI SUBMARINE – A REVOLUTION AT SEA

1. Padfield, War beneath the sea, p.459
2. Die wohl beste Beschreibung der Typ XXI- und Typ XXIII-Boote und ihrer Entwicklungsgeschichte stammt aus der Feder von Eberhard Rössler, der sie in mehreren Büchern höchst kenntnisreich beschrieben hat. Einen schnellen Überblick bieten auch die websites http://de.wikipedia.org/wiki/U-Boot-Klasse_XXI und http://de.wikipedia.org/wiki/U-Boot-Klasse_XXIII.
3. u.W. = unter Wasser
4. ü.W. = über Wasser
5. Waller, Derek; The U-Boats that Surrendered
6. Barlow, From Hot War to Cold, p. 162 ff.
7. ebd.
8. ebd.
9. Rössler, U-Bootbau, Bd. 2, p. 455
10. GUPPY: Greater Underwater Propulsions Power

### CHAPTER 5
### GERMANY BUILDS SUBMARINES AGAIN

1. UK National Archives, Public Record Office, CAB 80/101
2. Stuve, in: Fazination See, pp. 202, 203
3. http://www.dubm.de/u-boote_der_ddr.html
4. Ausführliche Schilderung seiner Tätigkeit in: Nohse/Rössler, Konstruktionen für die Welt, p. 21 ff.
5. Stuve in: Faszination See, pp 206/207
6. ebd., p. 207
7. Rössler, Geschichte des deutschen U-Boot-Baus, Bd. 2, p. 506
8. DER SPIEGEL 18-2008, pp. 50,51
9. Brüsseler Vertrag vom 23.11.1954, Artikel 2 und Anlage III zum Protokoll Nr. III
10. http://einestages.spiegel.de/static/topicalbumbackground/23226/als_die_atom_bombe_platzte.html
11. Brief Udo Ude, ehemaliger Entwicklungs- und Vertriebschef der HDW, vom 23. Juli 2012 an Verf.
12. Telefonat Verf. mit Prof. Abels am 2. März 2012
13. Rössler, Die neuen deutschen U-Boote, p.184: Die Vergleichsstudien zu den Projekten IK 20 und IK 24 sahen den Einsatz eines Babcock-Reaktors beziehungsweise eines MAN-Wahodag-Reaktors vor.

### CHAPTER 6
### SUBMARINES "MADE IN GERMANY"

1. Stuve, in: Faszination See, p. 208
2. Nohse/Rössler, Konstruktionen für die Welt, p.53
3. http://de.wikipedia.org/wiki/U-Boot-Klasse_207
4. Karr, Neue Boote für die südafrikanische Marine, MarineForum 10/2005
5. Ritterhoff, Upgrading Diesel-Electric Submarines, p. 56 ff
6. Bergande, Versatile Modernisation Concepts for Class 209, p. 80
7. SSK Dolphin Class Submarine, Israel in: naval-technology.com
8. Krause, Fakt oder Fantasie, MarineForum 7/8-2015

### CHAPTER 7
### THE SECOND GERMAN REVOLUTION IN SUBMARINE CONSTRUCTION: THE FUEL CELL

1. zit. nach Pressemeldung HDW vom 7. April 2003
2. Rössler, U-Bootbau, Bd. 2, p. 525
3. Rössler, Die neuen deutschen U-Boote, p.184
4. vgl. Kapitel 5: Deutsche Atom-U-Boote?, p. xx
5. Gabler, Submarine Design, p. 80
6. "Kieler Howaldtswerke AG are able to offer an extensive choice, beginning with the 90 t small boat and ending with the 1000 t submarine. Besides the highly developed Diesel electric propulsion common today, we would like to refer to the most interesting solution of the „Walter-propulsion", which was developed during the second world war for boats with an extreme high underwater performance. This concerns a propulsion plant working without atmospheric oxyden by using high concentrate hydrogen peroxide, a gas steam mixture for driving the turbines."
7. Nohse/Rössler, Konstruktionen für die Welt, p. 115
8. Graumann, Der Walter-Antrieb; p. 38/39. http://de.wikipedia.org/wiki/Walter-Antrieb
9. Gabler, Submarine Design, p. 79 f
10. Klein, Regensdorf, Wittekind, Zartmann, Closed Cicle Diesel in AIP, p.3 ff
11. http://de.wikipedia.org/wiki/Stirlingmotor#Geschichte
12. Nohse, Submarine Propulsion, p.7
13. HDW Wasserstoff-Energietechnologie, p 3-5
14. Nohse/Rössler, Konstruktionen für die Welt, p. 117 ff
15. HDW Wasserstoff-Energietechnologie, p. 7
16. Nohse/Rössler, Konstruktionen für die Welt, p. 118
17. Fuel Cell Technology, ohne Seitenangabe
18. HDW Wasserstoff-Energietechnologie, p. 8
19. Siemens AG – Marine Solutions: SINAVY Permasyn

20  Lorenz, Electrical propulsion systems, p. 65 ff

### CHAPTER 8
### THE FUEL CELL EMBARKS

1  Nohse/Rössler, Konstruktionen für die Welt, p. 108
2  Cameron, Not a single submarine seaworthy. 10.06.2011
3  Schütz, Type 212, p. 8

### CHAPTER 9
### THE CLASS 212A BECOMES REALITY

1  Schütz, Type 212, p. 8
2  http://de.wikipedia.org/wiki/U-Boot-Klasse_212_A und andere Quellen. Tatsächlich ist die Tauchtiefe militärisches Geheimnis. Hier handelt es sich also um Spekulation.
3  HDW-Prospekt „UBoot Klasse 212A" mit Angaben von Rössler, Die neuen deutschen U-Boote, p. 206
4  UBoot Klasse 212A
5  UBoot Klasse 212A; Stockfisch, Zweites Los der U-Boot-Klasse 212A, p. 69 ff
6  Stockfisch, Zweites Los der U-Boot-Klasse 212A, p. 70. Ausführlich zu Zeiss-Sehrohren: Schlemmer, Vom Turmsehrohr zu Optronikmast.

### CHAPTER 10
### HDW'S CLASS 214 SUBMARINES – FUEL CELL TECHNOLOGY FOR THE WORLD

1  Dinse, Manolemis, Class 214 submarines
2  nach HDW/TKMS-Angaben – Class 214 Submarine und HDW Class 214 Submarine, und http://de.wikipedia.org/wiki/U-Boot-Klasse_214

### CHAPTER 11
### STILL ON PAPER: HDW CLASS 210MOD AND CLASS 216 SUBMARINES

1  Hauschildt, Class 210mod, p. 26ff, Das U-Boot der Klasse 210mod, p. 18ff.
2  HDW Class 210mod Submarine – Datenblatt
3  Zweiwege-Paketdatendienst von INMARSAT für die Kommunikation per Telex, Telefax oder Datenübertragung (Internet)
4  Global Maritime Distress and Safety System (GMDSS)
5  Electronic Chart Display and Information System (ECDIS; deutsch Elektronisches Kartendarstellungs- und Informationssystem)
6  Die Bootsbeschreibung folgt im Wesentlichen Kohsiek, Hauschildt, Die Klasse 216, p. 18 ff.
7  HDW Class 216 Submarine – Datenblatt

### CHAPTER 12
### TOMORROW'S SUBMARINE TECHNOLOGY TODAY

1  HDW (Hsg.), Silent Fleet. Inzwischen fünf Ausgaben
2  Diehl BGT Defence, U-Boot-Flugkörper IDAS
3  AUV = Autonomous Underwater Vehicle
4  UUV = Unmanned Underwater Vehicle

# Bibliography

Australian Submarine Corporation: *Role of submarines.* In: http://www.asc.com.au/aspx/Role_of_Submarines.aspx. (o.J.)

Barlow, Jeffrey G.: *From Hot War to Cold. The U.S. Navy and National Security Affairs, 1945 – 1955.* Stanford, CA 2009

Bergande, Matthias: *Versatile Modernisation Concepts for Class 209.* In: Naval Forces, Special Issue 2011, Vol XXXII, Bonn 2011

Blair, Clyde: *Der U-Boot-Krieg* – 2 Bde. (Bd. 1: Die Jäger, 1939-1942; Bd. 2: Die Gejagten, 1942-1945). München 1998

Busley, Carl: *Die modernen Unterseeboote.* In: Jahrbuch der Schiffbautechnischen Gesellschaft, Bd. 1, p. 63 - 124. Hamburg 1901

Cameron, Steward: *Not a single submarine seaworthy.* In: The Australian. 10.06.2011. Sydney 2011

Diehl BGT Defence: *U-Boot-Flugkörper IDAS.* In: http://www.diehl.com/de/diehl-defence/produkte/lenkflugkoerper/idas.html

Dinse, Reinhard, Ioannis Manolemis: *Class 214 submarines – HDW's response to today's international warfare scenarios.* Mskr. 2006

Fulton, Robert: *Torpedo war, and submarine explosions.* New York 1810

Gabler, Ulrich: *Submarine Design.* Bonn 2000

Gannon, Michael: *Black May.* New York 1998
Graumann, Dirk: *Der Walter-Antrieb.* In: SONAR 19/2004

Hadley, Michael: *Der Mythos der deutschen U-Boot-Waffe.* Hamburg 2001

Harris, Brayton: *The Navy Times Book of Submarines. A political, social and military history.* New York 1997

Hauschildt, Peter: *U-Boote „Made in Germany" – Bestandsaufnahme und Ausblick.* In: Marineforum 6-2010, p 4 ff. Bonn 2010

Hauschildt, Peter: *Das U-Boot der Klasse 210mod – Hochleistung auf kompaktem Raum.* In: Marineforum 12-2010, p. 18 ff. Bonn 2010

Hauschildt, Peter: *Class 2010mod – a future-orientated submarine design.* In: Naval Forces, Special Issue 2011 – Vol. XXXII, p.26 ff. Bonn 2011

Herold, Klaus: *Der Kieler Brandtaucher.* Bonn 1993

Hess, Sigurd, Guntram Schulze-Wegener, Heinrich Walle (Hsg.): *Faszination See – 50 Jahre Marine der Bundesrepublik Deutschland.* Hamburg, Berlin, Bonn 2005

Howaldtswerke-Deutsche Werft GmbH (Hsg.): *Silent Fleet*, 5th Edition. Kiel 2011

Karr, Hans: *Neue Boote für die südafrikanische Marine.* In: Marineforum 10/2005. Bonn 2005

King, Mike: *The Global Submarine Market 2011–2023.* In: http://www.companiesandmarkets.com/MarketInsight/Defence/Global-Submarine-Market/NI8829. Amsterdam 2014

Klein, Manfred, Uwe Regensdorf, Dietrich Wittekind, Carlos Zartmann: *Closed Cicle Diesel – Priciple and Application.* In: AIP – Air Independent Propulsion Systems. Hsg. TNSW, HDW, IKL zur UDT 1993. Cannes 1993

Kohsiek, Sven: *Class 216 – Cutting edge technology for long mission profiles.* In: Naval Forces, Special Issue 2011, VOL. XXXII, p. 22 ff. Bonn 2011

Kohsiek, Sven, Hauschildt, Peter: *Die Klasse 216 – U-Boote für den weltweiten Einsatz.* In: Marineforum 1/2-2012 – p 18 ff. Bonn 2012

Koldau, Linda Maria: *Mythos U-Boot.* Stuttgart 2010

Kraft, Jakob: *Als die Atomträume platzten.* In: http://einestages.spiegel.de/static/topicalbumbackground/23226/als_die_atom_bombe_platzte.html. Hamburg 2011

Krause, Joachim: *Fakt oder Fantasie – Lässt Israel in Kiel U-Boote für nuklear-strategische Aufgaben bauen?* In Marineforum 7/8-2015. Bonn 2015
Kürsner, Jürgen: U-Boote – Relikte des Kalten Krieges? Neue Züricher Zeitung 25.1.2011

Lorenz, Jan-Hinrich: *Submarines – unseen but on scene thanks to electrical propulsion systems.* In: Naval Forces, Special Issue 2011, Vol XXXII. Bonn 2011

Mallman Showell, Jak P.: *The U-Boat Century – German Submarine warfare 1906-2006.* London 2006

Nechaj, Oleg: *Neue Atom-U-Boote: „Vorteil durch russisches Know-how".* radio Stimme Rußlands 01.08.2012 – http://german.ruvr.ru/2012_08_01/83649786/2012

Nohse, Lutz, Eberhard Rössler: *Konstruktionen für die Welt.* Herford 1992

Nohse, Lutz: *Submarine Propulsion – Conventional and Outside-Air-Independent.* Sonderdruck Naval Forces No. IV 1982 für IKL. Bonn 1982

Ostersehlte, Christian: *Von Howaldt zu HDW.* Kiel, Hamburg 2004

Padfield, Peter: *War Beneath the Sea.* New York 1998

Reuter, Karl-Erich: Permasyn Motors: *A New Propulsion System for Submarines.* In: Naval Forces, Subcon '95 – German Submarine Technology. Bonn 1995

Ritterhoff, Jürgen: *Upgrading Diesel-Electric Submarines by Retrofitting FC Plants.* In: International Defence Technologies: German Submarines – Today and Tomorrow. Bonn 1997

Ritterhoff, Jürgen: *Class 214 – A new class of air-independent submarines.* In: Naval Forces, Special Issue 2/99, pp. 101 - 105. Bonn 1999

Rohweder, Jürgen: *Beständiger Wandel – In 175 Jahren von Schweffel & Howaldt zu ThyssenKrupp Marine Systems.* Kiel/Hamburg 2013

Rössler, Eberhard: *Geschichte des deutschen U-Bootbaus,* Bd. I und II. Augsburg 1996

Rössler, Eberhard: *U-Boottyp XXI.* Bonn 2002

Rössler, Eberhard: *U-Boottyp XXIII.* Bonn 2002

Rössler, Eberhard: *Die neuen deutschen U-Boote.* Bonn 2009, 2. Auflage

Schlemmer, Harry: *Vom Turmsehrohr zum Optronikmast – Geschichte der U-Boot-Sehrohre bei Carl Zeiss.* Hamburg, Berlin, Bonn 2011

Schütz, Heinrich: *Type 212 – The German Navy heading for the next generation of Submarines.* In: Naval Forces, Conference proceedings Subcon '95. Bonn 1995

Siemens AG – Marine Solutions: *SINAVY Permasyn – small, reliable, and difficult to trace.* Siemens-Prospekt 2013

Stockfisch, Dieter: *Zweites Los der U-Boote Klasse 212A – Verbesserungen und Weiterentwicklungen.* In: Europäische Sicherheit und Technik. Februar 2012 p.69 ff. Bonn 2012

Stuve, Christian: *The increasing importance of conventional submarines in future operational Scenarios.* In: Naval Forces, Special Issue 2011, Vol XXXII. Bonn 2011

Sun Tzu: *On the art of war.* Deutsche Übersetzung aus dem Englischen, Version 1.0, © Guido Stepken. 2005

Techel, Hans: *Der Bau von Unterseebooten auf der Germaniawerft.* Berlin 1923

Thiede, Frank: *Zukünftige maritime Operationen – Anforderungen an die Fähigkeiten konventioneller U-Boote.* In: Marineforum 9-2011. Bonn 2011

Van der Vat, Dan: *Stealth at Sea: The history of the Submarine.* London 1994

Waller, Derek: *The U-Boats that surrendered.* In: http://ahoy.tk-jk.net/macslog/TheU-BoatsthatSurrendered-2.html. Melbourne 2011

Waschin, Heinz G.: *Brennstoffzelle und Permasynmotor – Der erste außenluftunabhängige U-Boot-Antrieb.* In: Wehrtechnischer Report 5/2004. Bonn und Frankfurt a.M. 2004

Wolf, Jim: *U.S. to mull more bombers, submarines for Pacific.* Washington Post 01.08.2012. 2012

Worcester, Maxim: *The Role of the Submarine in the Fight for Naval Supremacy in the Pacific.* Institut für Strategie- Politik Sicherheits- und Wirtschaftsberatung. Berlin 2010

**COMPANY BROCHURES**

*Class 214 Submarine – No limits but the endless sea.* HDW Broschüre. Kiel 2011
*Fuel Cell Technology* (Hand-out von HDW und TNSW), Mskr. Kiel/Emden 1988

*HDW Wasserstoff-Energietechnologie.* HDW-Prospekt. Kiel 1996

*HDW Class 214.* Data sheet. ThyssenKrupp Marine Systems. Kiel 2013

*HDW Class 210mod Submarine.* Data sheet. ThyssenKrupp Marine Systems. Kiel 2013

*HDW Class 216 Submarine.* Data sheet. ThyssenKrupp Marine Systems. Kiel 2013

*U-Boot Klasse 212A – Ein Spitzenprodukt der deutschen Unterwassertechnologie.* HDW brochure. Kiel 2011

**INTERNET (WITHOUT AUTHOR NAMES)**

*A German success story.* In: http://www.asiapacificdefencereporter.com/articles/98/A-German-Success-Story. Sidney 2010

*Not just a powerful weapon.* In: http://www.asiapacificdefencereporter.com/articles/118/Not-just-a-powerful-weapon. Sydney 2011
*The role of submarines in Warfare.* In: http://www.asiapacificdefencereporter.com/articles/104/The-role-of-submarines-in-Warfare. Sydney 2010
Submarines make sense. In: http://www.noac-national.ca/article/submarinesmakesense.html. 1997

*SSK Dolphin Class Submarine, Israel.* In: http://www.naval-technology.com/projects/dolphin/. (o.J.)

*The Top 10 Best Diesel-Electric Submarines in the World.* http://www.youtube.com/watch?v=8rTpwPTHenA . (o.J)

*U-Boot Klasse XXI.* In: http://de.wikipedia.org/wiki/U-Boot-Klasse_XXI. (o.J)

*U-Boote der DDR.* In: http://www.dubm.de/u-boote_der_ddr.html. (o.J)

*U-Boot Klasse 207.* In: http://de.wikipedia.org/wiki/U-Boot-Klasse_207. (o.J.)

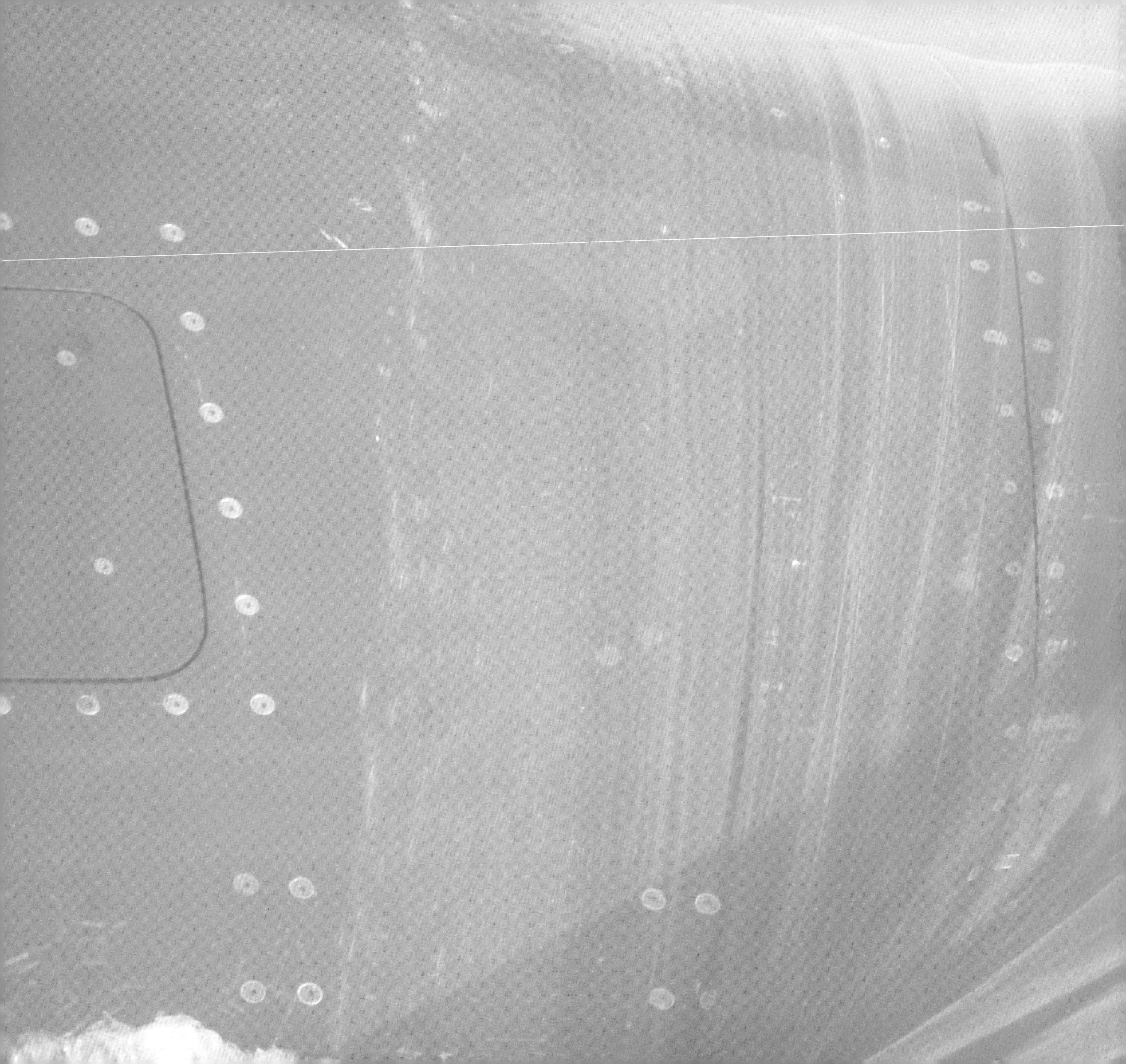